Garters and Grit:

Stories from Galena and Jo Daviess County, Ill.

by ***Becky Sisco***

Sisco Publishing Company, Dubuque, Iowa

ISBN 0-9778594-0-1

Sisco Publishing Company
1205 Pamela Court
Dubuque, Iowa 52003
563-582-7570
gartersandgrit@mchsi.com
www.gartersandgrit.home.mchsi.com

Table of Contents

Foreword

I grew up on a farm near Farley, Iowa, just 35 miles from Galena, Ill. and 20 miles West of the Mississippi River. I was aware of Galena and some of the other towns in Jo Daviess County, Ill. only to the extent that I memorized their names during a family trip to Chicago. Back then, Chicago's Riverview Amusement Park, Brookfield Zoo and Wrigley Field held much more interest for me.

I only began to get to know the area during the late 1970s, when my husband and I would poke around the antique stores in Galena and stop along a few roads to take pictures. I lost touch with the area for nearly 10 years, after we moved to St. Paul, Min. in the mid-1980s.

In 1993, I returned to the area, after the Telegraph Herald in Dubuque, Iowa hired me as a reporter. My beat was Jo Daviess County. I reported on everything from city council meetings, to court cases, to business start-ups. I also wrote personality features and stories about the local history. Often, on my days off, I explored the back roads of the county, purposely getting lost and finding ghost towns, cemeteries and abandoned farms.

Like most people who discover Galena and the surrounding area, I fell in love with it. Like others, I thrill to the natural beauty and history.

More important, I feel comfortable with the people. Because I had lived in both rural and urban settings, I almost immediately felt connected with them. Most people were born and raised in Jo Daviess County, but many moved there from the Chicago metropolitan area.

I also love and respect them. They are smart, friendly, industrious and sometimes contentious. Virtually to a person, they care deeply about their community. Although they sometimes disagree, they manage to pull together and make things happen.

This book is about just a few of these people, their histories and their contributions to what future generations will call "history."

I thank them for sharing their stories with me.

Thanks also to the many historians, amateur and professional alike, who both helped me with my research and let me rely on their work: Daryl Watson, Scott Wolfe, Steve Repp, Susan Gordy, Joann Schultz, Robert Kleckner, Barb Tousey, Terry Miller, Carl "Skip" Schwerdtfeger, Gerald Speer, Jeanette Graves and Lucille Broshous. Thanks also to the staff at the Jo Daviess County Circuit Clerk's Office—Sharon Wand, Joan Lincoln, Sheila Winter, Dawn Speer, Kim Einck and Kathy Phillips. They were always friendly, knowledgable and helpful.

In addition, I want to express my appreciation to my copy editors—my husband Dick Sisco, Maggie Gallivan and Richard Landis—who helped me make this book what I wanted it to be. I am also grateful to my friend and fellow author Jane Guill, who advised me on marketing the book.

Finally, thanks again to Dick, who bailed me out when I had computer problems. He also gave me limitless love and support while I wrote this book and helped me to keep my eye on the practical side of making a book.

Becky Sisco

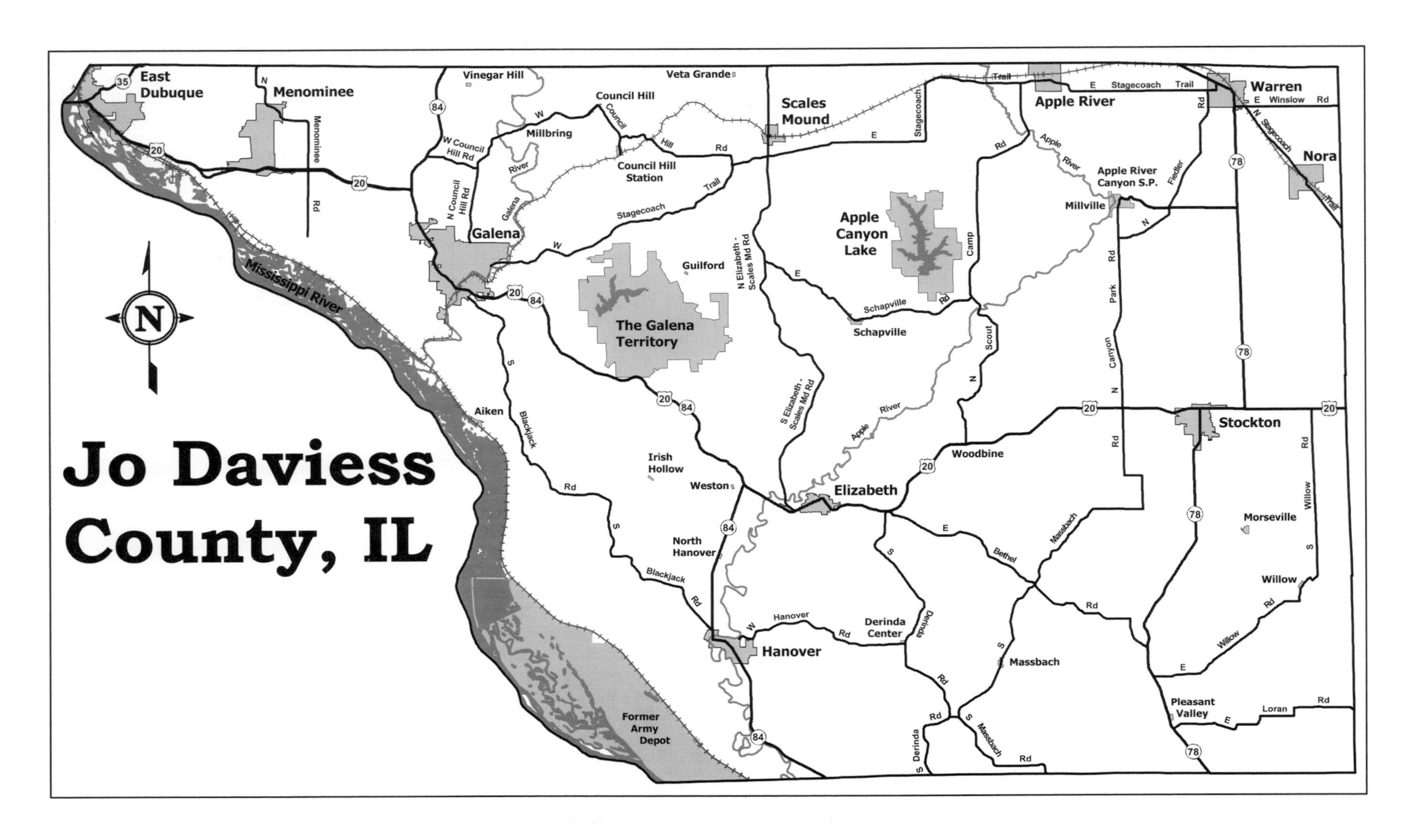

From the Jo Daviess County Highway Department

Famous People

Archie Lieberman

"I really came out here to be changed." *Archie Lieberman*

The year was 1954, and the air was cold enough to make your face hurt. Archie Lieberman had driven out to Jo Daviess County from Evanston, Ill. He met young Bill Hammer at the corner of Stagecoach Trail and Hammer Road. From there, the 12-year-old directed Archie to his parents' farm, where Archie would photograph Bill's older sister, Janet, who had won a national sewing contest.

Archie remembers his first encounter with the boy as though it took place yesterday. "Billy Hammer said to me, 'Do you like to work?' I said, 'Yeah.' He said, 'Good, because that's all we do around here,'" he says with a chuckle.

Archie, who freelanced for such magazines as "Life" and "Look," was on assignment for "This Week" magazine. Although it was only a one-day job, it would change the course of the photographer's life.

"I went down there and made these pictures," he says. "All of a sudden, the food smells and all those farm smells came back to me." During the Depression years, Archie had lived in a farming community.

Archie liked the Hammer family immediately. They were honest, humble and hard working people. They were good people, he says. "There is a comfort quality in being around really good people."

Archie would return to the Hammer farm many times. "I always had to come back here, where the world made sense. I would stay at the home place on the second floor in the spare bedroom, and I would smell the wonderful smells."

While there, he got to thinking about the cyclical nature of things,

"I was making a picture of young Bill, who was walking beside his father on a tractor, and I thought, 'What would happen if I photographed this kid as he grows up, gets married and has a family of his own?'"

Archie then began to work on "Farm Boy," a 20-year project that followed Bill photographically into his early 30s. Archie now considers the book to be one of his best projects, and I can see why.

One of my favorite photos shows Bill and his dad Willis at the kitchen table. Bill, with his T-shirt sleeves rolled up and revealing the emerging muscles of a soon-to-be man, is reaching for an ear of corn. Willis, in a buttoned-up work shirt, is slicing into a stick of butter. Both are grinning, as only two people who have engaged in hard work before sharing a relaxing moment can. When I look at the picture, I see it as a unique moment. Yet, I get the sense that it has repeated itself over and over in farm kitchens across America.

Most of Archie's photos are like that.

Archie always told his photography students to watch for what they see from "the corner of the eye." It is during those unplanned moments, when something grabs your attention and you don't exactly know why, but you take a picture anyway, that you get some of your best shots.

With some photos, you never will know what led you to take it. He points to a shot he took of Bill walking at night with his girlfriend, Dorothy Hickman. "How the hell did I have the sense to make a picture like that and then find it and put it in this book?"

As great a photographer as he is, Archie says, he is not creative. "Only God can create." Photographers are "discoverers," he says.

Archie also advises his students to get to know and understand the lives of their subjects. "What I did with the Hammers is insinuate myself into their lives, which I've always been embarrassed about."

Embarrassed or not, Archie believes one of his greatest achievements was to become so much a part of the Hammers' lives that they hardly gave a thought to his being there. One of his most gratifying moments occurred a few years after Bill married Dorothy and they returned home with their first baby. "Dorothy puts the baby in the crib, and I'm crouching in that little room, and Dorothy says, 'God, this is the first time I've been alone with him.' And I'm in the room hearing that!"

"Archie was always there taking pictures — at weddings and graduations and during planting and harvest time," says Janet. (Janet later married Bill Brickner and now lives in Scales Mound.) "Archie was very easy to have around and very willing to stay in the background. He never had us pose for pictures."

In 1974, the same year the book was published, Archie and his wife Esther bought property in Jo Daviess County. They became permanent residents in 1984.

Many people from the city have moved to Jo Daviess County after falling in love with its beauty and its more relaxed lifestyle, but for Archie it was something more. "I really came out to be changed," he says. "I wanted to become more real, to have what the Hammers had, to have a sense of belonging to the land."

Hammer Road

He says Willis and Bill knew before he did that he would make the county his home. "One time we went into Elizabeth, and they pointed out all these places. 'That's going to be your plumber. That's going to be your barber,' they said. They found this house for me."

The Liebermans live in a big, old farmhouse a mile or so down the road from Schapville. It has been updated and filled with cozy furniture. Surrounded by rolling cornfields and timber, it is Archie's favorite place to be. "I like looking over the barn and fields, where I can see for miles."

Willis and Bill are gone, but Archie and Esther have remained close friends with Janet and her family. "They have been to all our kids' weddings and our grandkids' graduations," Janet says. "The book came out a long time ago, so this wasn't just for the book."

Now in his late 70s, Archie is not so sure he is the person he thought he would become. "I really don't have the goodness of the Hammers," he says.

He says it was "selfish" of him to uproot Esther in order to move to the country. "She gave up a really lovely home in Evanston and friends to come out here. I came out here and gave up nothing. This is what I wanted."

"But I just had to do it," he adds.

Although he might not be the person he thought he would become, Archie has found a sense of place. "I used to say to the Hammers, 'You live in such a beautiful place.' They would say, 'Well, we live here, so we don't really notice.' I am that way now. I live it and I breathe it."

Archie stopped shooting pictures a few years ago. He says he has made every picture he wants to make. Until recently he taught photography at the University of Dubuque in Dubuque, Iowa. "I was a great photographer, and then I became a great teacher," he says.

He also reads, listens to National Public Radio and is catching up on the movies he missed during his busiest years. "I just saw 'The Blues Brothers' the other day."

The photographer says he feels accepted wherever he goes and enjoys chatting with people at the local grocery store. He feels honored to have been invited to join the 330 Club, a gun club in Dubuque, Iowa. "And I like our hospitals and doctors," he says. "I like our post office."

He feels something he never felt in suburban Chicago. "I feel as though Jo Daviess County embraces me."

"I am just an ordinary person with an ordinary life."

Dorothy Hammer

Ever since reading Archie Lieberman's book, "Farm Boy," in the early '90s, I wondered what happened to the Hammer family. Like many people, I wanted to know how the book ended.

Archie's beautiful 1974 book about the Scales Mound farm family touched a chord, partly because I grew up on a farm.

For more than 20 years, Archie traveled to the farm two or three times each year. He photographed Bill Hammer as he grew up and as his mother Mildred marked his height on the barn door. He captured Bill and his dad Willis choring together and in the old farm house.

He also snapped Bill with his first girlfriend, Dorothy Hickman.

Bill eventually married Dorothy, and Archie attended their wedding. Later he followed the young couple as they went into farming with Willis and as they gave birth to three babies.

At the end of the book, Bill and Dorothy were struggling to keep the farm going. Bill had taken a job in town, but farming remained his primary interest.

Bill told Archie: "What I really like about it is when you're alone, like when you spray corn. You're by yourself and you're just constantly looking at a beautiful picture. It isn't the same every day. The trees are blowing different, there's fresh air and the different seasons."

Dorothy said, "On our honeymoon we drove to California. We didn't stay as long as we planned; we came right back here. We do that all the time when we take trips; we can't wait to come back. It's so unreal to be gone. That's the unreal world. We know where life begins and ends here. Life goes on here."

I wanted to see whether Bill and Dorothy were able to hang onto the farm, whether the old farm house still was standing and what became of their three children.

I especially wanted to know more about Dorothy. I liked the honest, open way she expressed herself in the book. I wondered what it was like for her to have Archie hanging around taking pictures during her early married years.

I finally met Dorothy in the summer of 2004. A mutual acquaintance introduced us at the annual Stagecoach Festival in Scales Mound. I liked her the moment I met her. She had a warm, ready smile.

When I told her I would like to interview her for my book, she seemed embarrassed about being singled out. Once, for Archie's book, was enough.

"I am just an ordinary person with an ordinary life," she said.

It took a bit of cajoling, but Dorothy graciously agreed to an interview. A few weeks later, I drove down Hammer Road to the home she and Bill built in 1981. The old farm house is gone — Dorothy said it would have cost as much to fix it up as to build new — but the old barn still stands. Dorothy can see it from her home, which overlooks the valley where Bill was born and raised. She cherishes the picture her aunt painted of the barn, which hangs over her fireplace.

Dorothy Hammer

In many ways, Dorothy was right about having an ordinary life. Like the people she grew up with, she was raised on a farm, graduated from a small high school and married a local farm boy. Together she and Bill raised three children and ran the farm. Now Dorothy works three days a week for an insurance agency.

But there is something special about Dorothy. Partly it is her smile. She said she hates her smile, because she shuts her eyes whenever she smiles. Yet, she cannot help but smile.

She surrounds her home with delphinia, daisies, purple cone flowers, Oriental poppies and holly hock. She generously shares cuttings from her plants with her friends, yet apologizes because she hasn't pulled all the weeds. Along the fence line, hidden between her lilac bushes, she has created "pictures," using assorted objects, including the old mailbox from her and Bill's place.

"I think she is incredible," her daughter, Jayne Kleckler said. "She is one of the strongest people I know. ... She had to find out how to be independent."

Dorothy told me that Bill died in 1990, after struggling with heart disease. She felt lost without him but, with the help of family members and friends, she has made a new life for herself.

"She has had to become a different person because of that," Jayne said.

As though a prelude to what would come, Dorothy told Archie the year she turned 30, "I heard once that one door is never shut that another one isn't opened to you. This is always true. It seems like one phase of your life ends, but another whole new one is always waiting."

Dorothy was in eighth grade and Bill was a sophomore in high school when they went on their first date. He was "cute," Dorothy said. He drove a nice car, was a good basketball player and was a "nice guy."

"He was a little on the wild side, my parents would have said. But I wouldn't have. He drove his car fast and drank a little beer, but nothing bad."

They dated for awhile, then broke up and then got back together again. By that time, Archie had started working on his book. He took his first picture of Dorothy and Bill when they were about 15 and 17, as they leaned over his car, talking.

"Archie was so different," Dorothy said. "I had never known anyone who just took pictures."

In the photo, Dorothy is smiling, with her head turned toward Bill. Her eyes are not completely shut.

"That's one of my favorite pictures." She remembers the day it was taken.

Dorothy said she loved her life with Bill, helping him with the haying and feeding the calves. "We were never without something to do," she said. "To this day I would rather be outside."

They got along well and seldom fought. "The only time Bill and I would have a problem was when we would get our car stuck in the snow while going up the hill. We had to pull it out together, and he always had these signals, which I could never quite figure out. It got so where we would leave the car at the top of the hill."

Jayne said Dorothy and Bill were inseparable. "Their relationship was very important to them, and their relationship came first. You couldn't play one against the other."

The couple's first child, Jim, was born in 1962, and Archie showed up at the hospital. "He followed us when the nurse carried the baby out to the car," Dorothy said. She said she felt a bit flustered. "Here I am with a new baby, and I hadn't been around babies that much."

Judy was born in 1963, and Jayne in 1965. Archie continued his visits, and the years went by.

When Archie's book came out, Jim was 12, the same age as Bill when Archie started his project.

"I think Bill thought it was a lot of hoopla being made about somebody or something that was not that important," Dorothy said. "I think a lot of area people probably thought, 'What's so different about them from anybody else?' And that's what we thought, too."

"Now I think it is a great thing," she added. "It captured a way of life that isn't around too much anymore. ... There are so few family farms left around here."

Now and then readers stop to look for the old farm place. Once a couple from Minnesota dropped by, and Dorothy and Bill spent the afternoon giving them a tour of the area and talking about farming.

Now, when she goes to garage sales, Dorothy looks for copies of "Farm Boy." "I want all the grandchildren to have copies."

Bill and Dorothy Hammer (1960) (photo by and courtesy of Archie Lieberman)

Shortly after the book was published, the couple's financial situation improved. They bought a farm near Schapville, and Archie helped them move. They also rented some land. But they worked hard.

"Maybe that's why Bill died so young—he worked so hard," Dorothy said.

In 1980, at age 39, Bill suffered a heart attack and underwent surgery. "After that, he tried to take it easier. He quit milking and raised beef cattle. He lived on medication."

As happy as Dorothy was to have Bill by her side, the next 10 years were tough. "It was an anxious time for the kids and I. We worried if he wouldn't come back from feeding the cattle at a certain time. I would go out and look for him."

In December of 1990, Bill's health took a turn for the worse, and he was hospitalized. "Christmas day was sad," Dorothy said. "He talked about selling the cows. On the back of a menu we wrote down how many cows we had and what kind of price we should get."

The next day she completed the paperwork for selling the farm.

Twice over the next two days, Bill stopped breathing and was resuscitated. After the first time, Bill told Dorothy, "I'm not worrying about dying anymore. There's nothing to it."

That has given Dorothy comfort.

Bill died at 5:30 p.m., Dec. 27, 1990.

With the help of her son Jim, Dorothy continued farming until the farm was sold. They sold the cattle and hay and auctioned the machinery.

Dorothy got busy. She helped Jim on his own farm—he has three children and runs a dairy operation in Wisconsin—and went to work for her cousin, John Cox, of Galena, who then was a member of the U.S. House of Representatives. She maintained his campaign data base.

"She just stepped in and took over," Cox said. "She is one of the most intelligent high school graduates I know. Dorothy can do anything, in my opinion."

Dorothy also helped raise money for the ball park in Scales Mound. "That filled my time and got me busy and around people," she said.

Dorothy focuses on how her friends and family members were always there for her. "I had a lot of help along the way. People showed up at just the right time."

One of her favorite possessions is a picture of her with her friends and singer Kenny Chesney at the 1994 Dubuque County Fair. It sits on a buffet, along with the picture of her and Bill leaning against Archie's car.

Dorothy has been there for her friends and family members, too. When Judy was diagnosed with Hodgkin's disease, Dorothy helped her and comforted her.

On a moment's notice, she will drop what she is doing to watch her grandchildren, Jayne said.

Dorothy gives her boss, Steve Stadel, much of the credit. "He gives me a lot of flexibility" And she appreciates it.

Jayne likes the fact that Dorothy seldom, if ever, takes a mother-knows-best attitude toward her and her siblings. Rather, she respects their decisions, treats them as individuals and seeks out their opinions.

"All three of us kids have a different relationship with her," she said. "She seems to know us all well enough to know how to be, what to say and what to do."

One thing Dorothy herself has noticed is that, as she gets older, material things become less important to her. In that way she has become more like Bill, she said. "He was content with where he was and what he had."

Famous people at the DeSoto House Hotel

With a river wide enough to handle steamboat traffic and a population of 6,000, Galena in 1850 was, in many ways, the commercial center of Illinois. It needed a big hotel, and that became the DeSoto House Hotel, which opened in 1855. The DeSoto has run ever since, despite the fact that Galena has lost much of its commercial importance.

Many historic figures stayed at the DeSoto, according to Scott Wolfe, hotel historian. Here a few, which he described:

Abraham Lincoln, July 1856: A candidate for presidential elector, he spoke from the DeSoto House balcony in support of John C. Fremont, Republican candidate for president.

Stephen A. Douglas, August 1858: His most memorable of several visits to Galena, this one occurred two days before his debate with Abraham Lincoln in Freeport. He spoke before one of the largest political gatherings ever in Galena.

George B. McClellan, March 1860: This future commander of all Union armies during the Civil War, then was vice-president of the Illinois Central Railroad Co.

Ulysses S. Grant, summer of 1868: A frequent visitor, Grant made the hotel his presidential campaign headquarters during the canvass of 1868.

Tom Thumb (Charles Stratton), March 1877: This diminutive protegee of P.T. Barnum visited Galena on at least five occasions.

"Ulysses Grant deserves better."

Steve Repp

About 80,000 people visit the Ulysses S. Grant Home in Galena each year; that is, the home where Grant lived after the Civil War and before his election to the presidency. Few visit his other home. Few know about his other home.

In 1860, Grant, a military drop-out, would-be farmer, none-too-successful real estate broker and failed candidate for county engineer in St. Louis, moved to town to work in his family's leather business. He, his wife, Julia, and their four children rented a home.

That was in April, just seven months before Abraham Lincoln was elected president and 12 months before the first shots were fired at Fort Sumter, beginning the Civil War.

The home they rented was a two-story brick home on South High Street. It rented for about $100 per year, and Grant made about $60 per month, according to local historian Steve Repp.

Built in 1859, the home was new when the Grants moved in. It hardly has changed since then.

"The Grants saw the same pine boards we're looking at now," Repp says as he shows me around.

The wood moldings are solid but plain. The entrance hall is long and narrow with a simple, open staircase hugging the wall. The parlor and other rooms are cozy, not grand.

Although none of the furniture, drapes, wall paper or rugs are original to the home, they accurately represent the furnishings of Grant's era. Most of the furniture was made between 1850 and 1880, according to Repp, and the owners have selected reproduction colors and patterns for rugs and walls.

Repp, who has studied Grant's life for many years, says he can feel Grant's presence there. He can imagine Grant tousling with his sons after returning home from work and reading to Julia after the children have gone to bed.

He quotes from Julia's autobiography: "After the little ones had retired, our evening was spent by the Captain (Ulysses Grant) reading aloud the papers which were teeming with interest just then, after which he read aloud some interesting book until eleven o'clock, and I was happily employed in sewing for my little ones and listening to that dear voice doing so much to amuse and entertain me."

Because the home has the patina of age, I find it difficult to think of it as new and modern, as it was when the Grants moved in. Grant does not talk about the home in his autobiography, "Personal Memoirs of U.S. Grant." However, it was during his stay there that his second military career began. As soon as the call went out for Union volunteers, he attended a meeting at the Jo Daviess County Court-house in Galena.

Grant wrote: "Although a comparative stranger I was called upon to preside; the sole

Grant's rental home (circa 1880, courtesy of Steve Repp)

reason, possibly, was that I had been in the army and had seen service. With much embarrassment and some prompting I made out to announce the object of the meeting. ... A company was raised and the officers and non-commissioned officers elected before the meeting adjourned. I declined the captaincy before the balloting, but announced that I would aid the company in every way I could and would be found in the service in some position if there should be a war. I never went into our leather store after that, to put up a package or do other business."

Soon Grant arranged to have uniforms made for the company. He drilled the volunteers until they were assigned to a regiment. Soon he himself went off to war.

The home remained a rental home for many years, according to Repp. Now a part-time Galena resident owns it.

Repp stays close to the place, keeping an eye on it for the owners. Often he stops by to make sure everything is in order. When asked, he gives tours of the home.

He likes having that connection with Grant, whom he deeply respects. But some people might say his respect is misplaced.

Historians in a C-SPAN survey recently ranked Grant 33rd best out of 41 presidents. They gave him especially low marks in administrative skills, economic management and "vision." When the Wall Street Journal polled the Federalist Society, society members ranked Grant at 32, just a notch above Richard Nixon. History professors in a 1994 survey conducted by Siena College in Loudonville, N.Y. ranked Grant 38th, or fourth from the bottom.

"He deserves better," Repp says. "I would probably put him between 10 and 15. I am not saying he was the greatest president, but he surely should be in the teens."

Repp notes that the 18th president served during one of the worst times in the nation's history. After the Civil War, the nation was deeply divided. Families were devastated by the war, and the country was in economic turmoil. "Our national problems were more than one president and his administration could solve."

He notes that, despite these problems, the country expanded, reduced the war debt and began to heal under Grant's administration (1869 to 1877). "He brought stability to the country," Repp says.

Many of Grant's descendants also believe that history has given the president a bum rap. When they visited Galena in June of 2000, they said he has been portrayed unfairly as a hard-drinking, cigar-smoking man who accomplished little during his presidency.

Grant's rental home today

"He was a hero, and he was for the people," Julia Grant Castleton said.

Clarissa Emely Gear Hobbs, who volunteered as a nurse during the Civil War, agreed. She said this in a letter to her grandchildren: "Always remember, my grandchildren, that it was the silent General Grant, quietly enduring scorn and calumny of those higher up, who called him drunkard, unfit to command, till in the greatness of his soul, he overcame his surroundings of lies, and the great Lincoln found out all his noble qualities and exclaimed to his cabinet, 'Gentlemen, at last we have a general to lead us,' and he was made commander-in-chief, and quietly and silently he led the 'Union Forces' to complete victory, never showing any self-glory for a moment." Civil

The 1977 edition of the Encyclope-

Steve Repp in Grant's rental home

dia Britannica also came to Grant's defense. It states that the positive aspects of Grant's presidency too often are overlooked amid the scandals surrounding some of his appointees. "Grant supported amnesty for Confederate leaders and protection for Negro civil rights. His veto of a bill to increase the amount of legal tender currency (1874) diminished the currency crisis during the next quarter century."

Besides, says Repp, every administration has scandals, and none of them touched Grant personally.

Repp believes Grant himself was an honest, humble man. "He wasn't one to talk himself up, but knew how to get the job done," he says. "He didn't stand out in a crowd. He was described as being shy, to a certain degree, until you got to know him better. Then people found what an interesting talker he was."

In his book, Grant spoke openly about his failures, as well as his success, during the Civil War. Although he was considered a great strategist, he makes it plain that his strategies did not always work as he had hoped.

He also was amazingly forthcoming about the strengths and weaknesses of the commanders who served under him, as well as the generals he fought against.

Likewise, he did not hesitate to air his grievances with the higher-ups. Before Grant was commissioned to run the show, Major-General H.W. Halleck seemed to be the bane of his existence. Grant wrote that, at one point, Halleck ignored him "as much as if I had been at the most distant point of the territory within my jurisdiction; and although I was in command of all the troops engaged at Shiloh I was not permitted to see one of the reports of General Buell or his subordinates."

I can't help but like the guy for admitting that he was a mediocre student at West Point, that all he wanted to do after graduating was to teach math at the academy (but the Mexican War intervened) and that he was kicked out of the Army. (Halleck had sent orders that did not reach Grant, and when Grant did not comply, Halleck relieved him of duty and placed him under arrest. Within a few days, however, the mess was straightened out.)

It is also touching that, years after winning the Civil War and serving as president, he still seemed embarrassed by an incident that occurred when he was a young man on leave from West Point. According to his autobiography, "the conceit was knocked out" of him after he rode through the streets of his hometown feeling handsome and cocky in his military uniform, and a stable hand imitated him. The man wore a pair of pants the color of Grant's uniform with a white cotton military-like stripe loosely sewn down the side.

According to Repp, Grant did not put much credence in military protocol. Often he wore civilian clothes. "He was like a working man's general," Repp says.

Repp also believes the general was a dedicated family man, to the very end. Even though he was dying of cancer and in severe pain, he completed his autobiography so that his family would have an income after his death.

Finally, Grant was much more interested in peace than war, Repp said.

At the end of his life, the commander-in-chief said this about the Civil War: "...our people have proven themselves to be the most formidable in war of any nationality. But this war was a fearful lesson, and should teach us the necessity of avoiding wars in the future."

"The pendulum will swing the other way."

Terry Miller

Many of the 80,000 people who visit the Grant Home in Galena each year ask about the weird wallpaper in the front entrance hall.

The wallpaper, designed in a marble-block motif, is not original to the house but faithfully represents the 1860s, when the home was built, according to Terry Miller, Illinois Historic Sites coordinator in Galena. But you wouldn't want it in your living room. Much 1860s-type wallpaper was designed with frequently repeating patterns so that small sections could be cut out and easily replaced if damaged, Miller said. This paper was put up during a major renovation that began in 1989.

The rest of the wall coverings and carpets are more tasteful but tend to be appropriately busy, too. The carpet in the parlor is a replica of the carpet that was there during Grant's day and was made on the same loom as the original carpet, according to Miller.

About 90 percent of the furniture belonged to the Grants, including Grant's favorite easy chair, an overstuffed olive green chair that sits in the corner of the library.

The inside feels warm and homey, as it should be, Miller said. He said he is not after a "museum" look.

"I don't know if many people come to Galena just to see Grant's home, because there is so much here," Miller said. "But there seems to be a resurgence of interest in Grant, ever since a PBS (Public Broadcasting System) documentary was done a few years ago. And people are fascinated by the Civil War."

That certainly is true around Galena. In 2002, the Spirits of the Museum, a volunteer group for the Galena/Jo Daviess County Historical Society, re-established the annual Grant Birthday Celebration. The celebration usually involves Civil War encampments, period dance classes and a ball.

Each month, except during the summer, a group of people who call themselves the Civil War Roundtable gets together to discuss the Civil War.

Foyer in Ulysses Grant Home

They learn from each other and sometimes debate.

Likewise, several Civil War re-enactments are staged throughout Jo Daviess County and the surrounding area each summer.

Recently Miller's office commissioned 87-year-old Lily Tolpo, of Stockton, to construct an 8-foot statue of Grant's wife, Julia Dent Grant, to be placed on the lawn of the Grant Home.

Miller is excited about the project. "Only 2 percent of statues erected in the United States are in honor of women," he said. He noted that Dent Grant was the first president's wife to be called "First Lady" and the first one to write an autobiography. He said she was very popular while she was in the White House and hosted a large dinner each week.

Tolpo said it is the first statue of a woman she has made for public view, and she likes Julia. "Julia was short, a bit on the chubby side and cross-eyed," Tolpo said. "She could have had her eyes fixed, but General Grant liked her just the way she was, and that's the way she stayed."

"She was very loyal to her husband and was there on the battle front as much as possible," Tolpo added. "She was not one to put on airs, even though she came from an upper-middle class home."

The statue will face Grant Park, just a block away, where there is a statue of Ulysses Grant.

Sooner or later, Miller hopes to build a $10 to $12 million interpretive center across the street from the Grant home. It would contain a display area, audio-visual center, gift shop, room for artifact storage and a research library. According to Miller, his office has more than 30,000 artifacts and more than 450 books written about Grant.

The building project has some political support, but the state's budget went into crisis mode about three or four years ago, and money for historic sites was cut. Miller had to cut his staff from seven people to four and even reduce museum hours. (He is responsible for the Old Market House, the Washburne House and the General Store as well as the Grant Home.)

However, he feels certain that some money will free up. "The pendulum eventually will swing the other way," he said.

References

Brickner, Janet, interview, 2005.

"C-SPAN Survey of Presidential Leadership," www.americanpresidents.org.

Dimke, Jamie, "A Chronological Timeline of the Life of Ulysses S. Grant," Galena State Historic Sites.

"Federalist Society--The Wall Street Journal Survey on Presidents," www.opinionjournal.com.

Grant, Ulysses Simpson, "Personal Memoirs of U.S. Grant," 1995, Dover Publications, Inc., New York.

Hammer, Dorothy, interviews, 2004.

Hobbs, Clarissa Emely Gear, "Memories of the Civil War: 'I Am Going, Too,'" Galena Historical Society.

Kleckler, Jayne, interview, 2004.

Lieberman, Archie, interviews, 2004.

Lieberman, Archie, "Farm Boy," 1974, Harry N. Abrams, Inc., Publishers, New York.

Miller, Terry, interview, 2005.

Repp, Steve, interviews, 2004 and 2005.

Repp, Steve, "Ulysses S. Grant: The Galena Years," 1994, Steve Repp.

Siena Research Institute of Siena College, "Historians give good grades to Clinton presidency," Jan. 11, 1995 at www.siena.edu.

Telegraph Herald, "President Grant's Descendants Gather at Their Galena Roots," June 10, 2000.

Tolpo, Lily, interview, 2005.

"Ulysses S. Grant," Encyclopedia Britannica, 1977, Helen Hemingway Benton, Publisher, Chicago.

Farming

Tom Arnold

"Now that I've been around a bit, I feel like Dad. This is a great place to be." ***Tom Arnold***

A sign at the end of the long lane leading to Marcella Arnold's home identifies the property as a Century Farm. The land has been in the Arnold family since 1886, when Fred Arnold bought the first 80 acres. Today Marcella's son, Tom, owns the remote farm.

Tom can trace his family's history in Jo Daviess County back four generations to the mid-1800s. Since then, each generation has made different choices under different circumstances, but a strand of adventure, hard work and ingenuity ties them together.

Tom's great, great grandfather, Heinrich Arnold, was born in Germany in 1825. He grew up in a well-to-do family and got a good education. He fell in love with Augusta Schap, a young working-class woman who, as far as Tom and Marcella can tell, worked on the Arnold family's estate. Heinrich wanted to marry Augusta, but her father said no: The class difference was too great. So Heinrich boarded a passenger ship to New York City.

Tom Arnold

Once in the U.S., he staked a claim to an acreage in Guilford Township and headed west to Jo Daviess County. He farmed and saved his money. Then he sent Augusta a ticket to America.

When Augusta arrived in Woodbine, Heinrich was nowhere to be found. He lay in bed sick and unable to travel. Ten days passed before a neighbor happened by, whom Heinrich sent to fetch Augusta.

"Imagine what she must have felt," Marcella says. "She probably thought Heinrich stood her up." Augusta did not understand English. She never did learn how to read or write the language.

The couple had several children. Their eldest son, Fred, was born in 1859. Because Heinrich died in 1866, Fred grew up fatherless and poor. He quickly learned how to take care of himself. He hired himself out to other farmers and, when he got to be a young man, he moved to Idaho to become a miner.

After mining for seven years, Fred came back to Jo Daviess County. He married Mary Emma Durisch and bought the land north of Elizabeth, where Marcella lives. Later he added more land. He and Emma had five children, including Tom's grandfather Arthur. After Mary Emma died, he remarried.

Fred became a local mover and shaker. He raised beef cattle, planted crops, sold milking machines, established a creamery and started a grain elevator. As though that wasn't enough, he got some local investors together and organized the

Woodbine State Bank. (The banking company no longer exists, but the building remains.)

A stock promoter from Iowa had talked about starting a bank, but Fred thought he could do it himself.

"I could not see the idea of paying someone a big stock-selling commission, when it was not necessary; so I decided to do it myself," he told a reporter for the Northwestern Illinois Farm and Industrial Journal in 1930. "I laid the proposition before a few of the boys, and it went over easy."

"He was a kind of wheeler-dealer," Tom says. "The chase was probably more interesting than the money. I heard a story—and I don't know if it's true—that Fred was out sorting cattle one time and lost his wallet. He had $5,000 in it and sent his hired man out to look for it."

In 1916 Fred turned the farm over to Arthur.

Arthur, then 28, was still single and loved to travel. At age 26, he had gone to England and Portugal and then sailed to South America, where he lived for about a year. He learned Spanish along the way and worked in a railroad machine shop in Cordoba, Argentina.

In a letter to his friend, Walter Grube, of Elizabeth, Arthur wrote, "Very near everything is much different than in the states, more like much we hear our people tell of the 'old country.'" He liked the cities and the way the white plaster-covered homes contrasted with the green trees and cactus hedges. He said the people treated him with courtesy and kindness. However, he loathed the mosquitos and could hardly wait for a frost that would "put them out of commission."

After Arthur settled down on the farm, he married his housekeeper, Ruth Roberts, and they had two children, including Tom's father Wayne. Like his father, Arthur raised beef cattle. He traveled out West to buy the cattle and had them shipped to Woodbine by rail. From Woodbine, he would drive them, on foot, to the farm. By all accounts, he was a successful farmer.

But he never lost his wanderlust. In 1950, he persuaded Ruth to travel to Florida and then on to New Mexico.

Arthur was a man who thought he could do just about anything, according to Marcella. While in New Mexico, he underwent hernia surgery. As soon as he was released from the hospital, the story goes, he walked dozens of steps up to his doctor's office to pay his bill.

Arthur never returned to Jo Daviess County. He died in 1951 while in New Mexico.

Marcella believes he wore himself out. "Some of the things he did just weren't realistic."

Before leaving for Florida, Arthur had sold the farm to Wayne. Wayne was only 24 and had just married Marcella in October. He was leery of taking on such a major responsibility, but he believed he should follow his parents' wishes.

This suited Marcella. Marcella had grown up on a farm and had always hoped she would marry a farmer. She wasn't afraid of hard work and she liked being close to nature.

Wayne, too, loved nature and shared with Marcella a deep respect for the land. The two made a good life for themselves composed of hard work and short outings. At one time, they raised beef cattle, had a dairy herd, ran a hog farrow-to-finish operation and grew cash crops.

Meanwhile, the couple raised four children—Tom, Keith, Verlyn and Linda.

Conservation minded, Wayne used contour strips and rotated his crops to retain the nutrients in the soil and to prevent erosion. He renovated the pastures for better beef grazing. He planted seedlings along the stream banks to hold the soil in place. He also kept his cattle out of the timber and tore out noxious vegetation to encourage a diversity of plant life and to help the walnut and oak trees mature.

Wayne was one of the first farmers in the soil and water conservation district to try no-till planting.

Marcella, who was taught to take care of the land, supported Wayne in his efforts. In 1986 the governor named the couple the Conservation Farm Family of the Year.

Wayne was surprised by the award, according to Marcella. "He said, 'We've done this for a long time, and I didn't think anyone noticed.'"

But no one else was surprised.

"I remember in 1988 the Ag Stabilization and Conservation Service mandated that you have a conservation plan," Tom says. "I went in and asked

Jerry Misek (soil conservation service director) what I should do and he said, 'Your dad had a conservation plan in 1952.'"

But Wayne used fertilizers, herbicides and pesticides. Like many farmers during the 1950s and '60s—including my dad—he took pride in helping to feed the world. Using chemicals seemed the best way to increase yields, and farm experts encouraged their use. No one knew just how many problems they could create.

Besides working hard, Wayne and Marcella worked smartly and economically. When they went into dairy farming, Wayne built his own milking parlor. He did so not only to keep the cost down but also because he enjoyed tinkering.

"He was a lot like his dad," Marcella says. "He had these projects and ideas in his head. He always wanted to make things simpler."

One time he built a bunker silo. He embedded hooks into the concrete walls, which were poured while on their sides. Once the cement dried, he chained the hooks to his tractor and pull the walls upright.

Tom says his dad was "creative." "He would see something in a magazine and then modify the idea for himself."

Wayne died of cancer in 1988. Marcella wonders whether the chemicals caused the cancer.

Marcella has stayed on the farm because she likes it there. She likes the peace and quiet in the country, where no one can see what you're doing. She likes the way the Apple River flows peacefully through the property. Her favorite spot is on top of a hill overlooking the river, the bottom land, the collection of red and white farm buildings and the timber beyond.

She doesn't mind living at the end of a rugged, nearly 2-mile lane that sometimes becomes flooded in the spring. "I'm satisfied."

She has remained active, serving on the conservation board and as president of the Jo Daviess County League of Women Voters. I often ran into her at community meetings.

Tom owns the farm now and lives on the next hill over with his wife Jessica and three children—Vanessa, Cody and Andrew. When Wayne became ill, Tom helped out. Later he took over. "I had to make the decision whether to forget farming or jump in. I always had it in the back of my mind that I would come back."

Tom has not always farmed and has not always lived in Jo Daviess County. Like his ancestors, Tom had to try a few other things first. He worked as an electrician, a delivery driver, warehouse manager, apartment manager and musician. He lived in San Diego for eight years, where he was a keyboard player in a top rock band.

But he had always liked being outdoors and fondly remembered the independence he felt while growing up. "Now that I've been around a bit, I feel like Dad. This is a great place to be."

Tom farms the 280 acres that Fred owned, plus another 200 acres Wayne and Marcella bought during the late 1970s. Like his parents, he is doing all he can to preserve the land.

Tom rotates his tillable acres between hay and corn, planting corn only every fifth or sixth year. He limits his corn production to the amount he needs to feed his livestock and does not grow soybeans. He said too much soil erodes from corn and soybean crops. Eventually he hopes to finish his beef cattle on grass and reduce the amount of corn he grows.

He also limits his use of pesticides, herbicides and fertilizers, continues to manage the timber as his father did and participates in the conservation district's stream stabilization program. "I like working with systems and trying to make them work together, like ecological and farm systems."

In addition, he uses no hormones, antibiotics or animal by-products in animal production. He has hogs, beef cattle, turkeys, chickens and sheep.

Like his dad, Tom does things as economically and efficiently as possible. "I always felt if I couldn't make a living on 480 acres, I couldn't make a living on 4,000. But it's a tough life. It's hard to make ends meet."

Last summer I rode along with him as he baled hay with a four-cylinder diesel, 35-year old Massey Ferguson tractor and an old John Deere square baler. Every row or so, he had to stop the tractor, get off, and unplug and adjust the kicker, where the bales were sticking. Then he would start up again. The small, rectangular bales would land willy-nilly into a wagon he pulled behind.

Tom finds it amusing that, as a youngster, he begged his father to get a modern baler that would produce the rectangular-type bales that he makes today. Now his kids want him to buy more up-to-date-equipment to make the large cylindrical bales now seen across the countryside.

Tom says he will buy a new baler sometime soon. But balers are expensive, and he will get along with the old one as long as it still runs.

The farmer has also inherited his father's creativity. His creativity shows itself in the way he markets his products. Instead of growing crops or raising livestock to be sold through the open commodities market, he has his livestock butchered and sells it either directly to consumers or to companies that market to natural-foods stores or restaurants.

He began by selling sides of beef and pork off the farm and advertising in the local newspapers. After customers said that was too much meat, he reduced the amount to 20-pound packages. Later, he heard about a buying club in Chicago which was looking for a meat supplier. He contacted the club, and members started coming out to the farm to buy.

"Then I started thinking, 'The city sounds like the place to do business.'" So, he bought a refrigerated trailer and started delivering his products. About every six weeks he e-mails his 150-plus customers, asking them for orders. Then he fills up his trailer and heads into suburban Chicago. "Every time I go in, I have more customers."

Marcella Arnold

Recently he started selling his chickens to a delicatessen in Pecatonica.

"I juggle the production and the marketing. But I enjoy the mix of being on my own, working with my family and working with the public."

As his children have gotten older, they have been able to help. Eventually, Tom would like them to take over. "I hope I establish enough of a blueprint so that they can take this to the next level."

But he has no idea whether any of them will follow him into agriculture to become the sixth generation of Arnolds to farm in Jo Daviess County.

"It's too early to tell."

"'Direct marketing' is just a neat, fun buzzword."

Cory Cassens

Tom Arnold and his family are unusual in that they live on a traditional family farm and, unlike most of us, know where their food comes from.

The rate at which family farms are disappearing staggers the imagination. In 1840, farmers made up 64 percent of the U.S. labor force. That was at a time when the federal government was selling land out "West," and people like Heinrich Arnold were buying claims to farm land in Jo Daviess County.

Now less than 3 percent of the U.S. working population does farm work, according to the Bureau of Labor Statistics, and many of those do not work on traditional family farms. The bureau expects the number of farm workers to decrease even more—by 15 percent between 2002 and 2112.

In 1910 (the earliest year for which data is available) the U.S. Department of Agriculture counted 235,000 farms in Illinois. The number dropped to 77,000 by 2000. The number of acres in farm production dropped from 31.7 million in 1950 to 27.5 million in 2000. This drop occurred even though the U.S. Department of Agriculture expanded its definition of a farm.

The loss of farmers and farmland is not a particularly new phenomenon, however. The trend began almost as soon as European settlers began arriving in America. Between 1790 and 1850, the percent of the working population engaged in farming dropped from 90 percent to 64 percent.

The decline started with the introduction of labor-saving methods and devices. In 1793, Eli Whitney invented the cotton gin to separate cotton fiber from the cotton seed. The machine could do the work of 50 people. A few years later a Scottish engineer named Andrew Meikle designed the threshing machine to separate grain from a plant's stalks and husks. Later, in 1819, the invention of the iron plow with interchangeable parts made it easier to prepare the soil for planting. And the reaper, patented in 1834, made quicker, easier work of cutting grain.

Meanwhile, people relied more and more on horses to pull the equipment used in planting, cultivating and harvesting crops.

During the Civil War of 1861 to 1865, men left farms in large numbers to join the fight. This created more demand for modern machinery so that, by the time they returned, many men had been replaced by machines like the reaper.

As fewer farmers were needed and the Industrial Revolution went into full swing, many moved to the city and took manufacturing jobs, in some cases producing the very equipment that had taken their place.

In turn, the demand for increased food-production capacity grew. Producers no longer raised livestock and crops just for themselves, their families and local community members, as Heinrich Arnold did. They raised large "cash crops" to be sold through third parties to strangers in large cities, as Fred, Arthur and Wayne Arnold did.

The federal government encouraged education and research to help farmers become more efficient and keep up with demand.

Meanwhile, mechanical improvements continued, and, in the early 1900s, the tractor was developed to the point where it became a practical tool. Arthur was probably the first of the five generations of Arnolds to use a tractor, but he also relied on draught horses.

During the late 1800s, the production of some farm commodities began to outstrip demand—a trend which has affected all or most commodities at some point—and has caused commodity prices to drop. In addition, natural disasters, such as droughts or grasshopper infestations, have taken their toll. With each incident of a price drop or natural disasters, waves of farmers have fled to the city.

The best years for family farmers occurred between about 1910 and 1920, when Fred Arnold sold out to Arthur. An increasing urban population and many European nations, then embroiled in the first World War, needed food, according to the Economic Research Service of the U.S.D.A. Once the war ended, however, European farm production resumed, and the demand for U.S products dipped.

Despite an extensive system of federal price supports, which began in 1924, overall profit margins have narrowed during the past 80 years.

In order to survive, farmers have had to become increasingly efficient and productive. In most cases that has meant narrowing their focus on fewer commodities while increasing production. By the 1950s, when Wayne Arnold bought his dad's farm, producers also were relying on plant hybrids, chemicals and equipment improvements to increase their yields and profitability.

But all the mechanical, chemical and biological technologies—not to mention land—are expensive. Therefore, the profit squeeze has continued. In 1997 farmers received less than half the income in relation to their expenses than they received in 1910, according to the U.S.D.A.'s National Agricultural Statistics Service.

The number of family farms continues to shrink. Vertically integrated companies have taken over much of the poultry, pig and beef cattle production. In 1998, David Diedrich built the first large-scale hog-confinement facility in Jo Daviess County.

"In order for producers to survive, the prices they receive for agricultural products must improve," said Cory Cassens, executive director of the Jo Daviess County Farm Service Agency. "They already have done about as much as they can to reduce the cost of their inputs."

But they probably won't receive higher prices, because consumers don't want to pay more, and the U.S. government doesn't want to reduce farm imports from other countries, he said.

In 1965, after beef prices went south, my dad, the late Joseph Friedman, starting selling life insurance part time and, in 1967, my mother went to work in a toy factory. Later, Dad got a job at John Deere. Little did my parents know that they would be part of a nationwide trend.

According to Cassens, at least one member of most Jo Daviess County farm families works off the farm.

Some farmers, like Tom Arnold, have been trying to buck the grow-bigger-to-survive trend by diversifying their crop production, creating products for niche markets, such as the organic market, and/or marketing their products directly to consumers.

"I have come full circle," Tom said. He noted that, in many ways, he is doing things like his great, great grandfather did them.

He sees specialized, large-scale production as a "race to the bottom" for the lowest prices.

But niche markets are both limited and fickle, according to Cassens. Likewise, the northwestern Illinois climate is good for only so many crops. "For crops, it's corn and soy beans, with forage and small grains."

Yes, producers can earn money through niche or direct marketing, but they cannot make their entire living that way, Cassens said. "'Direct marketing' is just a neat, fun buzzword."

Threshing day (people, date unknown, courtesy of the Galena Public Library Historical Room)

He wishes he could be more optimistic, but he does not see the situation changing. "Everybody wants rural production to be there, but they want farmers to do it on their own and to keep the prices down."

"In this way I am being true to myself."

Daryl Watson

I walked into the Galena History Museum and up the creaking stairs to the office where Executive Director Daryl Watson works. As I poked my head through the door, he looked up and motioned for me to come in and sit down.

While Daryl finished a phone call, I glanced over his desk, stacked with neat piles of folders and photographs. Then I looked around the room, taking in the bookcase, old roll-top desk, file cabinets, chair overflowing with papers and slides, photo-reproduction stand, video equipment and a watercolor of a barn. My eyes finally rested on the slender, middle-aged man. He was wearing wire-rim glasses and a flannel shirt.

Daryl ended his conversation and leaned back. He folded his hands on his desk, and asked mildly, "What can I do for you, Becky?"

As usual, I had come with questions. But not the usual questions, such as: What were the lead miners like? How did the pioneers treat the land? Or, What role did small-town railroad depots play in their communities?

I wanted to know what makes Daryl Watson tick.

Daryl Watson

I have known Daryl since 1993, having interviewed him many times for the Telegraph Herald. Each time, he has fascinated me with stories and insights about the people of Jo Daviess County. He always seemed interested in my own observations, turning my interviews into two-way conversations.

The conversations would flow easily from topic to topic. One moment we could be talking about early farm practices and the next about contemporary American culture. The time always went quickly, and I would want to pick Daryl's brain all day. But there were always deadlines to meet.

Over time, I learned that Daryl grew up on a farm and earned a Ph.D. He lives alone on a small acreage near Apple Canyon River State Park, where he has been restoring the old farmhouse and buildings.

This highly educated man had returned to his agrarian roots and, so it seemed, was living history in both his work life and his personal life.

I wanted to know why.

"I do it for my own satisfaction, and in this way I am being true to myself."

Like all of Daryl's answers, his response led to dozens more questions. But I had to be patient. Daryl isn't one to go on about himself.

Within minutes, he was talking about Greek Revival architecture. Apparently, his farm house contains elements of the style, such as cornice returns. Cornice returns are an embellishment added to the bottom of the triangle formed by the two sides of the roof and the area beneath it. The design element adds just enough ornamentation to place the house a notch above the typical, strictly utilitarian farmhouses of the day.

"Nowhere else in the world did the Greek Revival style evolve as it did in America."

Franklin Blackstone, originally from upstate New York, built the home shortly after 1852. If he was like many migrants from New England and upstate New York, he was fairly well educated and independent minded. Perhaps he did some mining to bring in extra income. ...

So, maybe we should go back to the beginning, like tell me about his childhood.

Daryl is one of seven surviving children His father, George, died when Daryl was 9. "He was a man of few words. He was pretty serious and kept his nose to the grindstone."

Maybe we're getting somewhere.

Daryl's grandfather, George, Sr., was college educated and taught in the public school system. He could name nearly all the constellations. He loved to learn.

"The family was always curious. We were a poor family, but we were rich in education."

"I hated school, by the way. I hated mathematics."

An unsolicited personal remark!

However, like his siblings, Daryl was studious and quiet. Although he hated school, he enjoyed history. When he entered college, he double-majored in history and geography. He did his graduate work in historical geography and earned his way through college with part-time work and teaching assistantships.

So, what is historical geography? And why did he hate school?

"It is how people change a place through time. It has to do with how we humans come to view our environment — our place — and make it ours. It also has to do with the movement of people and the evolution of places.

"Historians often look at people and political events but don't look at their interaction with place."

For instance, people first came to Galena to mine lead. They cut timber for housing and other structures. Some cleared land for farms. The population rapidly grew, and the area bustled with economic activity. However, the cutting and clearing created erosion, which helped cause the Galena River to silt in. Steamboats could no longer get up the river to Galena, so much of the trade activity faded. Between that and the fact that the most easily accessed lead supply was disappearing, many people no longer had a means to support themselves. Galena's population, which was around 14,000 in 1857, dwindled to less than half. (Today it is about 3,500.) By the end of the century, the area had become primarily an agricultural community.

"Not only do we change the land, but it changes us."

This is fascinating stuff — and I long to hear more — but what brought him back to Jo Daviess County?

After earning his Ph.D., Daryl thought he might go into teaching. However, his dissertation advisor knew that Frank Einsweiler, then mayor of Galena, was looking for an administrative assistant/zoning administrator. "I didn't know Frank Einsweiler from a bale of hay."

But Daryl met with Einsweiler and liked his thoughts about historic preservation, so he went to work for the city of Galena. He stayed on for six years.

"It wasn't a bad fit. I was able to do a lot of good work dealing with preservation. But nothing in college teaches you how to deal with the public, how to deal with the press, or how to deal with neighbors who don't get along."

If there is one thing he learned, it was this: "Many people who are wonderful neighbors are anything but that if someone tries to trample on their personal property."

Meanwhile, Daryl volunteered for the Galena/Jo Daviess County Historical Society. In 1987, the society's board hired him as the museum's executive director. His first priority was to improve the society's financial situation. Then it was to build membership.

Now the job entails plenty of interesting work, such as preparing exhibits and talks and finding answers to people's questions about their homes' histories. During the 1990s Daryl helped start an annual "cemetery walk," whereby local actors portray scenes from the lives of people buried in the historic Greenwood Cemetery in Galena. A few years ago, he helped open a blacksmith museum.

But much of what Daryl does centers on fund raising, which doesn't interest him as much. "It's a never-ending process." But every job has its downside, he said.

"If I can help impart to others — particularly young people — a sense of history and its value, then I can feel good about that."

Things are starting to fit together.

Meanwhile, Daryl bought his little farm, which he had known as a child. He lived close by and occasionally helped the owners, Joe and Lillie Battig. The Battigs milked cows and raised crops. They used older equipment but kept the place looking neat and tidy. With its white house and big barns, it fit the image of a traditional family farm.

But by the time Daryl bought it, the farmstead had been abandoned, and the buildings were in terrible shape. Water had seeped into the house, and the basement was filled with mud. Part of the foundation was crumbling, and the floor joists were rotting. "Most people would have lit a match to it or bulldozed it."

Why didn't he?

"A simple little farm house has far more history than you can imagine." He knew that, although the house had been covered with asbestos siding, it was very old and resembled many of the farm houses built in the county — and that meant something to him. It stood for some of the people who made Jo Daviess what it is today and who, in turn, were shaped by the local landscape.

So, doing most of the work himself, Daryl dug out the basement, poured a floor, installed two large beams to shore up the house, doubled some of the joists and re-roofed and rewired the house. He also added a wing and moved a wall.

He described the structure: "It's a two-story upright with a gable end facing the public road and a one-and-one-half story wing that comes out from the side. The wings were always less in height to the central section. The wing has a porch that faces the road. The porch is a uniquely American institution. Also, it was not uncommon for a family to add a second wing later. The style peaked during the 1840s and '50s."

With its simple but somewhat rambling style, the house seems to suit Daryl well.

Daryl also went to work on his barns and other outbuildings. Projects have included roofing; replacing boards, windows and doors; stabilizing foundations; and fixing cracked cement. And, of course, painting. Just as Daryl is about to finish his last major project, his buildings will need another round of painting and repairs. As icing on the cake, Daryl is assembling an old-fashioned windmill.

I had no idea he was so handy.

Daryl feels pleased about returning a large dairy barn to an agricultural use. His brother stores farm machinery there.

He said it is important to save the old barns. They provide familiar landmarks, or reference points. "Somehow, they have become part of the landscape, like old oak trees."

They give people a sense of stability, which comes in part from familiar objects and places. "They give us something we call 'roots,' a way to pay attention to something older than ourselves."

Daryl points out, however, that he does not live his life in the past, nor would he wish to have been born before computers, modern medicine, centralized heat and easy chairs.

On the other hand, he tries to bring some values from the past into his contemporary life. He resists the temptation to become overly busy or spread himself too thin. He doesn't clutter his home with lots of things. "And I will never, ever get any kind of electronic scheduling device."

So why didn't he like school?

"For me, I could learn more back at the farm by creating some new thing to entertain myself. It could be as simple as making a dam in the creek or working on a bicycle. I was perfectly able and capable — particularly with coming from a large family — to accomplish things and find things out on my own."

"Most of the local people were against the lake."

Vern Livesay

Changes in Jo Daviess County have directly affected farmland. During the late 1960s and early 1970s, thousands of acres went out of production and were incorporated into one of two resort communities.

Apple Canyon Lake

The year was 1969, and a quiet man by the name of Harvey Branigar from Medina, Illinois decided to convert 14 farms near Apple River into a resort. His company, the Branigar Organization, would dam Hell's Branch, a stream that fed into the Apple River. That would create a 400-acre, 70-foot deep lake in the middle of the resort.

To many residents in rural Jo Daviess County, the idea seemed absurd. "A lot of people thought it would never work, to have the lake fill up to 70 feet deep," said Sharon Webster, who worked as a secretary to

Branigar's local land salesmen.

Vern Livesay, who had moved to Galena the year before, had never heard of the Branigar Organization. But, on April 3, 1969, before there was a dam and before there was a lake, he became a salesman for the company. "Cows were still grazing on the land."

The resort, which was to be called Apple Canyon Lake, would feature a 9-hole golf course, a club house with a swimming pool, a marina, a trail system, camping facilities and a restaurant, as well as a lake.

Did Livesay ever worry that Branigar would not make good on its promises?

"At first you wondered."

Although most sales and promotion assaults would center on the Chicago metropolitan area, Livesay was to focus his efforts on wealthy people living in Jo Daviess County and Dubuque, Iowa.

At times it was a tough sell. "Most of the local people were against the lake. They said it was going to flood the whole county, affect our rainfall and raise the water table. They came up with all kinds of things."

Branigar was pricing lots at $3,000 to $25,000, depending on the size and location, and that was a lot of money in 1969. The farmers who had sold land for the project thought they were getting a remarkable deal when they received $200 to $300 per acre.

But the economy was good. Livesay sold his first lot to a Dubuque jeweler, and many more sales followed. With up to 30 sales representatives working at a time, all 2,722 lots sold within five years.

"Every Sunday morning at 8 o'clock, we had to report to the office. We had to go out and walk the perimeter of every new lot as it was developed. We had a big tent up, and they would serve us scrambled eggs and pancakes. They would buy 12 dozen eggs and throw them into a cement mixer. Even local people came and had breakfast.

"By the time we sold the last lot, I could tell you how many trees and rocks were on each lot." (Later he established Lakeside Realty to handle property resales.)

There were a few snags. At one point, the Army Corps of Engineers made contractors tear out part of the dam they had built, not because there were problems but because no one from the Corps was present during its construction. Crews worked 24 hours a day to complete the dam by the 1970 New Year.

But Branigar fulfilled most of its promises. The lake filled up, and most of the other amenities soon became realities. Today Apple Canyon Lake is a Mecca for fishing, boating, hiking, golfing and snowmobiling. The lake ranks as one of the cleanest and best fishing spots in the state of Illinois.

At first, most buyers just camped at the lake on weekends. A few built simple A-frame

Apple Canyon Lake, viewed from the South (circa 1972, courtesy of Vern Livesay)

homes.

They raised eyebrows among local residents. "The farmers perceived them as rich snobs from Chicago," Webster said. However, as they attended local church services, shopped in area stores and spent evenings in local pubs, they became accepted.

At first, about 50 new homes were built each year. Then, for many years, the rate slowed to about 10 per year. More recently, it has gone back up, according to Webster, who now owns Lakeside Realty.

Land prices slumped during the 1980s, but now some lots, especially those on the lake, sell at a premium. Recently, one went for $235,000. "If you told the farmers back then that some of their land would go for that, they would think you were out of your mind." But some lots go for as little as $6,000, depending on the size and location.

Now Apple Canyon Lake has about 850 homes, and about 200 owners live there full time. It has become a closely-knit community with book clubs, garden clubs, golf leagues, coffee klatches, exercise groups and even boccie-ball teams.

"I always tell people you can be as active or inactive as you want to be."

Bruce and Arlene Wilke, who bought property during the early years and moved there in 1993, have noticed some changes over the years. "The new people want everything to be like it is in the city," Bruce said.

But living at Apple Canyon Lake still beats city living. "I don't have neighbors close to me. We like the quietness, the lake and the people. The people are friendly."

The resort contains a tangle of roads and dead-end streets interspersed among hills and trees. Even Livesay loses his way, now that he is retired. "The first day I drove to Apple Canyon Lake, I had a hell of a time finding it. Now, 35 years later, I get turned around."

Bill and Mary Jane Reddy

The Galena Territory

After the Branigar Organization succeeded with Apple Canyon Lake, it went to work on The Galena Territory. The first lots went up for sale in 1975.

East of Galena and just off U.S. 20, "The Territory," as people call it, is different from Apple Canyon Lake.

"The emphasis at The Galena Territory was going to be on horseback riding," Livesay said. He sold land at the resort community for about a year before starting Lakeside Realty. "They built a big air conditioned stable, but nobody was interested in horses back then, so they switched the emphasis to golf courses."

Today The Territory's resort core, Eagle Ridge Inn & Spa, boasts three 18-hole golf courses and one 9-hole course. The newest one, The General, features a hole with a 180-foot elevation from the tee box to the green. Green fees run as high as $170.

The Territory contains a lake, but the lake is smaller and commands less attention than the one at Apple Canyon Lake.

Bill Reddy was a chief in the Chicago fire department, and his wife Mary Jane was a full-time homemaker in 1977, when they stumbled across The Territory. While on their way to visit their daughter at college, they saw the now-familiar rock wall and sign at the resort entrance.

"I thought it was an amusement park," Mary Jane said.

After seeing an ad for land in their newspaper, they decided to take a look.

"We liked the hills. We love mountains and we're campers," Bill said. "This was as close as we could get to the mountains and not be in Colorado."

Besides, the Reddys were almost finished paying off their mortgage. They figured they might as well invest $175 per month, an amount equal to their mortgage payment, in land. They bought 1.875 acres and, in 1978, began to build a home.

The couple hired a contractor to put up the frame but did the rest of the work themselves, including the wiring, plumbing, heating, roofing, siding and inside finish work. Their children helped.

Work went slowly, only as time and money allowed. "Mary Jane has a name for the house. She calls it Eventually. Eventually, we will do this or eventually we will do that." Although they have built an addition, they still need to finish the ceiling in the basement.

The home is warm and attractive with a brick fireplace filling one wall. The Reddys can view the wide valley below from their living room window.

Besides working on their house, the Reddys organized several social functions. They became active in the Natural Area Guardians, a local nature group. Mary Jane joined the home extension service, and Bill served on The Territory's architectural review board.

Meanwhile, Bill helped establish a volunteer fire department. At first, the county didn't have a 911 service, and volunteers did not have pagers. "All we had was the siren at the firehouse. Whenever we heard the siren, we would call the other volunteers. Then we would all go to the firehouse and call the sheriff's office to find out where the fire was. I didn't always hear the siren unless the wind was right."

They also got to know area farmers, and Jane started quilting with a group of farm women. Now they are working with other Territory residents to restore an old one-room school house in The Territory.

The Reddys found the area farmers warm and welcoming, but the people who lived in town generally were less accepting. The couple would see bumper stickers that said "I am not a transplant" or "I am a native Galenian." "At first, when we went into town, we didn't say we were from The Galena Territory," Mary Jane said. "We just said we lived in the country."

The Galena Territory

"Everybody looked at us as though we had a lot of money. In our situation, that wasn't the case," Bill said.

"I have to admit that some (Territory residents) seem to have such deep pockets that they don't know what to do with their money," Mary Jane said. She noted how huge some of their homes are.

"People have to build the biggest house they can," Livesay said. "If one person builds a house that's 3,000 square feet, the next has to build one that's 4,000 feet."

Bill said he cannot blame locals for being resentful. "The people who moved out here had a big impact on land values." Prices went up throughout the county, and most residents couldn't afford to buy property.

On the other hand, those who sold land got a good price, Bill said. He also pointed out that many transplants have helped raise substantial money for local charities and improvement projects.

Although Apple Canyon Lake and The Galena Territory were both built as resort communities by the same company, they differ. While owners at Apple Canyon Lake seldom rent out their property, The Galena Territory functions, in part, as a playground for weekend guests. Many homes were built specifically for rental, a week or a day at a time. Eagle Ridge alone lists about 500 homes for rent. The Territory contains 3,270 lots with 2,022 homes.

This has caused friction at times. Full-time residents, which include about 370 households, have complained that weekend guests have thrown rowdy parties and disturbed their otherwise peaceful neighborhoods. But lately, Eagle Ridge and other rental agencies have been cracking down, the Reddys said.

Another difference lies in the fact that the board of Apple Canyon's property-association must take a vote among owners before raising dues or undertaking major projects. But the board at The Territory can take action without such approval.

Recently, The Territory association built a $3 million addition to the club house. The Reddys think that was too much.

There are other problems. The Reddys' feel they are paying double for security—through their association dues and through property taxes. Yet, The Territory is not adequately patrolled, they said.

However, they believe it is a wonderful place to live. Natural beauty and meticulously groomed golf courses surround residences. At night, the stars shine brightly in the dark, country sky. Bluebirds nest in birdhouses that Bill and others have built. Members of the community help each other out.

"We still love it out here," Bill said. "I don't know anywhere else we could go where we would be as happy."

References

Arnold, Arthur, letter to Walter Grube, April 12, 1914.

Arnold, Marcella, interviews, 2004 and 2005.

Arnold, Tom, interviews, 2004 and 2005.

Bellis, Mary, "A History of American Agriculture 1776-1990," www.inventors.about.com.

Cassens, Cory, interview, 2005.

Eagle Ridge & Spa Web site, www.eagleridge.com.

Economic Research Service of the U.S. Department of Agriculture, "U.S. Farm Policy: The First 200 Years," Agricultural Outlook, March 2000.

Houghton Mifflin, "Cotton Gin" in "The Reader's Companion to American History," www.college.hmco.com.

Livesay, Vern, interview, 2006.

NationMaster.com, "Encyclopedia: Threshing Machines," www.nationmaster.com.

National Agricultural Statistics Service of the U.S. Department of Agriculture: "2002 Census of Agriculture - State Data," www.nass.usda.gov.; and "Trends in U.S. Agriculture," www.usda.gov.

Northwestern Illinois Farm and Industrial Journal, "A Big Man in a Small Town," pp. 4 and 5, August, 1930.

Reddy, Bill, interview, 2006

Reddy, Mary Jane, interview, 2006.

U.S. Bureau of Labor Statistics, "Industry at a Glance: Natural resources and mining," www.stats.bls.gov.

Webster, Sharon, interview, 2006.

Wilke, Bruce, interview, 2006.

Commerce

Jeff Graves and Rod Smith

"We did fine, and Irwin's dad did fine." *Aimee Bishop*

Irwin and Aimee Bishop

The couple keeps the lights off, except when there are customers. "We have to watch the expenses," Irwin explained.

Irwin and Aimee took the business over from Irwin's father Orville, who started it in a storefront across the street in 1905. In 1916, Orville built the current store.

"This building will be one of the most up-to-date of its kind in this and surrounding country," the Elizabeth Weekly News reported in March of that year. In April, Orville was "spending a couple of days in Chicago picking out the newest styles in clothing and furnishings."

But the store hasn't changed much during the past nine decades. "About the only thing that has changed is that it is self-service now," Irwin said.

"Years ago, people would come to the counter and give you a list, and the clerk would go around and pick everything up," Aimee said.

For awhile, the couple experimented with providing credit to their customers, but that was a mistake, according to Aimee.

In addition, the Bishops have cut back significantly on the number of grocery items they carry. Most of the store is dedicated to good, sturdy boots and shoes, such as Red Wings and Wolverines; work clothes; casual wear; and housewares.

Last year the couple installed a new green

A young couple, who appeared to be from out of town, walked into the O.M. Bishop Store. "If you need the light on there, put it on," Aimee Bishop told the couple. The pair switched on a florescent light, looked at some boots and then left.

It was a quiet mid-week summer afternoon in Elizabeth. A smattering of shoppers criss-crossed Main Street. A few dropped by the O.M. Bishop Store (also known from the sign over the place as Bishop's Busy Big Store) to pick up such items as a gallon of milk or shoe laces, or to say hello to Aimee and her husband Irwin.

Between customers, Aimee looked for the 16 books of the Bible in a word puzzle.

Bishop's is a long, narrow general store with old wooden floors. Most of the lights hang from round, white glass fixtures, the type you don't see much anymore. A worn Skoal decal on the checkout counter proclaims, "A pinch is all it takes."

awning with white lettering out front.

But you won't see brightly lit, color-coordinated displays at Bishop's. The store is virtually devoid of modern merchandising tricks. Items are stacked on long rows of grocery shelves.

Shelves behind the counter hold photographs of the couple's two sons and their children. One son lives in Decorah, Iowa, and the other in Dubuque. There also is a World War II photo of Irwin in his Army uniform.

The store has been Irwin's life. He has always worked there, except for three years when he was with J.C. Penny and the following three years when he served in the Army. After completing his Army duty, Orville needed him in the store.

"Irwin is 86, and he still wants to come up here every day," Aimee said. "We don't come up on Sunday anymore though. We're here Monday through Saturday. We get here about 9 and go home when we get tired. That's usually about 3:30."

Aimee said she would rather stay home. "But our son says if we ever took Dad out of here, he would never make it."

She needs to help Irwin, on whom the years are taking their toll.

Although the store hasn't changed much, times have. The streets used to be packed on Wednesday and Saturday nights, when the farmers came to town. Farmers would bring in as many as 30 dozen eggs at a time to sell, Aimee said.

During the early years, Orville showed silent movies in the opera house upstairs. The Elizabeth Weekly Press touted the opera house: "A large stage with every convenience will be built in, with the best of heating and lights."

Nearly every week Bishop's featured some type of entertainment, whether silent films or plays. It was the place to be.

The Elizabeth Weekly News announced Jan. 29, 1930, that Bishop's would start showing talking pictures the following summer. "It just didn't pan out," Aimee said. "There already were too many movie houses."

Eventually, Orville removed the stage. Later there were dances and roller skating parties upstairs. "Now it's just storage," Aimee said.

But, all in all, the business provided a decent living, according to Aimee.

"We did fine, and Irwin's dad did fine."

"We work with each other, not against each other." Jeanette Graves

Elizabeth Garage Inc. is more than a car dealership and repair shop. It is a local meeting place. It also serves as a downtown promotion agency and historical archive.

Often customers stay to chat with one of the owners, Jack, Jeanette, Jeff or Jay Graves, as their cars are being repaired. Jeanette offers warm hugs, as well as rides home to people whose cars are in the shop. Occasionally people stop in simply to say hello or, like Daryl Steinhagen, who owns a barbershop across the street, to sell tickets to a fund raiser.

Usually the window in front is covered with

Jeanette and Jack Graves

hand-painted signs or flyers promoting the Spring Fling, Elizabeth Community Fair or some other local event.

Inside the waiting room are framed photographs, news articles and newspaper ads, depicting the shop's history and some of the town's past. If anyone has a question about who was who in or around Elizabeth, they can ask Jeanette.

Irvin Stadel and Jack Graves

The business has been in the Graves family since Jack's dad Les bought into a partnership in 1924. (He became sole owner in 1925.) The previous owner, Howard Vanderheyden, had died suddenly at age 30 of an apparent heart attack.

The 1915 building that houses the garage is much the same, even though fire nearly destroyed it in 1924. Jack's parents replaced the former Mansard-style roof (characterized by high sides and a flat top) with a barrel-shape roof, but the brick exterior remained. Old Buick and Pontiac signs hang out front.

Jack remembers going along with his dad in his wrecker during all hours of the day or night and in all kinds of weather, as Les helped rescue people.

He figures times were a lot tougher then than they have been for him. Les owned the garage throughout the Great Depression. But Les was an easy-going guy, Jack says. "People who knew him and worked around him have said I am exactly like him."

Les gave credit to his customers, and that practice has continued, according to Jeanette. She feels good about being able to help people during tough times, she says.

Les died in 1945 at age 41, when Jack was only 8. Ownership passed to Jack's mother Agnes.

"I have been told that Agnes stayed home only a week after Les died and then said, 'I had better get down and run that business,'" Jeanette says. Agnes operated the business until she died in 1971.

According to Jack, his mother was one of only three women in all of Illinois to manage an auto dealership. "Back then, that was like a person in their 40s trying to get into the White House (when U.S. presidents were older, gray-haired men)."

As Jack grew up, he became involved in the business. When he was a teenager, he and his mother would take the night train into downtown Chicago—to 1024 S. Wabash St., to be exact—to pick up cars. "We would get in about 11 o'clock at night and then drive home. Lots of nights we would come all the way out and never meet a car."

Jack chuckles as he tells the story about a customer who once admonished Agnes for letting "that little fellow" drive a car. "I was 14 at the time. I was short, real short."

Later, Jack became a body man for the garage, but Agnes maintained tight control.

"She didn't let me do anything," Jack says. "I wasn't allowed in the checkbook, but that probably was a good thing."

"She fired and hired," Jeanette adds. "She was tough. She wasn't an easy person to work for, and she really gave it to Jack." Jeanette has worked at the garage for 38 years and spent a few years under Agnes's management.

"But she was good at running the business because people liked her," she says. "She knew a lot of people from around Hanover and Stockton."

She also dealt with some heavy debt. Luckily, several area businesses gave her credit, and she managed to pay off the debt. Jeanette says she was always grateful to the people who helped her.

After Agnes died, Jack, Jeanette, Jack's sister, Jane Specht, and Jane's husband Marlo, became owners. Jane worked at the garage for awhile, and Marlo was county sheriff. Jack pretty much ran things.

In 1984, Jack and Jeanette's sons Jeff and Jay bought the Spechts' half, and the ownership has remained the same ever since. Jack is general manager, Jeanette and Jay are office managers, and Jeff is shop foreman.

Jeanette says she and Jack work well together. "We work with each other, not against each other."

Jeff and Jay's talents and interests are complementary, too. Jeff, who has dark skin and hair, says he has been a "gear head" from early on. "I have always liked cars. I guess I couldn't sing and I couldn't dance," he says.

Jay, who is fair-skinned, enjoys office work. He also sells cars and works part time for the Elizabeth Post Office.

"I would say that Jeff and Jay may be a little more serious than Jack and I," Jeanette says. "They are good little businessmen."

Three of Jack and Jeanette's grandchildren also work for the business—Matt Wand, Mark Wand and Darin Tippett. Jeff's son Cody also is taking an interest in the business and "likes to tinker around," according to Jeanette.

All in all, the business has been good to the Graves, Jeanette said. Once they had to take out a $50,000 mortgage, but they have paid that off. The sale of automobiles and maintenance service remains fairly steady. Customers come and go all day long.

Irvin Stadel has been doing business with the Elizabeth Garage for 57 years. "I bought my first automobile there when I came home from the service in 1948," he says. "It was a two-tone pink Chevrolet with a sloping back. It had a radio. Can you feature that? I had the world by the tail."

Stadel says he likes doing business with the Graves. "Jack treats me real good. The boys do, too," he says.

"Jack don't deal," he explains. "You can go in there and say, 'I've got this other model I'm looking at. What would be the difference?' He gets out the calculator and gives you a price. You either take it or leave it. I like that there is one price, and that's it. I never felt like Jack put the hooks into me."

The service is good, too, according to Stadel. "Jeff, he's a good mechanic. I go down in the morning and say something isn't right. He says, 'Bring it in this afternoon or tomorrow.' Then they take care of it. That means a lot."

It also means something that Stadel has known the Graves for a long time and that they are easy to talk to. "They are kind of like family. So many places you go, they (the business owners) are outsiders. With Jack and Jeanette, they belong to everything. Jack and I are both on the (Apple River) Fort board together."

"I would hate to see the Elizabeth Garage ever close," he adds.

Those are the kinds of comments that give the Graves satisfaction. "Jack's folks would be so proud to see this place continue," Jeanette says. "This business meant everything to them."

A second fire destroyed the Elizabeth Garage in May of 2005, but the Graves are rebuilding on the same spot.

"A large car went over the Grant Highway Thursday." Elizabeth Weekly News

The 1910s, the decade in which the O.M. Bishop Store and Elizabeth Garage were built, was an exciting time for the village of Elizabeth. Business was booming, and work was starting on Highway 5 (now U.S. 20). Automobiles were still new in rural communities like Elizabeth, and they captured people's imagination.

The business boom

Charles Eby, who grew up in Elizabeth, moved away and returned in 1915 for a visit, was so impressed by the changes he saw that he wrote a long piece for the Galena Gazette extolling the town's progress. Here are excerpts from what he wrote:

"Twenty years ago it was utterly impossible for the town to 'pull together' as a whole.

Elizabeth Garage (circa 1915, courtesy of Jack and Jeanette Graves)

If, by any miracle, an improvement did get through, it was—as the now condemned town hall was—upon a cheap foundation built by the cheapest method. Today they all are as one in their faith in Elizabeth, and build for permanency. Witness the two splendid bank structures—one of them unequaled in any town of its size in this section—the waterworks system, well graded streets, cement walks, and the electric light plant now being installed. ...

"Selfishness, snobbishness, envy—all are dying, in fact are just about dead; and their passing along with mudslinging and petty jealousies is making Elizabeth one of the most lovable as well as progressing towns in the country. ...

"I'll not say much about the recent improvements—only those now actually going ahead, most conspicuous of which will be the new garage which has been begun for the firm of Goldthorp & Wilcox. ...

"Bray & Goldworthy's new brick store will also be a conspicuous improvement, as will that of O.M. Bishop's adjoining. ...

"A half-block of Main Street, facing the railroad cut, and toward the depot on Myrtle Street, N.A. Gault is building a large new office and show room for the display of the Dodge car and the Ford, which he sells . ....

"Beautiful houses there are all over town, modern, and set in attractive lawns and gardens, housing contentment, happiness, prosperity ..."

Today Elizabeth is a quiet little town, but most of the storefronts are filled. Some businesses, such as the Elizabeth Market and Elizabeth True Value, cater to the local trade.

Merri Berlage, co-owner of the Elizabeth Market, a typical small-town grocery store, said Elizabeth is just far enough from Dubuque, Iowa and Freeport, Ill. to attract local residents. Locals rely heavily on the market, especially for last-minute items.

"We try to be a small-town store for everyone. But I know that we are a convenience store to a lot of people."

Although a Wal-Mart Super Center opened in January of 2005 in Galena, just 15 miles away, it hasn't cut much into the market's business. "It hit us for a couple of weeks or so. But everybody decided to come back."

She noted that many fairly young people—people in their 30s and 40s—own businesses in downtown Elizabeth and seem to be making a go of it.

A few stores, such as Eshelman Pottery, attract more tourists than locals. "A lot of people drop by as they pass through on Highway 20," said Laurel Eshelman, who co-owns the business with her husband Paul.

The Eshelmans started their pottery business in Elizabeth in 1988 and moved to Main Street in about 1990. Although they sell most of their work at art shows and through their Web site, they are seeing a gradual increase in walk-in business, both from tourists and local residents.

They chose to live and work in Jo Daviess County because property was cheap and the local schools had a good reputation.

"This is a wonderful community, and I love being a part of it," Eshelman said. "People take an interest in each other and support each other."

She also enjoys living in a rural community surrounded by such beauty. And, although Eshelman did not grow up on a farm, she feels she has much in common with local farmers. They know what it is like to be self employed, run a seasonal business, pay for their own health insurance and sometimes struggle to make ends meet.

The Highway

In 1916, Ill.-5, also known as the Grant Memorial Highway, stretched 190 miles from Chicago to East Dubuque, passing through Stockton, Elizabeth and Galena along the way. Then a dirt road, it went past the Elizabeth Garage and the O.M. Bishop Store.

The road was undergoing major improvements, including grading and surfacing. A group called the Grant Highway Improvement Association had formed to "keep up on every day in the year activity in the way of publicity and agitation, and maintain at Rockford an office with a salaried secretary who keeps closely in touch with the people of the communities along the route," according to the Elizabeth Weekly News.

In 1917, the Galena Daily Gazette reported that "the trip from Galena to Freeport and return (about 115 miles round trip) can be easily made in a day." At the time, the Grant Memorial Highway was "only fair" between Galena and Elizabeth but paved between Elizabeth and Stockton.

The Elizabeth Weekly News said plans called for a "model" highway that would be "20 feet in width, paved in brick and built to last a century."

When the road finally came to completion in 1926—construction was delayed during World War I and later because of inadequate funding and weather conditions—it was built of concrete rather than brick. The Weekly News said contractors followed "the most advanced principles of engineering science" and that road builders from around the world were studying the state's building methods.

Later it went into the federal highway system and became U.S. 20.

U.S. 20 and downtown Elizabeth

During construction, Elizabeth-area residents enjoyed watching workers blast rock and operate their large concrete mixers and steam rollers. They also speculated about just which route the road would take west of town.

Of course, the highway didn't last 100 years. Later it was widened to accommodate larger cars.

Now transportation officials and local residents again consider the highway to be inadequate. As early as the 1960s, the Illinois Department of Transportation recommended building a four-lane road between Freeport and East Dubuque. The highway would have passed through northern Jo Daviess County, but the National Environment Policy Act passed in 1969 required extensive study.

Meanwhile, population growth was occurring in the southern half of Jo Daviess County, and plans were scrapped.

In 1991, then-Congressman John Cox, of Galena, obtained $2.1 million in federal funding for a new transportation study.

Soon transportation officials reported that 20, with its hills and curves, was unsafe.

They said the state could either leave the road as it is, improve 20 or build a new four-lane road roughly parallel to it. They sought input from local residents and hired experts to study the potential impacts on air quality, plant and animal life and cultural and historic structures.

Early public meetings often were contentious. Some people accused transportation officials of already having their minds made up. A few weren't so sure the current road wouldn't do.

People cheered at a meeting in February of 1995, when Jane Sample said she wondered whether anyone besides people in the trucking industry would benefit from the four-lane highway.

Many also were concerned about the potential for loss of farmland, reduction of economic activity due to traffic bypassing towns, environmental deterioration and destruction of beautiful scenery.

A group of residents called the Freeway Watch Committee hired its own engineer to study the prospect of widening the existing road. Others asked IDOT to consider a route similar to that proposed during the 1960s.

The study wore on.

Most opposition eventually dropped off, as people concluded that the alternatives would not work or that safety was a legitimate concern. In September of 2001, when Ruth Mercedes Smith, the popular and highly respected president of Highland Community College, died in an auto crash on U.S. 20, opposition virtually ended.

In December of 2004, the transportation department published its final Environmental Impact Statement. It recommended a route known as the Long Hollow Freeway with the South Simmons Mound Variation. Now the Federal Highway Administration must approve the route, and approval seems likely, according to Jon McCormick, project engineer.

But money is a problem. Both the federal and Illinois state governments are strapped for cash and, so far, neither has allocated money for highway construction. Construction will cost an estimated $711 million, which is twice as much as estimated when the study began. A bypass around Galena alone will cost about $150 million, McCormick said.

A group called JDS/4-Lane Highway 20 Association has been lobbying Congress for money. John Cox, who heads the group, thinks it has made a good case. "We are telling representatives that we recognize we need to pay the bill, rather than simply saying, 'Give it to us but don't ask us to pay the cost,'" he said. "But the response in Washington has not been terribly enthusiastic about increasing taxes."

After 14 years, many people wonder whether the road will ever be built. But Cox said his group will succeed by keeping its name in front of Congress.

"I understand that some people—particularly taxpayers in Illinois—are cynical about ever getting the road built during their lifetime, but I am optimistic," Cox said. "Of

Elizabeth Weekly News, Aug. 7, 1930

The road-hog who refuses to keep to the right.

course, I expect to live a long time."

The Automobile

No one took automobile transportation for granted during the 1910s.

Each week the Elizabeth Weekly News reported the number of auto sales at local dealerships. For instance, it reported April 19, 1916: "Despite the rainy April weather we have had this week auto sales have jumped from two last week to five since our last issue. Goldthorpe & Wilcox (the predecessor to the Elizabeth Garage) seem to be in the lead this week selling two, one to Dr. R.E. Logan and the other to Louis Bohnhoff of Schapville. These dealers also sold a Buick to Paul Groesinger. R.E. Dawe sold a 1916 model Studebacher to Henry Hood who resides south of town. N.A. Gault sold a Ford touring car to Louis Miller of Schapville, making in all five cars for one week."

If expensive cars passed through town, that was news. "A large car went over the Grant Highway west last Thursday with a Des Moines pennant fastened on the top," according to the Sept. 8, 1915 edition of the Weekly News. "In fact the past week has witnessed a regular procession of strange automobiles through Elizabeth over the Grant Highway and most of the autos have been high-class touring cars, the expensive kind driven by professional chauffeurs. More fine touring cars have passed through Elizabeth this summer than in the preceding years combined."

Today newspapers report traffic accidents when there are injuries, but in 1916, the Elizabeth Weekly News covered near-accidents. It reported: "As we were walking down to the post-office one day this week we saw something that fairly made us sit up and take notice. It happened in the main business section of the town and in reality was a narrowly averted triple auto collision (at the crossing between Bishop's store and Blewett's hotel)."

Few laws governed drivers. However, as accidents occurred, citizens became more aware of the dangers of driving and began to demand regulation. After the near-miss described above, the newspaper's editors said drivers should be made to "toot their horns and go very slow around such places." They also suggested that "some rule be made" governing how drivers take such corners.

Paul Eshelman

The Weekly News warned its readers about the potential for accidents over the July 4 holiday. It periodically ran cartoons labeled "Drivers we hate to meet."

In 1921, the Illinois General Assembly authorized the Department of Public Works and Buildings to hire a "sufficient number of State Highway Patrol Officers to enforce the provisions of the Motor Vehicle Laws." The following year the Illinois State Police was created.

Of course, traffic continued to increase, both from routine travel and tourism. In 1921, the Grant Highway offered the shortest route between Chicago and Yellowstone National Park.

In July of 1929, the Weekly News estimated that an average of 2,500 vehicles drove through Elizabeth each day. Now that number is about 5,600.

"We are here for the lifestyle."

Ken Winge

No matter how often I drive into downtown Galena, I still take delight in the sight of the old brick buildings with their scrolly, neatly-painted trims. Although there are no neon signs—the city of Galena doesn't allow them—Main Street brims with color and interest.

Ken and Sandy Winge

The first building inside the floodgates, to the right, stands alone. None of its four walls appear to be perpendicular.

The funky old structure houses Galena River Wine and Cheese, a homey, friendly shop stuffed on one side with yummy cheeses from around the world and tasty crackers, dressings and spreads. The front counter beckons with big cookies and homemade caramels.

Chris Ludescher, who participates in local theater, often works behind the counter. He offers a big hello and tells me about his latest play.

The other side of the store features an assortment of wine and beer.

Ken and Sandy Winge own the shop. Like many downtown Galena store owners, they transplanted themselves from the Chicago area. But the Winges have been around long enough now to have seen many changes on Main Street.

Before 1977, the Winges barely knew that Galena existed. Friends of theirs had bought a Victorian home on Bench Street, just part way up the hill from Main, and invited Sandy and Ken out to Galena to help them restore their home. Once the Winges got a taste of Galena, they couldn't get enough of it. They spent several weekends with their friends and, in 1979, bought a home next door.

At first, the couple used their Galena home only on weekends. "After coming out here for two or three years, we said, 'You know, we really love Galena. Why not just move here?'" Ken said. "I was kind of burned out. I had been in the investment business in Chicago."

The couple liked the beauty, history and slower pace of life. But they needed a way to support themselves and their children. They decided to open a shop on Main Street.

"We literally walked the streets with our friends, saying, 'What kind of business does Galena not have?'" Ken said.

Galena did not have a music store or a cheese shop. The Winges decided to open a cheese shop. "I said, 'We can at least eat our mistakes.'"

The Winges and their friends bought the building, which was constructed in the mid 1800s. The Winges used a quarter of the building and called their business the Galena River Cheese Shop.

Neither had managed a retail business, and their shop didn't sit in the best location.

"When we bought the building, we were kind of out in the sticks," Sandy said. "Ours was the only business on this end of Main Street."

Ken estimated that 25 to 30 percent of the downtown storefronts were empty, with about half—including an insurance agency and a plumbing shop—catering to local people. The other half appealed to tourists.

"People said, 'You will never make it.'"

Fortunately, building costs were low. Ken remembers that the DeSoto House, a historic, three story hotel in the heart of downtown, was up for sale for $100,000. "That was the highest number being tossed around for anything. It was like going back to the 1930s, in terms of price."

The couple restored the building and opened the cheese shop June 19, 1982. "We had a lot of pretty slim years," Ken said. "But we decided a long time ago that we are here for the lifestyle, not to make a lot of money."

The Winges were happy. "I remember feeling for the first time that my vote counted," Sandy said. "We could get involved in things."

Sandy acted in her first play and became involved in various arts groups. She and Ken became active in the Galena Area Chamber of Commerce and helped launch "The Galenian," a publication that lists businesses and events in the Galena area. They also volunteered for their church and the Galena/Jo Daviess County Historical Society. Ken even considered running for city council.

"I could walk to work, which was just four blocks away," Sandy said. "If I had time, I would walk along Main Street and talk with all the shop keepers along the way. There was a feeling of openness and friendliness."

On Sundays, they would close at 3 p.m. and play volleyball in the park with their friends.

Eventually, Galena Cellars Winery opened a store across the street, and other businesses followed suit, bringing more activity to the Winges' part of town. Four or five years after opening their shop, the couple expanded their business. In 1990, they took over the entire building and added wine and premium beers. They renamed the store Galena River Wine and Cheese.

Now they enjoy a healthy business.

"Our interest in fine wine and food preceded the Baby Boomers' interest, so we were lucky," Ken said. "We are about five years older than the Baby Boomers, so we have been at the leading edge with bringing in things that appeal to them."

During the 23 years they have been in business, the Winges have seen the mix of downtown businesses change, with about 90 percent now geared toward tourists.

Most of the storefronts are full, but it is much more difficult to own a business than before. In 1980, one could rent a small storefront for as little as $50 a month. Now rents can exceed $1,000 per month, and businesses need to sell more product in order to succeed.

To survive, business owners must be more serious about their business and keep longer hours. Ken remembers people posting signs on their front door that said, "Open by chance or by appointment." "You couldn't do that now. A lot of gift shops, especially on the North end of town, stay open until 8 or 9 o'clock at night."

Once there were many antiques shops, but now gift shops dominate the scene.

The Winges still enjoy their business, but plan to retire within the next couple of years. "There are too many other things we want to do as well," Sandy said.

They have never regretted their decision to leave Chicago and move to Galena.

"We have been very blessed in the way of life this has given us," Sandy said. "We have received everything we needed and sometimes more than we expected."

Peck Building

"I am very sure that Galena will not die on the vine."

Frank Einsweiler

The Peck Building, where Ken and Sandy Winge run Galena River Wine and Cheese, might not exist today if Galena had gone the way of urban renewal, as so many cities and towns did during the 1960s.

It was 1970, and the city had hired a consulting firm to study the downtown district. By that time, Main Street no longer had the number of barber shops, clothing stores and grocery stores it once had. Many of the buildings, most of which were built between 1860 and 1890, were in poor repair. Downtown was dying.

Galena was not getting its share of the local retail dollar, the city's Planning Coordinator Bruce Kriviskey told the city council, according to the Galena Gazette. Although tourists accounted for some downtown sales—they shopped primarily in a few antique stores—local business was much more vital to downtown's future, he said.

Kriviskey warned that, if downtown lost the local trade, "the voids will be filled by cheap rental businesses and develop the Honky-Tonk character of Old Town in Chicago."

Shoppers are "repelled by old looking facilities and dust in display areas," consultant Ron Bussey of Barton/Aschman Associates in Chicago said.

Furthermore, if something did not change soon, the more successful merchants would move to the outskirts of town, consultants said.

The only way to save downtown was to make room for more modern and convenient retail facilities, along with more parking. More locals would shop there, which would bring business back downtown and to the rest of Main Street. New facilities should include a supermarket and a couple of "variety stores," plus a new hotel, they recommended.

That would mean removing 22 of downtown's 181 historic buildings. In 1968, 85 percent of Galena, including the downtown area, had been placed on the National Register of Historic Places. Buildings on each end of Main Street would be removed, and the center of town would become a pedestrian mall.

In addition, low-interest loans and preservation grants would be available to refurbish remaining structures.

Mayor Robert Buehler wholeheartedly endorsed the plan, calling it a "planned program for rehabilitation, restoration and beautification of downtown." It would not only

Downtown Galena, looking to the north

preserve downtown, it would ensure Galena's economic future, he said. He had even bought the old carousel from the Riverview Amusement Park in Chicago and planned to place it on one end of Main to attract people to Main Street.

Without such a plan, downtown would "fall down through deterioration," he said.

Councilman Francis "Dutch" Powers agreed. "Do you want us to leave it like it is?" he said. "I walked the streets the last three weeks, and we have a lot of crummy buildings."

Downtown Galena, looking north

Besides, for every dollar the city would spend, it would receive $3 in federal and state money. How could the city refuse?

But many residents were skeptical. "I am very sure that Galena will not die on the vine," Frank Einsweiler wrote in a letter to the editor of the Galena Gazette. "The kind of Galena that you and some others envision may die on the vine, but the real grand Old Lady herself will be here long after you and I are six feet under."

Others were furious. They liked neither the plan nor the way it came about. Dozens of people signed their names to a full-page ad in the Galena Gazette. "We like it here now," the ad said. "Let's maintain our national importance. People will not come to see where buildings have been. Vacant lots make a poor tax base. Relocate—where? Why did our study change from PRESERVATION to URBAN RENEWAL? Who decided this? FIGHT URBAN RENEWAL."

In March of 1970, John Hilbert, who had worked for the city, started an underground newspaper called "Northwestern Territory." "People have not been impressed by the dark suits and haughty pronouncements of the young inexperienced experts," he wrote.

The solution, he said, was to "take pride in what we have, what no one else has, and, if we are not ashamed of ourselves, we can turn our disadvantages into advantages simply by firmly believing in ourselves and the physical set-up we have here."

That was not all. In a flyer titled "How to kill Galena, Ill." Russell Kirk wrote: "All these lunatic idealogues (Vietnam War protesters) who have got into the habit of blowing up the city hall and the colleges' administration building don't worry me overmuch; probably we'll catch and imprison most of them. Our more efficient vandals are certain people in positions of power and wealth who consider themselves Civic Improvers."

More than 1,000 people signed a petition saying they lacked confidence in Beuhler's leadership.

Meanwhile, Beuhler complained to the Galena Gazette: "You only hear one word from people opposed and that is 'demolition." He also reminded Galenians that the local historic district was designated during his watch.

Although Beuhler faced heavy opposition, he had the city's best interest at heart, according to Jo Ann Turner, who worked for the city from 1968 through 2001. "Mayor Beuhler loved this town," she said. "He loved it because it was so European looking. He loved the hills. He loved everything about it."

She believes the opposition was especially strong because Beuhler, a wealthy businessman who had moved to Galena from metropolitan Chicago, was an "outsider."

In the summer of 1970 a group of citizens petitioned the city council for a referendum. Frank Vincent offered the city a check for $500 to pay for it. (He sold headstones at the Vincent Memorial Shop on Main, in a building that briefly housed the Jo Daviess County Courthouse in the 1800s.)

The city council first dismissed the idea of a referendum, but in a later meeting, agreed to hold the election.

Hilbert was at that meeting. He wrote that "for a few brief moments the mayor was speechless, sitting there twisting his gavel in his surprised hands."

Meanwhile, seeing a need for compromise, the Galena Chamber of Commerce proposed an alternate plan that would take out fewer buildings but still would fall under the federal urban renewal umbrella.

The referendum took place in late September. When asked whether Galena should "preserve and restore downtown by undertaking with state and federal assistance, an urban renewal program...," 1,361 residents voted no, and 340 voted yes. It was a thundering defeat for urban renewal.

For several years, nothing happened, and Beuhler sold the carousel.

"At the time you could have shot a cannon down Main Street and not hit anybody," Turner said.

In 1973, Frank Einsweiler was elected mayor. A retired contractor, who ironically had made a living in new construction (mostly for institutions), Einsweiler was a strong preservationist.

He started making his mark a few years later, after the back of the Coatsworth building at 126 S. Main St. caved in. The building had housed J.R. Grant's leather shop, where Ulysses S. Grant worked before the Civil War.

Although residents had adamantly opposed urban renewal, they pressured Einsweiler to tear the building down. But Einsweiler, who was fond of saying that Galena's future depended on its past, refused.

"I remember saying to him, 'Why don't we just tear it down?'" Turner said. "But he said, 'Jo Ann, the Coatsworth Building is the key to renewing downtown.' I think he thought that, if the building was restored, then people would see what could be done."

Frank Einsweiler (circa 1980, courtesy of the Galena History Museum)

"He was absolutely right," she added.

The Coatsworth was rebuilt and, soon thereafter, the city obtained a grant to help developer Wally Koch restore the DeSoto House Hotel.

"Building after building was restored after that," Turner said. "Of course, it didn't happen overnight."

"I believe Galena would be a lot different if it weren't for Frank Einsweiler," she added. "He always amazed me. He could see so far ahead."

Daryl Watson, who was administrative assistant and zoning administrator from 1978 to 1984, called the period a "turning point." "No one was quite sure if this restoration would continue or if it was just a blip on the screen," he said. But Einsweiler continued to "rattle cages" and look for state and federal grant money.

"And it wasn't just the government," he added. "There were individuals who took it upon themselves to make an improvement."

In 1983, the Galena/Jo Daviess County Convention and Visitors Bureau was formed, which also helped.

Improvements have continued, and property values have risen.

In 1997, the city began a $14 million

downtown-renovation project. It dug up the streets and sidewalks; replaced damaged water and sewer lines; buried electrical cables; re-paved the streets, adding decorative bricks to the sidewalks; built a short, attractive flood wall; and installed new, old-fashioned looking street lights.

"Early on it was a bit overwhelming, trying to get our arms around the whole thing," city Administrator Mark Moran said. For him the tough part was completing the paperwork for issuing bonds. "It doesn't sound like much, but it is a lot of work."

Councilman John Rosenthal complained at a recent city-council-candidate forum that the city spent too much money "dolling up" downtown, while neglecting needed improvements to other city streets.

Many residents agree with him, but others believe the money was well spent.

Tourists love the place. With all the work that has been done and with strict building and sign codes, Main Street remains quaint yet fresh and inviting. It is filled with gift shops, art galleries, restaurants, furniture stores and dress shops.

Galena has become increasingly well known during the past three decades, and now attracts 1.3 million tourists each year from across the Midwest. According to the Galena/ Jo Daviess County Convention and Visitors Bureau, it ranks as Illinois' third highest tourist destination, next to Chicago and Springfield.

From 1983 through 2000, tourism grew substantially each year, said Nancy Breed of the visitors bureau. Then 9/11 and a recession hit. "The growth in numbers has flattened, but we haven't gone backward, as some tourist destinations have," she said.

For many years now, Galena residents have tended to avoid Main Street during weekends, when the tourists arrive. Some complain that downtown offers little in the way of products that meet everyday needs. The last downtown pharmacy closed in the spring of 2000. They also say it still is too difficult to find a parking spot.

Most of them shop at the west end of town, where there is a supermarket, a hardware store and, as of 2005, a Wal-Mart Super Center. Yet, they recognize that the local economy depends upon tourism.

Downtown merchants often complain that business is slow, especially from January through March, and that rents are too high. But shop owners have carved out their own niche by offering products and services that are unique to the rest of downtown. They also get a boost from local business and civic organizations that offer a wide variety of events and activities that appeal to both residents and tourists. Most shop owners seem to make a respectable living.

Meanwhile, competition runs high across the United States for tourism dollars. As Councilman Dan O'Keefe said, "Suddenly every town has become a 'historic town.'"

Most towns, however, pale in comparison with Galena, when it comes to their historic character. Unlike other towns, Galena does not need to fake history, Illinois' Galena Historic Site Manager Terry Miller said. "This is the real deal."

Primary businesses in downtown Galena

1900	1940	1970	2004
16 grocery stores	9 law offices	16 antique stores	25 gift shops
15 law offices	8 grocery stores	11 taverns	20 restaurants
11 clothing stores	8 taverns	7 real estate/insurance	16 clothing stores
10 taverns	8 restaurants	6 beauty salons	11 antique stores
9 barbers	5 department stores	4 law offices	10 art galleries
7 hardware stores	4 medical practices	4 clothing stores	9 real estate/insurance
6 medical practices	4 shoe stores	4 restaurants	8 bed and breakfast inns
5 saddlery shops	4 dry cleaners	3 barbers	5 taverns
5 hotels	4 clothing stores	3 drug stores	5 civic/fraternal groups
5 shoe stores	3 hotels	3 art dealers	4 law offices

References

Berlage, Merri, interview, 2005.
Bishop, Aimee, interviews, 2003 and 2004.
Bishop, Irwin, Interviews, 2003 and 2004.
Breed, Nancy, interview, 2005.
Cox, John, interview, 2005.
"Dubuque Area, Iowa," Dec. 2004, Polk City Directories, Livonia, Mich.
Elizabeth Weekly News: "Auto Sales Report," June 23, 1915, and Sept. 8, 1915; "Auto Sales Increase," April 19, 1916; "For a Nice Auto Journey," July 16, 1917; "Grant Highway Traffic Will Show Increase," May 21, 1921; "Elizabeth Residents Watch Road Work Sunday Afternoon," Feb. 13, 1925; "Howard Vanderheyden Dropped Dead," March 5, 1924; "Paving Work Progressing Rapidly," July 16, 1924; "Over Million Cars Registered in Illinois," July 23, 1924; "At Last!" Aug. 27, 1924; "Illinois Makes Highway History," Oct. 22, 1924; "Elizabeth Garage Burns Early Sunday Morning," Dec. 31, 1924; "Dissolved Partnership," Dec. 16, 1925; "Illinois Highways in 1925," Jan. 6, 1926; "To Install Talking Pictures," Jan. 29, 1930; "July 4 Dangerous Day," July 4, 1929; "War on One-Eyed Autos Declared," July 9, 1930; "Are You an Experienced Driver," Sept. 4, 1929; "The Auto Output," Oct. 2, 1929; "Drivers You Hate to Meet," Aug. 27, 1930.
Eshelman, Laurel, interview, 2005.
Galena Gazette: "Build New to Preserve Old," May 22, 1969; "Economist Predicts 'Improve or Die,'" Oct. 2, 1969; "Feasibility Survey Outlines City's Needs," Oct. 9, 1969; advertisement, Oct. 16, 1969; "Tempers Flare at Urban Renewal Meeting," Oct. 23, 1969; "Preservation of Downtown Galena: A Synopsis of the Urban Renewal Feasibility Study," Feb. 19, 1970; "Councilmen Vote To Continue Planning," Feb. 26, 1970; Letters to the Editor, March 19, 1970; "Schedule Referendum on Two Issues," Aug. 27, 1970; "Chamber Endorses Renewal Program," Sept. 17, 1970; "Urban Renewal Proposal Rejected By Voters," Oct. 1, 1970.
Illinois State Police Web site, www.isp.state.il.us.
Kirk, Russell, "How to kill Galena, Ill.," reprinted from unknown source, date unknown.
McCormick, Jon, interview, 2005.
Miller, Terry, interview, 2005.
Moran, Mark, interview, 2005.
Northwestern Territory: "Council Agrees Give It to the People," 1970; and "Hatchet Job," 1970.
O'Keefe, Dan, Galena Mayoral Candidate Forum, March 29, 2005.
Repp, Stephen, "Seventy Years on Main Street: A Business Directory of Galena, Illinois 1900 - 1970," 1989.
Rosenthal, John, Galena Mayoral Candidate Forum, March 29, 2005.
Telegraph Herald: "Road group seeks more information," June 15, 1994; "Groups to air U.S. 20 concerns," Aug. 25, 1994; "Officials seek residents' help on 4-lane U.S. 20 plan," Aug. 26, 1994; "U.S. 20 survey offered," Dec. 1, 1994; "Group pushes to save U.S. 20," Dec. 13, 1994; "Survey: Safety key on U.S. 20," Jan. 28, 1996; "U.S. 20 Scheme criticized," Feb. 24, 1995; "U.S. 20 study eyes 'cultural landscape,'" Feb. 27, 1995; "U.S. 20 meeting erupts," May 24, 1995; "U.S. 20 proponents drive for funds," June 7, 1995; "Group initiates drive for 4-lane road," May 22, 1999; "Highland Community College president dies," Sept. 7, 2001.
Watson, Daryl and James Clark, "A Timeline of Galena History," www.galenahistorymuseum.org.
Turner, Jo Ann, interview, 2005.
Watson, Daryl, interview, 2005.
Winge, Ken, interview, 2005.
Winge, Sandy, interview, 2005.

Hospitality

the late Tom Bruun

"I'm always here, except when I'm gone."

Tom Bruun *

Tom Bruun takes life as it comes.

"Nothing is really scheduled," he says. "Things happen as they happen around here."

Like the hog roast that happens once or twice a year at Council Hill Station.

"I butchered a 200-pound pig and had a hog roast a week ago Sunday," he says. "I never took a head count, but I imagine seventy-five to a hundred people showed up."

When Bruun butchers a hog, word spreads among his friends and neighbors. "It was just a fine get-together," he says. "I had only one zip-lock bag of pork left."

Most days somebody or other drops in—a tourist who is looking for an antique, is just curious or has gotten lost, or a neighbor or friend who needs something fixed or just wants to shoot the breeze.

Usually you can find Bruun somewhere around the place. He might be out back in a shed fixing an old ringer-type washer or the like, mowing hay, tending his garden, baking biscuits from scratch or sitting in his bent-wood rocker in the old Council Hill General Store. "I'm always here except when I'm gone," he says.

Bruun has been divorced for several years. His daughters are grown up and gone, so he "batches it," like he did before he was married. He was born and raised in the area and, at one time, owned a farm three miles away as the crow flies.

Whether or not he is around, people are welcome to stop by, have a candy bar or bottle of pop and take a load off.

"There's a kind of honor system here," says Roger Blum, who drops in on a rainy summer afternoon. "If you take a can of pop, you leave some money on the counter."

Among the other drop-ins throughout the afternoon are Lyle Skaggs, Mark Rosenthal and Bard Harmond. Rosenthal grabs a can of orange juice and lights up a cigarette. He says little and doesn't stay long. The other men's conversation roams idly from one topic to the next—the snowstorm of 1947, the tourists who have stopped by over the years, horses, chiropractic and the Amish, whose simple lifestyle Bruun deeply respects.

"Sometimes we even get into politics," Bruun says.

One of Bruun's four rat terriers, Shorty, scratches at the door. "You're the closest to the door, Roger," Bruun says. "I think he's trying to tell us something."

Blum gets up and opens the door. The frisky black-and-white dog shakes himself off, skips around the room and then settles at Bruun's feet.

That's the other thing about hanging out at the general store. Bruun doesn't expect visitors—especially the ones he knows best—to act like pampered guests. Sometimes they help him with his repairs or chop wood for his wood-burning stove. "If they're going to sit around and soak up some of the heat, they've got to help with some of the wood," he says.

But they don't mind. "You know that old saying, 'He'd give you the shirt off his back'?" Skaggs says. "Well, I think Tom would do that."

The conversation turns to little games the men have learned over the years, mostly in bars. Bruun pulls out some nails and tries to stack six of them in a certain way. "A carpenter one day showed me that."

Next, he sets two empty pop cans on top of a table, one sitting upright on the left and one on its side on the right. Then he puts one can on the floor beneath the upright can, placing it on its side, and sets another one upright on the floor beneath the one that's on its side. He asks me whether I think the distance between the tops of each of the pairs of cans is the same.

** Bruun died in 2005 at age 64. His daughters, Terri Bennett and Becky McGlynn, have taken over the store.*

I look up and down, from one can to the other, getting into the game and forgetting my role as an observer. "No," I finally say. "There is more distance between the tops of the two on the left."

"How can that be?" the men say, goading me on. "Look, in both cases, one is on its side and one is standing up straight."

I look again, wondering if I really am right. I think so, so I rip a sheet from my notepad and make a little drawing to prove my point.

"Boy, you must really be smart," one of the guys says. "No one has ever gotten that one before."

I laugh, figuring they are messing with my head.

"You never know what you'll run into around here, what will transpire," Bruun says.

Tom Bruun

Time passes. The rain stops and starts again. A train approaches, passing about 15 yards from the store. Its whistle blows, and the bells at the railroad crossing clang. Council Hill Station started up in 1854, after the Illinois Central Railroad laid tracks through Jo Daviess County. There was a stockyard, a church, a school, a cheese factory and several houses. Now all that is left is Bruun's store, his sheds and a newer home built next door.

The setting is just right for the meandering conversation and idle games.

The old general store hasn't changed much since Bruun bought it, and it was empty for 20 years before that. The wainscoted ceiling and walls are still painted creamy yellow and leaf green, the colors of the Clover Farm Store, which it once was. But the paint has faded and peeled.

"I've talked about repainting it," Bruun says. "But everybody says, 'Just leave it the way it is.' They say you can see new buildings anywhere."

That makes Bruun feel good. He likes preserving a bit of history and sharing it with neighbors and strangers. "I get some grandparents who come in and say it looks just like it did when they was kids," he says. "Once it's gone, it's gone."

It represents a time when people knew the real meaning of work and didn't think they needed so many things, he says, as the Amish are to this day. "They are happier with less. They're not trying to keep up with the Joneses. They live a simple life."

"I don't need a four-wheeler, a motorcycle, camper or mobile home. I don't have an air conditioner, and I still heat with wood."

He chuckles as he tells about the customer who called one time and asked him to fax something. He doesn't own a fax machine and probably never will. "I do have a telephone and a television though. I'm not going to say I'm a hermit."

The store contains an assortment of old stuff—a roll top desk, a working wood stove, some old light fixtures, photos of Council Hill Station, which were printed from some old glass negatives, old ledgers from the store, stacks of papers and books. A clock that was original to the store still runs. In addition, there are a few contemporary T-shirts and caps, which Bruun sells.

The area around the store is strewn with everything from rusted railroad cars to a pile of tree trunks. Bruun shows me the stuff in his shed—a sleigh, some harnesses, a wine press, an old cook stove, etc.— some things he is fixing and some he will get around to fixing someday, or sell as is if anybody wants it.

"I'm kind of known as a pack rat."

"I'm going to go get something, and you tell me what it is," he says, inspired. Soon he returns with something made of worn leather. I shrug my shoulders, as expected.

"This is a goat harness! You've got to drive down the road quite a ways before you'll find another goat harness."

"If somebody comes through and wants it, I'll probably sell it."

As supper time approaches, everyone heads for home, leaving Bruun to tinker with his antiques and settle in for the evening. Maybe some of his buddies will be back tomorrow, maybe not. Either way, Bruun will be content.

"What is here seems far more real."

Bill Barrick

A narrow gravel road takes you to the Inn at Irish Hollow. The inn is outside of shouting distance from any neighbors, in the middle of what one might call "nowhere."

Many world-weary travelers have retreated down the narrow path to be held in the warm embrace of the inn. Owners Bill Barrick and Tony Kemp extend the same hospitality they believe Nina Semrow showered on her customer-guests many years ago when it was the general store and the neighborhood gathering place.

As one crosses the threshold into the old general store/inn, you begin to feel the cares of the 21st Century slip away.

The store looks much as it always did. There are shelves filled with fruit jars, books, tin containers, old Coca Cola bottles and candy that is sold by the pound. The old mail boxes — the store served as the local post office — sit atop the old counter, with the names of some of the local postal patrons still visible, along with an old-time coffee mill and an arcane cash register adorned with swoops and swirls of brass. A set of dish towels, hand-embroidered with "church on Sunday," "wash on Monday," "iron on Tuesday," etc., hangs from a rack in the back of the store. Hand-painted letters on the large front windows still advertise "General Merchandise" and "Groceries, Tobacco."

The sound of soft classical music and the smell of cranberry muffins baking waft in from the kitchen in back. Years ago the sound of trains passing and the smell of livestock from the busy stockyard across the road would have filled the general store. But the tracks were torn out during the late 1960s, and the stockyard is long gone.

Soon Bill and Tony appear, both wearing butcher's aprons tied neatly over jeans and casual

Inn at Irish Hollow

shirts. They proffer warm handshakes and welcoming smiles. Return guests receive hearty, warm hugs.

Tony and Bill bought the general store in 1989. Built about 1880, it has living quarters in back and above.

"We walked in here and said, 'This is it,'" Tony said.

"There has always been a warm feeling here," Bill said. "It feels like this place was always a happy place."

"It is peaceful and restful," Tony said."I believe a residue of energy can be left in a building. The energy here was a calming, determined and focused energy."

The two, who are domestic partners as well as business partners, then lived in Chicago, where they sometimes struggled with the frenetic pace of life. Tony worked for the Chicago Hilton and Towers and had just been given a promotion and a raise. "I got the worst feeling inside," he said. "I thought, 'They are going to own me.'"

Bill was a casting director for a movie production company. "I hated the film business."

They had driven to Jo Daviess for a weekend getaway. They were so captivated by the red barns and hilly countryside that, although they had never considered living in the country, they began to look for property the following day. In order to make a living in their newly-discovered haven, they would operate a bed and breakfast inn. After looking at as many as 50 properties, both in Galena and in the countryside, they bought the general store.

Although the building felt right and they never doubted their decision to buy it, Bill and Tony knew they had plenty of work to do and that they were going against the odds.

"We came out here with zero dollars," Tony said. Besides having no money, they were only in their middle 20s and had no financial backing.

"We didn't question it, but everybody else did," Tony said.

"We weren't taken very seriously initially." Bill added. "Country inns really weren't being done at the time."

They began to renovate the building, with an eye toward retaining its character while making it comfortable for today's guests. Virtually nothing had been changed since 1936, when Nina's husband died, so the couple had to redo the plumbing and wiring. They added seven bathrooms and painted and decorated.

Besides renovating the old general store, the couple has built three stone cottages on the hill behind the store. Decorated with natural materials in warm colors, they feel as cozy as the inn. But they are spacious with 21st Century conveniences.

Bill Barrick and Tony Kemp

"We needed to reconfigure everything while retaining the essence of how it was." Bill said.

They also thought a lot about what they liked about various places they stayed and what people visiting the Galena area would like. They designed an inn and, while doing so, recreated themselves, they said.

Although they have had some tough years, they have managed to build a successful business in the middle of nowhere.

"One thing we did have was a lot of determination," Tony said.

"We both tend to be designers and creators," Bill said.

Now they see Jo Daviess County as a land of opportunity and the inn as a place for personal reflection and growth.

"There is so much opportunity to create yourself around here," Tony said. "Here I can get inside myself and allow what truly is inside of me to come out. I can find clarity and see something actually being created."

Bill agreed. "What's here seems far more real," he said. "My perception is that it is easier to find what's really you when your environment seems more real."

Tony and Bill pick berries from the land surrounding the inn and make their own syrup and preserves. They like to cook with natural ingredients, focusing on those that are in season. They believe such fresh ingredients not only are more nourishing but also help give them and their guests a closer connection to the land.

"We live in a perfect four-seasons area." Bill explained.

As inn keepers, they want their guests to experience the same peace, warmth and quiet reality that has helped them sort out their own thoughts and feelings and to "create" themselves.

"We want it to be elegant,yet comfortable," Tony said.

Bill said they provide world-class service without being ostentatious.

"I get the feeling of being taken care of in a very elegant way," said Val Gee, a guest from Chicago. She described a gourmet picnic lunch that Tony and Bill had packed for them. "We were sitting on the porch watching the birds and taking one thing out of the basket after another."

"It is like coming home—to a family atmosphere," Val's husband Jeff said. "There is an amazing peace and tranquility here."

During a previous visit, the Gees developed the idea for a book they eventually wrote, called "Super Service: Seven Keys to Delivering Great Customer Service ... Even When You Don't Feel Like It! ... Even When They Don't Deserve It!"

The inn provided both the tranquility the couple needed to develop the idea and the kind of service they wanted to describe in their book. "The book probably would not have happened if we hadn't been here," Jeff said.

That is exactly the kind of experience Tony and Bill want their customers to have. "This is not about us," Tony said. "Once people get here, it is about them and their comfort."

"I was always running away to my little house."

Sharon Fallbacher

World War II had just ended and Sharon Fallbacher was four years old when her family moved from their small white home in the town of Highwood, Ill. to Chicago. She was not happy with the move.

Once she entered kindergarten, she frequently ran away from school. "They would lock me in the boiler room at school, because that's the only way they could keep me from running away," she said, as we sat at her kitchen table. "I was always running away to my little house."

This went on for about two years. "Then they told me about Suzanne Degnan, who was cut up and different parts of her were thrown in the sewer." Six-year-old Suzanne Degnan was killed Jan. 6, 1946. A college student, William Heirens, was convicted of the murder.

"That's what they had to do to get me to stop," she said.

For just an instant, as she described her experience, Sharon seemed sad and vulnerable. But she usually seems anything but that. Tall with broad shoulders, a husky laugh and no shortage of opinions, she is a woman who seems to take her life straight up.

I believed her when she said house and home have been important to her, ever since her family left the small town of Highwood. She and her late husband John renovated two homes in suburban Chicago. After discovering Galena—while looking for antiques and collectibles—they bought an 1842 miner's cottage and renovated it, too.

Later, when the house they referred to as "the big yellow house on Park Avenue" came up for sale, they bought it and immediately went to work on it. They took possession around Christmas of 1988 and had the 14-room house torn up by February.

They remodeled six bathrooms, replaced two furnaces, installed central air conditioning, replaced 57 windows, stripped 17 doors, installed 52 electrical outlets, had two chimneys rebuilt, had the roof replaced, had the kitchen remodeled, replaced the carpeting and other floor coverings throughout the house and hung 231 rolls of wallpaper.

John had to jack up parts of the house and pour new footings. "He spent months on his back digging holes to pour the cement."

Sharon Fallbacher

Meanwhile, they bought the old elevator doors from the Marquette Building in Chicago and then had the 400-pound souvenirs sand blasted and painted. John built an octagon-shaped pad, and the doors became the walls of a gazebo. He also built a roof for it, making sure it exactly matched the pitch of the roof on the house.

In addition, John built 16 shelves for the kitchen, where Sharon could display her large collection of Department 56 village pieces, including more than 200 houses and all the accessories that go with the set. The kitchen, with her little houses, is her favorite room in the mansion.

"I am fascinated with little houses." As a child, she read "The Little House" many times. Now she keeps a copy in each guest room.

Many unexpected expenses came up, but the Fallbachers met them with what became their mantra: "As long as we're this far in debt, we might as well ...'"

In 1989 they opened their home as a bed and breakfast inn and called it the Park Avenue Guest House. Things didn't exactly get off to a smooth start. "The week we opened, the sewer backed up into the basement, and I had a houseful of people."

But soon the couple worked the kinks out. Sharon has enjoyed both the home and being an inn keeper.

"I get to decorate, which I love." She has redone many of the rooms a second time. Recently she had an oak floor with inlay installed in the formal dining room and furnished it with mission oak furniture. And, of course, she tore off the wallpaper and replaced it with new.

"Now I have a reason to make 50 sets of place mats and to have every color of Fiestaware there is."

But Sharon's love for her place goes beyond the house. It reaches back to the people who built it.

While she and John were renovating the house, she often went to the Galena Public Library for a break. "It was warm, and they had bathrooms," she said.

While there, she began looking into the

Park Avenue Guest House

history of the house. She learned that James H. and Lucille Pratt Sampson first owned her property. First, they built a house next door. Later their son, Bias, and his wife Annie Greene Sampson built Sharon's house.

She read about the Sampsons and traced them to two living descendants, a granddaughter of Bias and the granddaughter's son. She gets a kick out of the fact that people referred to Bias as a "philanderer." And she finds it interesting that Bias died on the same day her mother was born.

Sharon said she does not know much about her own family history, so she "adopted" the Sampsons.

Her enthusiasm also carries forward to the people who later owned and rented the home, to her guests and to the friends she has made in Galena.

From 1916 until sometime during the 1980s, it was rental property. Sharon met many of the people who have lived there and has enjoyed their stories.

"Dave Philips and his family lived here," she said. "He set the place on fire."

That's true, Dave said. "I was only two years old. We were playing with matches and caught the bed on fire."

Dave said he doesn't remember much about living in the house, but he does remember the spanking he received after the fire.

"And now I'm a captain on the Galena Volunteer Fire Department! John always got a charge out of that," he said.

"After 17 years, people still ring the doorbell and say they used to live here," Sharon said.

Although Sharon sometimes becomes frustrated with local politics and property taxes—she makes no bones about it—she loves her little community.

"I feel safe and secure," she said. "I know so many people. With my being a widow, they watch out for me."

People of all ages and incomes live in her neighborhood, which she likes. It is different from her former neighborhood in Arlington Heights, Ill., where "everybody was the same age, had 2.1 children and planted the same trees."

After John died in 2000, many people asked her whether she would move back to the Chicago area. Her answer: "No."

"I have two lifestyles going on here."

Wendy Heiken

On Friday afternoons, when most of her guests arrive, Wendy Heiken appears at the front door in a full, floor-length dress, which is high at the neck and nipped at the waist. A hoop skirt spreads into a large circle around her laced-up shoes.

Wendy's dress reflects what she believes to be a more genteel time, when people knew how to be gracious and when multi-tasking wasn't a virtue.

Often she leads her guests into the parlor, where she serves them tea and relaxes them into the spirit of the late Nineteenth Century. When the weather is hot, she takes them on the veranda for lemonade or champagne.

Wendy owns a bed and breakfast inn called Annie Wiggins. She is in her seventh year as an inn keeper in Galena. The inn she operates has seven guest rooms and was built in 1846.

Wendy believes most of her guests are taking a break from an otherwise hectic lifestyle or trying to forget their problems for awhile. "They carry a tremendous amount of stress," she says. "I think everybody is exhausted. I get the sense their lifestyles are harried and frenzied."

She wants her guests to get a sense of how gracious and slow life used to be. "My goal is to give them a very unique and historical experience. I'm not there yet, but that's my goal."

Tall, with dark hair and light, translucent skin, Wendy moves gracefully in her period clothes. She has a friendly demeanor and a calming voice.

But Wendy's genteel manner belies her own hectic life. "In reality, this is a tremendous amount of hard work."

Wendy's week begins at 4 p.m. on Friday, when her guests begin to arrive. "Every weekend, it's 14 strangers, who I hope will become friends."

Besides welcoming them, she answers their questions about what to see and do and where to eat around Galena.

Each day she serves breakfast, which includes such scrumptious treats as pumpkin bread pudding with bourbon sauce or apple pie with Brie cheese and Canadian bacon. On weekends, she takes on the persona of the Widow Wiggins as she gives "ghost tours" of the city, describing strange deaths and unexplained appearances.

Monday is wash day, when she strips all the beds and lugs basket after basket of laundry down to the basement to be washed, dried and folded. During the rest of the week she cleans, shops, gardens, sews and entertains more guests. When Friday afternoon comes around, she does everything all over again.

She tries not to let her guests see much of her day-to-day reality. "I have two lifestyles going on here."

Wendy also tries to give her guests something she never had—a home where she could always feel comfortable and safe. Her mother was an alcoholic. Her father, a truck driver, frequently was on the road. "When Daddy was home, it was a safe place to be. If not, it wasn't."

Wendy Heiken

In addition, she is a "frustrated re-enactor," Wendy says.

She said she became interested in Civil War history during the early 1990s, when Ken Burns produced a series about the war for public television. Later one day, she was flipping through the TV channels when she saw a re-enactment of the Lincoln-Douglas debates. The TV camera panned the crowd that was listening to the debate and picnicking in the park.

"All the people were dressed in period clothes. Everything was perfect, down to the dishes," she says. "The Internet was just getting started, and I learned there was this wonderful hobby out there called 're-enactment.'"

Eventually she moved to Galena with her husband Bill, who had grown up nearby in northeast Iowa. She discovered how much Civil War history was in Galena and how much of it was kept alive. She learned that organizations sometimes hosted period events.

"I wanted that to be part of my lifestyle. I don't know where else I would have the opportunity to live out my fantasies."

They bought their B and B in 1998. It was built by Darius Hunkins, who built railroads and moved to Galena in 1838 with the Illinois Central Railroad. Rumor had it that he built the home two stories high and later raised the house and built another story beneath in order to prove his engineering prowess. However, Daryl Watson, executive director of the Galena History Museum, said that is unlikely.

"The first year we were in the house, I hated this place," Wendy says. The toilets leaked, the wallpaper sagged and the floors were covered with green shag carpets. But she and Bill got the plumbing fixed, ripped off old wallpaper and replaced it with fresh wallpaper and paint, took out the carpeting and filled the home with rococo (mid-Victorian) furniture.

"I love this place," she says.

Wendy wracked her brains, trying to come up with a name for her inn. One day "Annie Wiggins" popped into her head. She loves the name. "It is old-fashioned and whimsical at the same time."

Annie Wiggins Guest House

She seems especially to love the clothes that go with the age, and she sews as often as she can. "I just cut out three new dresses."

During the 1860s, women wore "outrageously bold prints and colors," which "nobody in their right mind" would wear today, she says. She loves the bold fabric, including her red and yellow plaid cotton and her purple, red and royal blue plaid taffeta. "I tell people, 'The uglier the fabric, the better the dress.'"

Wendy Heiken

"I am going to make a gown out of purple polka dot."

Her collection of period clothing includes two work dresses, six day dresses, two black mourning dresses (for the Widow Wiggins), one tea gown, three ball gowns and several bonnets. "This gets very addicting."

She calls one of the ball gowns "notorious." Cut low and worn with a waist-cinching corset, it gives new meaning to the term "hour-glass" figure.

Although 1860s day wear was "buttoned up," ball gowns were a different story, she says.

Wendy is doing her part to ensure there are more period events in Galena and, happily, more places to wear period clothing.

In 2000, she re-instated the annual Grant Birthday Celebration, which had taken place every year until about the 1950s. The celebration includes a ball, of course. She also co-founded the Galena Historical Dance Society, which meets monthly to learn period dances.

Each Monday evening, she welcomes other period seamstresses into her dining room, where they work and chat at a large table.

Wendy tries to talk me into making a corset because, she says, a reproduction dress will never fit properly without one. I tell her I will consider it.

In addition, she helps with lectures and demonstrations sponsored by the Spirits of the Galena History Museum, of which she is a member.

If she has her way, she will host more events at her inn. "I'm trying to talk Bill into letting me convert the garage into a ballroom. I think every house needs a ballroom."

"Ten years ago, people were happy with a bathroom down the hall."

Patricia Goldthorpe

If you think owning a B & B is a nice little enterprise for an eccentric little couple who has two or three extra little bedrooms in their pretty little Victorian home to rent, think again. It is a highly competitive, fast paced business that requires owners to keep up with the ever-changing demands of a finicky and sophisticated public.

"Ten years ago people were happy with a room and a bathroom down the hall," said Patricia Goldthorpe, co-owner of the Goldmoor Inn in rural Galena and member of the Visit Illinois board of directors. "Now they want whirlpools, fireplaces and kitchen galleys," she said. "Innkeepers are buying land and building from the ground up. That is so they can provide all those amenities."

Goldthorpe is no exception. She and her husband Jim have built several cottages on their property and plan to add more.

"On-site dining also is a huge trend nationwide," she said. Many tourists expect lunch and dinner as well as breakfast.

Furthermore, those who live in a world of fast food and frozen dinners want to learn about how their meals are prepared. "People want hands-on. They want to experience the life style of an inn keeper. They want to experience the lifestyle of the chef."

In response, the Goldthorpes plan to build a gourmet kitchen and offer cooking classes. "It will get down to where we will put people in a van and go to the farmers market," Goldthorpe said.

Wendy Heiken, who owns the Annie Wiggins Guest House in Galena, remodeled her 1842 mansion in order to provide private baths. She works hard to make her guests feel pampered and comfortable. "But the amenities quest sometimes makes me crazy," she said. "At what point is enough enough?"

For me, a room with a bathroom down the hall is enough. I fondly remember the first time my husband Dick and I stayed in a B and B. The inn was a refurbished Victorian mansion in Washington, D.C. and located in a seedy but soon-to-be gentrified neighborhood. Freshly painted homes stood next to sad, neglected structures with peeling paint and boarded-up windows.

We shared the bath with two other couples.

At breakfast, our hostess recounted her experiences of the night before. A member of a neighborhood watch group, she had armed herself with a walkie-talkie and hassled any drug dealers, pimps or prostitutes who dared to show up on her street. She told us about shouting, in colorful and uncordial terms, at a pimp who drove by. I liked her moxie.

For me, who lived in a safe neighborhood, just listening to her was an interesting and novel experience. The breakfast was great, and the room was elegant. The home was only a three-block walk to a Metro stop.

Now, with all the surround sound and jacuzzis, I have been priced out of the B & B market. It's Super 8 for me.

The entire tourism industry in Jo Daviess County must work hard to keep up its appeal to travelers, according to Nancy Breed, operations director for the Galena/Jo Daviess County Convention and Visitors Bureau.

In a visitor survey taken in 2003, the bureau learned that 65 percent of tourists want rest and relaxation, Breed said. But how they define that varies from person to person. For example, for some people it means pursuing outdoor activities, such as skiing, biking or hiking. Others consider shopping, spending a day at a spa or eating a good meal relaxing.

"We as a destination need to offer many different things that can trip that relaxation trigger," Breed said.

Destinations also must offer activities that appeal to every age group. This is much more true since 9/11, when visitors began traveling in larger groups. Many who formerly traveled in couples, looking for a romantic weekend away, are taking along the children, as well as grandparents, aunts, uncles and even neighbors, Breed said.

The word for that is "togethering," according to Katie Markese, public relations manager for the Illinois Bureau of Tourism. "If you are a hotel, you have to ask yourself: Do I have something to offer every member of the family? You have to make sure everyone is happy," she said.

The survey also showed that 72 percent of overnight guests were there on a repeat visit and that 90 percent planned to return within a year. That was good news to the bureau, because it means people enjoyed their stay. But it also presents a challenge. "If we are going to keep them coming back, we need to keep the product interesting and fresh," Breed said.

During the past two years, the city of Galena, with the help of the Galena Rotary Club, built a walking path along the Galena River levee. It also built a bicycle trail.

But a new trail doesn't pop up every day, so the local hospitality industry needs to keep coming up with new events—and it does. For instance, two Galena hotels, the Victorian Pines Ramada and Country Inn and Suites, organized an annual hot-air balloon festival. The Elizabeth Chamber of Commerce developed the annual Ride the Ups and Downs bicycle tour. The Galena Garlic Co. hosts an annual food tasting event. And the Apple River Fort in Elizabeth continually offers new living-history demonstrations.

"You can't stand still in this industry," Breed said.

Breed recently left the CVB to become director of the Galena History Museum.

References

Abstract for the Park Avenue Guest House.
Barrick, Bill, interviews, 2003 and 2004.
Blum, Roger, interview, 2003.
Breed, Nancy, interview, 2005.
Bruun, Tom, interviews, 2003.
Court TV's Crime Library, www.crimelibrary.com.
Fallbacher, Sharon, interviews, 2005.
Harmond, Bard, interview, 2003.
Heiken, interviews, 2004.
Gee, Jeff, interview, 2004.
Gee, Val, interview, 2004.
Goldthorpe, Patricia, interview, 2005.
Heiken, Wendy, interviews, 2004.
Kemp, Tony, interviews, 2003 and 2004.
Markese, Katie, interview, 2005.
Rosenthal, Mark, interview, 2003.
"Serial Killers A-Z," www.geocities.com.
Skaggs, Lyle, interview, 2003.

The Mississippi

Don Oliver

"I'm only three miles from town, but I feel like I'm on vacation."

Gini Appel

The people at Frentress Lake know they have it good.

"When I turn down the road to come here, I can almost feel my blood pressure start to drop," Gini Appel says.

At first sight, the river community doesn't look like much. From Heller Road, you get the back view of a string of cottages and homes, with their scraggly yards and mish-mash of styles. But, from Gini's porch, you can see the backwaters of the Mississippi River. A tree-filled peninsula spreads out before you in serene beauty. You can watch the river change colors with the passing clouds and rising and setting sun.

For as long as she can remember, Gini spent summers with her family at Frentress Lake.

"We were in the water, like all the time," Gini says. "We lived in our swim suits."

"We always had people down, even when it rained. If it rained, we kids would put our ponchos on and play in the puddles in the road. We were never bored."

They often built sand castles. "It was play in its basic form."

The children learned to water ski and taught countless others the skill. "You would literally stand on top of the water. I felt so tall. It was exhilarating."

They even enjoyed polishing the family's V-bottom aluminum boat. "To shine it, you took handsful of sand and rubbed it on. It would gleam, and we were so proud of our work."

Anise Bonnet, the oldest resident in the community, has similar memories. "We swam all day and, at night, we played games." Often she and her family built bonfires, roasted marshmallows and sang songs. In the winter, they skated on the ice.

"It used to be that people would move down here after school was out and then move back before school started. When everybody was gone, it was so quiet down here."

Anise's family lived at Frentress Lake year-round. Her parents owned the land and managed the resort. Now she and her son Steve own and care for the property. She does the bookkeeping.

Frentress Lake is named after the first white family—Eleazer and Diademia Frentress and their children—who settled permanently on the land. In 1827, Eleazer received a claim to 320 acres that lie along the river and continue north, past where U.S. 20 now runs. However, the family did not settle there at first. Instead, they headed north in a keel boat with 2-year-old Thomas, 4-year-old Lucy and another couple by the name of Camp. They landed at Cassville, Wis. and settled in a small mining camp.

According to "History of Jo Daviess County: 1887" the two women likely were the first white women to venture into that area. "It will require no very great stretch of the imagination to recognize in Mrs. F. a courage amounting to heroism, when she assumed the risk of placing her babes and herself beyond the pales of civilization and at the mercy of hordes of Indians."

But the Frentress family fled back to Galena on July 4, 1827, after three men from their camp discovered that a group of Winnabego Indians had attacked a boat nearby, killing one white man and wounding another. They arrived in Galena the next day, after traveling 50 to 60 miles by horseback and foot through timber and thick undergrowth.

At first Eleazer mined for lead and then farmed along the Galena River. A few years later, he built a log cabin on his claim near the Mississippi and began to work the land.

His family was about to move into the cabin, when news of the Black Hawk Wars arrived. It was May of 1832. "He unhitched his team from the plow, left it standing in the middle of a furrow, and hustled to Galena to join the forces that were being mustered," according to the history.

The wars ended by September, and soon the family moved into the cabin.

"The Frentress Cabin was a double one, built of round logs, and then 'scutched' down. There was a hall, or entry, between the two parts, and for many years it was regarded as the grandest farm house in all this region of country. Its doors were always open, and its beds and its table always free and welcome to everyone who claimed its hospitality."

Meanwhile, Diademia Frentress gave birth to more children.

"I try to keep her spirit alive," Gini Appel says. "I don't want this courageous spirit to be forgotten. I think she was a lady I would have liked a lot." A few years ago, she wrote a skit about the Frentress family, which she and her neighbors performed at one of the community's July 4 celebrations. "I just love telling her story."

Gini Appel

The cabin remained in its spot north of U.S. 20 until 2003, when the Dubuque County Historical Society bought it and moved it to the National Mississippi River Museum in Dubuque, Iowa.

During the late 1800s, Charles and Lizzie Heller bought 40 of the 320 acres that belong to the Frentress family's descendants.

The Hellers built a resort with 28 cottages, about 10 or 15 outhouses and a small store.

People rented the cabins, and the Hellers took care of the property. The resort passed down to the Hellers's daughter Elyse and her husband William Kroll and then to the Krolls's two daughters, Anise Bonnet and the late Helen Thurston. Now it is in Anise and Steve's hands.

Stories abound about how, during the Prohibition years, Chicago Mafia boss Al Capone and his mob would hide out at Frentress Lake and carry on illegal bootlegging activities. Anise remembers there being a tavern on the grounds, where people drank illegally. However, it is tough to say just how many of the stories are true.

Regardless of what took place during the 1920s and '30s, by the 1950s the resort had become a family-oriented community for local "river rats." Now most people seem to live the idyllic life that Gini describes.

"I am only three miles from town, yet I feel like I'm on vacation," Gini says.

"I feel like I live in the state of the Mississippi River," says Kate Fischer. She and her husband, Jerry Enzler, bought a home on Frentress Lake in 2001. "The river is almost like a skin with life coursing beneath it. When I am in a canoe out there, I am by myself—sort of. There are no humans, but there are all kinds of frogs and beautiful butterflies. There is so much life out there, it is awe inspiring.

"I don't need anything else. I think I could sit there forever—except I would need to jump in once in awhile."

Kate loves watching the daily, even hourly, changes in the river. "It makes Lake Michigan, which I grew up on, seem boring."

She even enjoys the spring flooding.

To Kate, life seems simpler on the river than it does in town. "In town I seemed to need a lot more things because I was inside more. It is remarkable how many fewer things I need out here. Besides, we can't store anything in our basement, because we would have to lug it out every spring.

Life seems easier, too. Our lawn is half sand and half weeds, so we don't get too hot and bothered about it. We're not out there trimming bushes, hedges and sidewalks. We don't have sidewalks."

She likes the people in the small community, too. "There are a lot of really accomplished people who live down here, but that doesn't matter. They are just one of the neighbors. This is a very egalitarian community."

Ruth Graham spent her first summer at Frentress Lake in 1992 and became a year-round resident in 2003. "It's a dream world right here. I am so content to get off work and go home. I never want to leave once I'm home. I never stop appreciating what we have."

Like Kate, she enjoys the people as well as the peaceful setting. "I became one of the group immediately."

The community remains quiet during the winter and still comes alive during the summer when people invite friends and relatives to stay.

Lately, it has been undergoing a transformation. Residents have replaced all but nine of the original cottages with year-round homes. The new structures are much bigger and higher off the ground. They give Frentress Lake less of a camp-like feel and more of a suburban look.

Now families own, rather than rent, the structures. However, they do not own the land. Instead, they hold five-year leases.

"We're probably the biggest fools in the world," Kate says. "But this is just about the only land (near the water) that's available and close to Dubuque. Our lawyer put it this way: 'As a lawyer, I would tell you that this is a stupid thing to do. As a human being, I would tell you that, if you don't buy the place, I will.'"

Kate trusts the Bonnets. They have always been fair with the home owners and have been good stewards of the land, she said.

Instead of worrying about the property arrangement, she feels concerned about the future of the backwaters. Frentress Lake is silting in faster than she would like to think.

If the U.S. Army Corps of Engineers receives Congressional and presidential approval to extend the locks and dams on the river, that will speed up the process.

But Kate will enjoy her place on the river as long as she can. "In March, when the river breaks up, thousands of eagles come through here. I have counted as many as 82 eagles in my five trees alone."

"I liked being out in the open with the wind blowing through my hair." **Babe Schubert**

Catherine "Babe" Schubert has lived a good life. She has never had a ton of money or owned a fancy place, but she has had Mother Nature. For most of her 94 years, she has lived the life of what folks call a "river rat."

Babe and her late husband, Bob, spent nearly every spare moment fishing the backwaters of the Mississippi River or hunting on the islands that dot the backwaters. Sometimes they roller skated and danced. They did their fair share of partying at one time, too.

They raised four lively children and nearly always had other people around—out-of-town hunters and fishermen, who spent weekends or days off in the Schubert home down by the Mississippi River. Locals stopped by to buy bait, rent a boat or to get their boat motors repaired.

Babe grew up in an outdoorsy family. From

as early as she can remember, her parents would walk down to the river with their bamboo fishing poles and Babe's older siblings in tow. Babe's mother would carry her in her arms. "She would nestle me down in the grass and she'd get a chance to fish."

Babe was a teen when she met Bob at a dance. He was a good dancer, and so was she, and they shared an interest in the outdoors. They married in 1928, when she was only 16 and he was 25.

"I had a wonderful husband. He was kind. He loved dancing. He loved fun. He loved outdoor sports. He liked everything. We always did everything together," Babe says. "He was good with the kids. He was a good father."

In 1955 they bought their place on the river southwest of Galena and moved down a year later. During the day, Bob worked at Kraft Foods. (Later he worked at an auto repair shop in Galena.) He built boats on the side.

Babe sold bait and took care of the hunters who slept upstairs in the Schuberts's humble two-story home. She would get up at 3 a.m. to fix them breakfast and later, when they returned, she would clean their ducks for $3 apiece. Often at night, she and Bob played poker with them at the kitchen table. The coffee pot was always on.

Babe Schubbert (circa 1935, courtesy of Babe Schubert)

"We used to drink quite a little bit, too. We lived fast, but it seemed like we didn't care. We just enjoyed ourselves all the time."

Whenever time allowed, they would fish or hunt for rabbits or quail. "Bob would call from work and say, 'Get ready.'"

Those were the days. "You don't live until you get out on the islands. You feel altogether different when you get out in the woods."

She speaks familiarly of places called Harris Slough, Spratt's Lake, Keough Slough, Fish Trap, and Dead Man's Slough.

In the winter, they would walk out onto the ice and fish. "I liked being out in the open with the wind blowing through my hair. I never wore anything on my head."

She says that spending time with your spouse in nature brings you closer. "You have more of a feeling for your partner. Making love in the woods is one of the best things you can do. And in a boat. An open boat, not a closed one."

She says some of the happiest days of her life were when she and Bob and the kids spent nine days camping on Hanson's Island. The family pitched tents, and she cooked on an open fire.

In 1959, Babe received a river boat pilot's license and became the first female fishing guide on the Mississippi.

Although she took the qualifying test more than 45 years ago, she can almost feel her nerves twinge when she thinks of it. The licensing agent was stern and seemed less than eager to grant her the license. "The guy stood there with his arms folded."

But she passed the test and, to this day, feels proud of her accomplishment. Babe operated a guide service for the next 25 years. She charged $7.50 per hour per fisherman.

Babe would take a small group—usually men—in one of several boats into the backwaters, where she figured the fish would be biting. Her favorite was a 16-footer that would go just about anywhere and was built by Bob and their son Butch in 1956.

Using a fly rod with a single-action reel, she would catch the first fish. Then she would let her customers take it from there. They caught bass,

Babe Schubert

bullheads, sunfish and crappies. "I never came back from guiding without bringing in a big mess of fish."

Bill Gilles can attest to that. Once, when they left the spot they had been fishing, they forgot to pull up the bag containing their catch. She turned around and headed back to the spot, determined to reclaim it. "She went and fooled around with a pole with a boat hook on it. Damned if she didn't catch that thing with all the fish in it.

"She could hold her own with the toughest of them, but she was a nice lady."

Babe and Bob made good friends among Babe's customers, including Bill Gilles. "All of us who know Babe love her. My kids love her," he says. "She is a person whom it is kind of a privilege to know. She is different and a real character."

He says the Schuberts's hospitality became legendary. "You could go down there anytime unannounced. You could go into the kitchen and have a cup of coffee."

"I've always been good to people," Babe says. "I like people. I don't shut myself away from them."

Although Babe knew the Mississippi River well and could handle a boat like a well-trained puppy, she never lost respect for the river. "It's mean out there in that river if you don't know it. When the wind comes from the South, you can get a good tossing around. ... You don't want to be out there when it's foggy."

Once, when she took two women up the river, a storm came up unexpectedly. "The sky was full of those white cumulus clouds." The wind blew 65 miles per hour, turning the Mississippi into a sea of white caps and deep green holes. From up close, the sprays of water looked like shattered green glass, she says.

Babe and her customers would have waited out the storm, but Babe's boat wouldn't stay anchored in the strong wind. They had to head for home. Using her expert boating skills, Babe brought the women back safely. "I went full blast coming in. That was a real ride."

Living where they did, the Schuberts often had to contend with flooding. During the big flood of 1965, the water swirled into the ground level of their home, rising above their knees. Discoloration in the kitchen wall still shows just how high the water got.

Babe quit guiding in the mid 1980s. Her boat was getting old and so was she. She and Bob continued to operate a boat rental and bait business. Bob fixed motors.

About 15 years ago, she stopped going out on the water. She felt she no longer could handle a boat safely and didn't want to be a "burden" to anyone else. As much as she loved fishing and motoring over to the islands, she has been content to remember the river as it was.

The river is changing, she says. "The river is getting so low that anybody who don't know it better not go on it. ... All the sloughs are drying up. ... Everything (all the wildlife) seems to have disappeared. ... You'll never see the river like it was."

In 1996, Bob died. Babe stayed in her home by the river and continued to sell bait. "I had one of the best bait businesses around."

A few years ago, her legs started giving out, so she got out of the bait business. Old friends continued to stop by to chat. She feels blessed to have so many friends and blessed by the fact that her mind remains sharp, her memories are mostly good and she still has all her teeth. "I don't think about dying, unless it just hits me. I just feel like I always felt."

She still has her memories and she still has Bob, in a way. She has made a mental promise to Bob that she will live to be 100. "Pa (Bob) is with me every day. There's always something I want to tell him about."

"I was out here every day last spring."

Don Oliver

It was still dark one late fall morning when I met Don Oliver for a morning of fishing. I treaded down the wooden dock toward the seasoned angler, whom I had met only once. A few people had suggested that, if I wanted to see what fishing on the Mississippi River is like, I should go with someone knowledgeable like Don.

We had planned to go out earlier in the fall, but the conditions weren't right. Don doesn't like to fish unless he has a good chance of catching some walleye.

Fall fishing hasn't been very good for the past few years, he said. "'93 was the last good fall." That was after record flooding.

I wouldn't have known. I don't fish.

The thermometer read 36 degrees, as he started his motor and edged his 16-foot Alumicraft out of its slip at Frentress Lake Marina. Once he motored into the main channel of the river, he sped up and headed across the way.

The first morning light shown dimly through a gray mist, which had settled over the water. The river took on a deep, steely teal tone.

"Some days you can't find your way out of here," he said.

I hadn't dressed warmly enough. I crossed my arms tightly over my chest, defending myself against the bone-chilling cold.

Don noticed my discomfort and lent me a heavy jacket. "The river is the coldest place in the world when it's cold. It's also the hottest place there is when it's hot."

"I used to fish out here in snowstorms, but not anymore," he added. "When I had customers, they wanted to go."

Don thought this trip would be his last for the year, and he wasn't looking forward to putting his boat away. "Winters are long."

During the winter, he and his wife Gerry usually spend a month or two in Florida, but he doesn't care for winter much, even there. All season long he looks forward to spring and to getting back on the Mississippi.

The fishing tends to be better then, he said. "I was out here every day last spring. It was the best spring in a long time." He showed me a picture of himself and another man with a stringer full of walleye.

The mist was thickening into fog as Don found what he thought might be a good spot. He slowed his motor, a 50 horsepower Evinrude, and coaxed his boat into an inlet between two islands known as Round Island and Schumacher's Island. "It looks like the wind is coming from the east."

He prefers to fish over the wing dams, which are underwater dams made of brush and rocks, where fish like to feed.

The fisherman switched to his trolling motor, an 8-horse Evinrude, picked up a rod and took a minnow from an aerated container. "Today I'm fishing with minnows. In the spring and summer, I fish with leeches and worms."

Don dropped his line in but didn't get a bite. "They're down there a little too far." His depth finder read 18 feet.

Without further ado, he started up his big motor and moved on. "I don't stay very long any place, unless I'm catching a lot of fish. Dead Man's

Slough is probably the only place where they'll be today, but I didn't have any luck there yesterday."

He said the water temperature was about 56 degrees, just right for catching something.

After finding a new spot in Dead Man's Slough, Don again threw out his line. I watched the last of the mist clear and the sun rise in brilliant shades of pink and gold. Soon something snatched Don's minnow but didn't take his hook. Don wasn't sure what kind of fish it was.

Don Oliver and his walleye

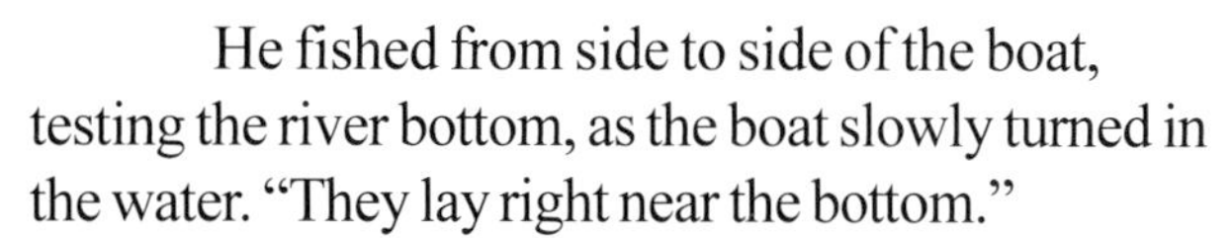

He fished from side to side of the boat, testing the river bottom, as the boat slowly turned in the water. "They lay right near the bottom."

I was starting to feel a bit bored and restless—I had decided long ago that fishing required more patience than I have—but I pretended to be interested. To pass the time, I took pictures and plied Don with questions. He obliged me with answers.

Don said he grew up near the river, but he didn't fish much as a boy. It was only after he started working as a lineman for Interstate Power Company, when an older co-worker invited him and another guy to fish with him, that he realized how much he could enjoy the sport. Before long, he bought a boat and motor.

Don said it took him four or five years to learn the art of fishing and to know and understand the river. "It takes awhile to learn which wing dam to fish at what river stage. And at first we didn't have trolling motors."

After he felt confident in his ability, he started a guide service on the side. Most of his customers were good, but he gave up the business a number of years ago.

Now, at age 77, he mostly fishes alone or with his son, Larry, and other family members. "Most of the friends I fished with have died."

Still, much of Don's life revolves around the sport, from eating his catch to making his own jigs. "I make four or five thousand at a time."

Eventually, he got another hit, and the fish jerked and swayed. "It's a dang bass," he said as he reeled it in. "I don't like to get 'em. I wish it would have been a walleye. Walleyes don't pull and go all over the water like that. They pull more deeply.

"A week from now, the walleye might be bitin' like crazy."

Discouraged, he motored back up the river, to a place called Nine Mile Island. Again, he let his boat drift as he fished from side to side. I could see that we weren't going to leave the river until he caught a Walleye. I wondered how long that would take, as my hands became increasingly numb with the cold.

By this time, the sun was up, and the sky was clear and nearly cloudless. Along the shoreline, the trees reflected into the now-blue water.

It didn't take long for Don to feel a tug on his line. Surely and steadily, he pulled in a one-and-a-half pound walleye, the fish he had been waiting for. It was about 19 inches long, so it was a keeper. He held it up for me to take a picture.

Having fulfilled his mission and sensing my restless state, Don headed back to the dock. "At least we didn't get skunked."

Don said he doesn't know why the sport appeals to him so much. "I just love to fish," he said.

"Even an experienced river pilot could be fooled."

U.S. Army Corps of Engineers

The Mississippi River is not the river it once was. Some people says it's changed for the better, and some say it has changed for the worse.

The longest river in North America and named after an Ojibwa Indian word meaning "Great River," the Mississippi stretches 2,552 miles from Lake Itasca, Minnesota to the Gulf of Mexico.

"It is not just folklore that people once waded across the river," the U.S. Army Corps of Engineers says in one of its brochures. Hundreds of islands and sandbars divided the water between Minnesota and southern Illinois, which is known as the Upper Mississippi River. When the river was low, some of the sandbars broke through the surface of the water.

That suited everyone just fine until 1823 when the first steamboat, the Virginia, traveled from St. Louis to St. Paul. For several decades, the steamboats carried loads of lead out of Jo Daviess County to other parts of the country. As they went, they burned huge quantities of lumber harvested from the islands and flood plains.

The Mississippi was a tough river to navigate. It was filled with snags and would change after every storm. The sand bars would shift, and trees would fall into the river, "so that even an experienced river pilot could be fooled." In short, the river was unpredictable and unkind to the steamboats. River pilots lived dangerous and sometimes short lives.

In 1854, the first railroad connected the east coast to the Mississippi, and it wasn't long before railroads crossed the river and became the chief mode of transportation. However, the population along the upper Mississippi was growing. People demanded safe, predictable river transportation to the Atlantic Ocean.

In 1878, Congress directed the Corps of Engineers to create a 4.5-foot channel. The Corps removed snags and blasted out or excavated rock. It built wing dams – small dams made of brush and rock that extended into the water from the shore – and closed off access to some of the sloughs to keep the river in the main stem and, thereby, cutting a deeper channel.

Twenty-nine years later, Congress authorized the Corps to deepen the main channel to 6 feet. It did so by building more wing dams, closing off more sloughs and periodically dredging the river.

The early 20th Century brought about the invention of the tow boat. The diesel powered machine could push almost 10 times as much cargo on barges than the steamboats could carry.

Mississippi River backwaters

Because the tows needed more water to navigate well, Midwestern commercial interests asked for an even deeper channel. The Corps came up with a plan to build 26 new locks and dams between St. Paul and St. Louis. (Three already existed.) This would create a series of "steps" up the river, with large pools forming near each "step" or dam. Congress approved the plan in 1930, and 23 of the new dams were completed by 1939.

After the water level rose, the pools covered many islands as well as thousands of acres of wet meadows and farmland. Now there are "lakes" in areas that used to be dry except during floods.

The project has made the river relatively safe and predictable. Now more than 25,000 commercial tows and 45,000 pleasure boats lock through the system each year, according to the Corps. Petroleum products and coal move up the river from the South, and corn, wheat, oats, barley and rye move down the river from the upper Midwest. Other common cargo includes liquefied methane gas, molten sulfur and anhydrous ammonia.

While the dams have deepened the river, they have also slowed the river, allowing silt to build up on the bottom. When the river is low, the tow boats stir up the silt, pushing it out into the backwaters. As a result, the backwater "lakes" are silting in at an average rate of about 1 centimeter each year, according to Mike Griffin, Mississippi River wildlife biologist for the Iowa Department of Natural Resources. "If a lake has only one foot of water, it has a life expectancy of only about 20 years."

However, without the lock and dam system, many of those lakes would not have existed in the first place, Griffin said. He also noted that, because the Corps owns most of the land within the Mississippi River corridor, development has been controlled there. What islands and peninsulas that remain have become reforested. This has been good for waterfowl and migratory birds. "With one continuous corridor of trees, there is just a tremendous variety of birds that travel that corridor."

But the barge industry has harmed some wildlife, he said. Tow boats churn up large amounts of water, killing many fish eggs.

Likewise, barges have brought zebra mussels to the Mississippi River from the Asiatic Sea – via the Great Lakes and the Illinois River. These mussels have colonized over native mussels living in the bottom of the river, endangering some of the river's 57 varieties of native mussels.

Now the Army Corps of Engineers wants to extend the current locks from 600 feet to 1,200 feet. That would allow tow boats to pull all their barges through in one pass, rather than having to unhook half the barges at each lock and make two passes.

This would not directly affect sedimentation, Griffin said. However, it would encourage additional barge traffic, which would speed up sedimentation in the backwaters.

Other factors have affected the river as well, Griffin said. For decades, farmers have tiled their fields in order to drain off excess moisture. When it rains, the water drains quickly from fields into streams and rivers that flow into the Mississippi.

Meanwhile, communities along the river and its tributaries have been growing and developing. Water pours off buildings and down parking lots and streets into city storm water systems, which dump into the river.

Because rain has less chance of soaking in, heavy thundershowers can result in more frequent and dramatic flooding than before.

The good news is that, since the passage of the Clean Water Act in 1972, companies have reduced the amount of pollution they allow into the river. Likewise, communities have built sewage treatment plants instead of dumping raw sewage into the river. With regard to pollution, "we're in pretty good shape," Griffin said.

References

Appel, Gini, interviews, 2003 and 2004.

Bonnet, Anise, interview, 2004.

Fischer, Kate, interview, 2005.

Graham, Ruth, interviews, 2003 and 2004.

Griffin, Mike, interview, 2005.

"History of Jo Daviess County: 1887," pp. 542 and 543.

Oliver, Don, interview, 2003.

U.S. Army Corps of Engineers publications: "The Mississippi and Its Uses," 2003; and "The Upper Mississippi River: Nine-Foot Channel Navigation Project."

Celebrations

Anthony Rayhorn, Karina LaFrancois and Janessa Klass playing volleyball and Mitch Allen at the Elizabeth Community Fair

“We don’t know who they are or where they come from.”

Ruth Graham

Every year at about 3:30 p.m. on July 4, people gather on Frentress Lake Road outside of East Dubuque on tractors, wagons or golf carts, on horseback or by foot, wearing hats or homemade costumes.

Usually members of the local volunteer fire departments show up with their engines, and a couple of deputies from the Jo Daviess County Sheriff’s Department bring a squad car and play a recording of “Bad Boys” for the crowd.

The 4 p.m. parade—same time, same place every year—has been going on for 13 years. Organizers Ruth Graham and Gini Appel sometimes lose track of just what year they started it.

The parade tradition began during the early 1990s when Ruth, who had lived in Connecticut, told Gini about the parades that her community out East held. Gini said she had always wanted to have a parade at Frentress Lake.

“We were soul mates,” Ruth said. So, the two spread the word that anyone interested in joining in was welcome. Just enough people showed up to call it a parade. It began with the people who own cottages or homes along a stretch of the Mississippi River backwaters known as Frentress Lake.

“The first parade lasted about 5 minutes. We had about four families,” Ruth says. The following year, a few more families participated and, the following year, a few more did.

It has grown to include friends, relatives and, during recent years, strangers. “Now men show up on their tractors, and we don’t know who they are or where they come from. But we fit them in. We will fit anyone in,” Ruth says.

“It just keeps getting better and better,” she adds.

The parade almost didn’t take place in 2005. It rained off and on during the morning, and organizers called it off. But, by mid afternoon, the rain had stopped, and kids who live in the community begged their parents to go ahead with it. So, word went up and down Heller Drive to let everyone know the parade would go on after all.

It was too late to call the fire departments and other non-resident participants back, so the parade was small. Without the heavy equipment, it was a lot like those of the early years, Gini said.

Like most years, Gini slung a long, red skirt with a blue waistband over her shoulders, looking like the Statue of Liberty in a toga. She sat in the scoop attached to Rod Zapf’s 1939 Ford Fergusson tractor, and Zapf lifted her above the crowd.

Jolene Osterberger sprayed her children’s hair red and blue and slipped homemade fire cracker costumes—large poster boards formed into cylinders and spattered with blue and red paint—over their heads. The children, Allie, Sammie and Jacob, winced as they were sprayed but proudly displayed their costumes afterward. They wore little hats with strands of silver paper shooting out the top like sparklers.

Dan Graham, known for his unusual attire,

Pam McKenna and Marlene, baby Luke, Rick and Dick Burgmeier

showed up wearing a jock strap over his shorts and holding a sign saying, "Support our troops." One year he wore a pair of water skis positioned over his bathing trunks so that he appeared to having nothing on underneath.

"He is a respected lawyer from Chicago," Ruth said. "I can't believe the dumb, stupid things intelligent people will do for this parade."

Participants waved and shouted to neighbors and friends, who sat in lawn chairs watching the menagerie go by.

Meanwhile, Steve Osterberger buzzed the crowd with his small seaplane. It looked for a moment as though he would hit the telephone wires.

The parade reminds Kate Fischer of growing up in Elm Grove, Wis., when Elm Grove was "barely out of the stage of being a pasture." The kids would wrap themselves in tin foil and call themselves monsters or put on their parents' clothes and call themselves hobos or clowns. Parades weren't overplanned or overdone."

"It's like Norman Rockwell," she adds. "I hate to say it, but it really is. It's not that Frentress Lake isn't in the 21st Century most of the time, but for 20 minutes, it is not."

Usually Kate's son Jason dresses up as Abraham Lincoln, but in 2005 he couldn't be there. "So this year, it was Katie Graham who went as Lincoln. It really doesn't matter who it is, as long as you have your stock characters."

Usually Ralph Tranel brings a surrey drawn by ponies, and Gerry Tranel rides his horse Chance. Parents pull their children in wagons, and people dress up their dogs.

However, there are variations. One year Katie Graham turned her 1980 Toyota Corolla into a "chia car." She covered the top with a layer of dirt and planted grass seed in late June. By the day of the parade, a 2-inch lawn had grown on it.

Ruth and Gini say just about anything goes, as long as it is "historical or hilarious."

Soon the parade was over for another year.

But the July 4 celebration doesn't end when the parade ends. People gather in Ruth's yard for a potluck. Later, seven members of the Graham clan put on a water-ski show, with all of them getting up on their skis at the same time. Apparently that is difficult to do.

Just before dusk a few of the folks perform a historical skit, a tradition they started in 1976 for the country's bicentennial. One year Jerry Enzler had just begun to read the Gettysburg Address when the seven skiers came around the river's bend.

Often, by 4 p.m., you can hear Ruth mutter to herself, "Never again," as she is busy directing traffic, making lemonade, setting up tables and keeping track of a houseful of guests.

But soon she begins to look forward to the next Fourth. The event is too much fun and provides too many good memories to stop making the effort.

Mark Brady, Mary Brady, Brian Brady, Emma Alveal and Grace Brady

"We're never going to let the weather interfere again. The parade must go on, even if it means having umbrellas over our heads."

Gini says the celebration gives her a way to pay homage to her country. "Children need to know about the people who have fought and died for this wonderful country, where we have the freedom to do things like this. Besides, nobody likes to celebrate like I do."

(Back) Vicki Hefel, Carol Feltes and baby Megan Hefel. (Front) Rachel, Nick and Ben Hefel

Gerry Tranel and horse Chance

Bill Anderson, Todd Malcolm and Kyle Malcolm

Rachel and Hannah Herrig, Ben Hinderman and Ralph Tranel

Jolene and Sammie Osterberger

Rod Zapf and Gini Appel

Charley Anderson and dog Sam

Gavin and Adam Fuller
and Brian Tschiggfrie

"You get more tired every year, but it's fun."

Lynne Hesselbacher

Sept. 13, 1930 turned out to be a great day for a parade and the conclusion of the 10th annual Elizabeth Community Fair.

The parade, which went through the center of town on the Grant Highway (now U.S. 20), consisted of the Elizabeth community band; a contingent of Civil War veterans; and floats from the Weston, Long Hollow, Hickory Grove, Mount Morely and Terrapin Ridge rural schools, the 4-H Club and the Pythian Sisters. Children from the Elizabeth Public School marched, room by room, and assortments of farm machinery, horses, new cars and cows brought up the rear.

The people from the community of Derinda, who portrayed cowboys and Indians, won first prize for their float. The "smallest girl on the smallest pony" was the daughter of Mr. and Mrs. George L. Ryder, and the "smallest boy on the smallest pony" was Curtiss Mitchell.

In 2005, the parade was canceled. People lined up along the side streets with their tractors and wagons, golf carts and cars, as dark storm clouds gathered from the West. Wayne and JoAnn Wand were there with the float they made in 1988, a representation of a Chicago Great Western Railway locomotive. A cardboard birthday cake sat on top of the cab in honor of the Elizabeth Lions Club, which was celebrating its 60th birthday. Wayne covered the cake with plastic, as raindrops began to fall.

The Precision Lawn Chair Marching Dads were ready to go, too, complete with lawn chairs and ugly shorts. "These would be the shorts on sale, the ugliest and the loudest," Duff Stewart said.

Meanwhile, John Eversoll tied a bunch of balloons onto a Cadillac limousine, which he borrowed from a friend. "The story is that it was being built for Elvis Presley when he died, and then the president of Cadillac drove it for awhile," he said.

John, Wendell Roberts, Carole Berlage and Janann Arand planned to represent the Elizabeth High School Class of 1955. They were in a festive mood, joshing each other and looking forward to their 50th class reunion that night. "Ours was the best class that ever graduated from Elizabeth," John bragged.

Soon the sprinkles turned into a downpour. People headed for cover, either in their cars or on townsfolk's porches, hoping to wait out the rain. But about 11 o'clock a county sheriff's deputy came by to let everyone know the parade was off. Not only was there rain, but high winds soon would follow. As the deputy drove down the street, a dagger of lightening flashed in the western sky.

If only the town had a longer parade permit! People were certain the weather would clear up by afternoon — and sure enough, it did. But the permit lasted only until Noon.

Some people headed for home, while others gathered in downtown restaurants. Soaking wet, I found a seat at Duallys Bar and ordered a cup of decaf and a grilled cheese sandwich. The bartender called me "Sweetie."

Soon the rain slowed to a drizzle and, by about 1 p.m., it had stopped.

Eventually, people made their way out to the Elizabeth Community Center, where other community fair activities were taking place. There were food tents, bingo games, rides for the kids, a dunk tank, live music and a threshing demonstration. Some young adults played volleyball in the sand.

The night before, the annual truck pull drew about 1,000 people. There was also supposed to be a semi pull, but the people from the semi club got mixed up on the date and didn't show up.

Inside the community center, area residents displayed home-grown vegetables, flowers and hand crafted items. Dororthy Ellinor brought four vases of flowers. She won a blue ribbon for her sweet peas and a red ribbon for another bunch. She also won blue and red ribbons for her quilts. She received $2 apiece for her first-prize entries and $1 apiece for her second-prize entries.

Nearby in the barns, 4-H members and their families prepared their steers for judging. Lyle Miller sprayed Justin Witt's steer, Schooner, with oil in order to make its coat shiny. Justin blew its hair forward with a blower.

Travis Schiess, a 13-year-old from Pearl City in nearby Stephenson County, explained what judges look for when evaluating steers. "The hair needs to be pushed up toward the head. It's important how they walk and how you train them. They have to walk nice. And body structure. They need a nice, level body with a long stride."

The activities at the 2005 fair did not differ greatly from those featured in 1930. Then there was a picnic, the community band played, and people brought their produce for judging and display.

Dorothy Dittmar

Several people competed in a pie-eating contest, with Floyd Handel taking first prize. Ralph Wilcox won a contest "requiring a whistle after eating a number of soda crackers." In addition, there was a "slipper-kicking contest," won by Mildred Rodden, an egg toss and a tug o' war.

John H. Byers, who was secretary for then-Congressman William R. Johnson, gave a speech promoting community spirit. "He advocated economy during the present times and buoyed up the spirits of his audience with words of optimism, stating that savings deposits are now growing in the United States banks, that the United States and particularly this section of Illinois is less depressed than most parts of the present day world and that after the over-production of the past few years has been used up, things will again take on a more prosperous aspect," the Elizabeth Weekly News reported.

Little did Byers's listeners know that the Great Depression had barely begun.

The fair itself provided a sense of optimism. The Weekly News reported that an estimated 4,000 to 5,000 people attended, making the 1930 celebration the best-attended fair to date.

Today the fair serves much the same purpose as it did in the beginning. "It provides a time for everybody to get together and a way for people to show off their produce," said Lynne Hesselbacher, president of the Elizabeth Community Fair Board. "It is about old fashioned community spirit and pride."

People who have moved away come back during the fair to see relatives and old friends. "Our grown daughter never misses a fair," Lynne said.

Each year the board finds a community organization or milestone to celebrate. This year it was the Lions Club, and next year it will be the volunteer fire department, which will celebrate its 85th anniversary.

Lynne, who has been on the board for 31 years, never begrudges the time she spends planning the event. "It's just fun being with the rest of the fair board. You get more tired every year, but it's fun."

Other board members, including Merle Gothard and Don Kautz, have also served on the board about 30 years. "Our joke is that, once you are on the fair board, you can't leave unless you get someone to take your place," Lynne said.

Justin Witt with steer Schooner

Travis Schiess with steer Frankie

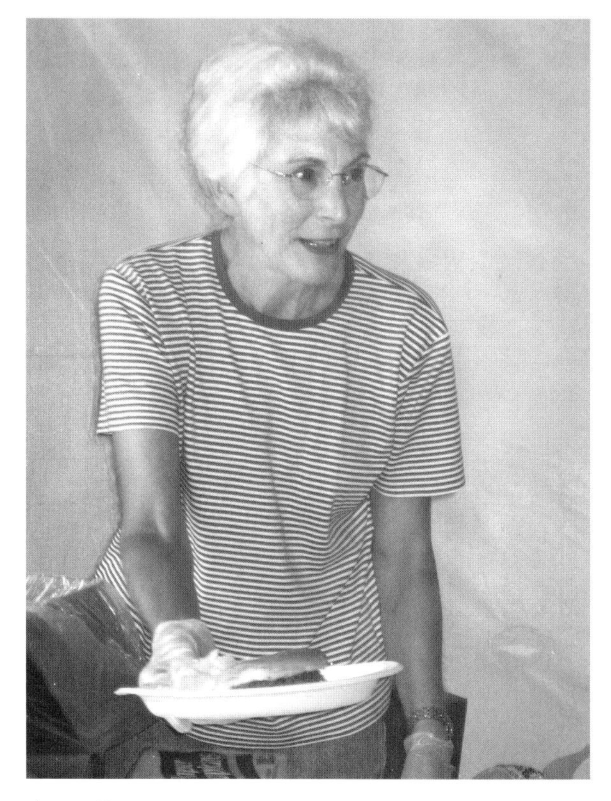

Ann Berry

John "Big John" Linicun and Lee and Loris Beyer

Wayne Wand

Dorothy Ellinor

"Hanover is a nice little town to come home to." ***Amy Butzow***

Amy Butzow grew up in Hanover and lives in Chicago. She returns home often and tries not to miss Mallardfest, the town's biggest celebration.

"Hanover is a nice little town to come home to. The best part is seeing old friends."

Amy remembers the freedom she felt as a child while riding around town on her bicycle and the feeling of being comfortable, safe and supported.

What is her favorite place in town? "Wherever my mom is."

Many others who grew up in Hanover return for the annual festival. Those who stayed in town also look forward to the weekend. And those who didn't grow up in Hanover but moved there later in life get a chance to meet people and learn more about their adopted community.

The festival begins on Friday evening with a community dinner. Afterward, the younger crowd meets up at a street dance or one of the local pubs.

The celebration continues on Saturday with a parade and fun, home-grown contests and activities. Groups of hearty individuals line up on each side of the Apple River, which runs through town, to play Tug of War. The losers wind up in the river. Golfers test their skills by teeing up on one side of the river and attempting to hit their ball across it.

And Mallardfest wouldn't be what it is without the duck retrieval. People buy plastic ducks, which are tossed into the river. Then Jeff Brueggen's yellow lab, Phoebe, dives in after them. The people whose ducks Phoebe retrieves first win cash prizes.

"Phoebe's a good old dog," Jeff said. "The dog works its butt off to get the ducks to shore."

Mallardfest got its name from the fact that Hanover claims to be "the mallard capitol of the world." It probably is.

About 50 years ago, Leo Whalen could see that the number of mallard ducks was declining, so he decided to start a mallard hatchery. He called it Whistling Wings. Now his daughter, Marianne Murphy, owns the business, and Marianne's daughter and son-in-law, Monica and Mark Klippert, help run the business.

Whistling Wings raises more than 200,000 mallards each year and sends them all over the country and around the world. Leo Whalen once gave Pres. Lyndon B. Johnson 50 mallards in return for a Lone Star LBJ hat. Some ducks are released into the wild.

Enter Bill Wolter, a member of the Hanover Chamber of Commerce. In October of 1970, he threw a party for members of the Hanover Chamber of Commerce at his home to show them how the organization could organize an Octoberfest for the community. Everyone had a good time, but there was no festival for the next several years.

Then, in 1975, Bill decided to throw another party to celebrate 10 years of being in business on Main Street. This time he invited the community, hired Kurt Roche and his band to play German music, lined up a few hay wagons and took Octoberfest on the road. The wagons of people

Kurt Roche

Ed Simon

stopped at each of the town's four bars and then when on to the VFW for a German meal and to Storybrook Country Club for a dance.

"A year later, Judy Guay, another chamber member, saw where it brought a lot of people into downtown businesses, so she decided we should have another Octoberfest," Bill said.

The celebration has been going ever since. Sometime during the early 1980s, the name changed from Octoberfest to Mallardfest. Later, the date was moved from October up to the third weekend in September. The weather has been perfect every year since then.

"A lot of people work on the festival year in and year out," Mark Klippert said. "From 11 o'clock on [on Saturday morning] it is pretty much in auto-pilot mode. It's almost like marriage. I just know that, at 3:30, Jeff will be there with his dog."

The festival has become a time for people to meet up with old friends, celebrate their heritage and get silly.

"I have three or four classmates who live elsewhere," Mark said. "They come back, and we reminisce."

Brenda Ferrell has lived in Hanover all her life. "I like the closeness and the friendships I have made." She also loves driving along the country roads that surround the town.

Ed Simon moved to the Hanover area 35 years ago and owns a horse ranch. He loves the beauty of the land and the friendliness of the people. "People wave to you when you go down the road."

"It was just something to do."

Donald Brauhn

Four adolescent boys climbed up a tree on Sherwood Avenue in East Dubuque on July 17, 1930. They didn't come down until 48 days later.

No, they weren't protesting anything. "It was just something to do," said one of their sons, Donald Brauhn, of Dubuque, Iowa.

Donald and David Brauhn and Cletus and Paul Murphy built a platform during June of 1930 and placed it in the tree. Donald and David, age 13, were twins. Their younger brother, Roger, would hoist a bucket up to the four boys. "Food would go up, and other stuff would come down, if you catch my drift," Donald's son said. "They played cards and were waited on, so it must have been like a penthouse up there."

When asked if his father was a character, Donald said, "To sit in a tree almost two months when you're 13, that's a character."

The boys might have stayed in the tree longer if a truant officer hadn't come by to remind them that school was to start the following day, the East Dubuque Register reported. "Only the appearance of the truant officer Tuesday night discouraged the boys from their determination to remain aloft longer." They climbed down just in time to dash off to school.

But they apparently beat a record, having sat in the tree 34 hours longer than the previous record holder, a youth from Des Moines, Iowa. They also topped the 922-hour record once held by a Milwaukee boy.

All three of the Brauhn boys have died, Donald said. He does not know what became of Cletus and Paul Murphy.

He said his dad served as an Army

machine gunner in the South Pacific during World War II and then became an electrician. During the last few years of his life, he worked for the city of Dubuque as an electrical inspector. He died in 1969 at age 52.

The tree remains, but the platform was removed after the tree sitters came down. The Brauhn boys' dad needed the wood.

References

Appel, Gini, interviews, 2003, 2004 and 2005.

Brueggen, Jeff, interview, 2005.

Butzow, Ann, interview, 2005.

Elizabeth Community Fair, July 23, 2005.

Elizabeth Weekly News: "Elizabeth Community Fair Sept. 18th and 19th," Sept. 12, 1923; "Third Community Fair Proved Big Success," Sept. 24, 1923; and "Tenth Annual Elizabeth Fair Is Big Success," Sept. 17, 1930.

Ellinor, Dorothy, interview, 2005.

Ferrell, Brenda, interview, 2005.

Fischer, Kate, interview, 2005.

Graham, Ruth, interviews, 2003, 2004 and 2005.

Hesselbacher, Lynne, interview, 2005.

Klippert, Mark, interview, 2005.

Mallardfest dinner, 2005.

Simon, Ed, interview, 2005.

Telegraph Herald: "Residents flock to Mallardfest," Oct. 21, 1994; and "Preparations under way for Mallardfest," Sept. 7, 2004.

Witt, Justin, interview, 2005.

Wolter, Bill, interview, 2005

Politics

I. Ronald (Ron) Lawfer with reporters (courtesy of Ron Lawfer)

"I didn't want to be in Congress just to tell my grandchildren I was in Congress."

John Cox

John Cox

When John Cox ran for the U.S. House of Representatives in 1990, he said Congress should pass a one-time income-tax surcharge to help save the savings and loan industry, which was struggling.

Voters didn't like the idea of a tax increase any better then than they do now. Cox's advisers warned him that such a statement could cost him the election. "My whole campaign was in an uproar," the former Congressman says.

Cox already had one major strike against him: He was a Democrat in District 16, which had never sent a Democrat to Congress.

But he knew that Americans would have to pay for part of the S & L bail-out, one way or the other. Better now than later, he thought.

Cox also talked about the budget deficit, which was $221 billion that year. The national debt stood at nearly $3 trillion. He suggested several options for reducing the deficit and paying off the debt—raise "sin" taxes, start up a national sales tax, increase the tax rate on the wealthiest Americans and/or cut defense spending. Each of those ideas could have turned off important voters—and campaign contributors—but Cox was steadfast.

"I said, 'We can't add to the national debt and just pretend it's going to go away.'"

How refreshing. Today the Bush Administration refuses to talk about deficits except when cutting programs for poor people. During a 2004 presidential debate, George Bush blamed deficits on the stock market and did not acknowledge the role of tax cuts or the war in Iraq. But I digress.

Although Cox trailed his Republican opponent, John Hallock, by a 2-to-1 margin in August before the election, he won the House seat with 54 percent of the vote. He attributes his victory to his honesty, knowledge of the issues, campaign style and dumb luck.

Cox says he has always taken an interest in politics. As early as 1956, when he was 9, he thrilled to watching the political conventions and rooted for John Kennedy to become the Democratic vice presidential nominee. As a young man attending college during the mid-1960s, he majored in political science, and he knew he wanted to become involved in public service.

After college, he returned to his hometown of Galena, ran for Jo Davies County state's attorney and won. He figured he would go for a second term there, then run for Congress. Next he would run for the U.S. Senate and finally make a bid for the presidency. He had it all scheduled out.

But, as time went by, Cox gave up his dream of building a life in politics. After serving two four-year terms as state's attorney, he started a law practice. By the late 1980s, Cox had three children, all still in school. He was enjoying his involvement in the Galena community, together with his wife Bonnie. His practice was thriving.

However, he continued to keep up on

current issues, reading several newspapers each day and watching television news commentaries. "Every Sunday morning I argued with the TV."

In 1989, after then-U.S. Rep. Lynn Martin decided not to run for re-election — she ran for the Senate instead — Illinois Central Committeeman Carl "Skip" Schwerdtfeger asked Cox to run.

"John had a nice combination of idealism and practical politics," Schwerdtfeger says. "That's pretty rare. A lot of politicians out there are hard and cynical, but John is not hard and cynical."

At first Cox said no. He thought it would be too hard on his family, but Bonnie and the kids encouraged him to run. "They said, 'You will always regret it if you do not do this.'" So, he ran.

Cox nearly ran his legs off. He spent so much time on his feet, going from door to door, that he lost more than 30 pounds. He folded over his pants in back and hid the gather under his jacket because he didn't have time to buy a new suit.

"I would start the day by looking at my schedule, and I would see all those meetings and appointments. I would get so stressed and depressed. But the day would go by at lightening speed."

Cox says people reacted well to him because he told the truth and kept his campaign positive. He urged them to become involved in politics, regardless of their political leanings.

I suspect people also were attracted to his passion, his reassuring voice and to what one reporter called his "boyish good looks." He had a thick, dark head of hair—which has since turned silver-gray—and an engaging smile.

Toward the end of the campaign, however, Cox almost answered the siren call of negative campaigning. The Democratic Congressional Campaign Committee had produced a TV commercial highlighting the votes that his opponent, John Hallock, had cast against state programs for senior citizens. It was willing to spend $5,000 to run the ad. Cox knew Hallock had later voted in favor of similar programs, but he told the committee he was willing to go ahead with the ad. He would just run it by Bonnie first. Bonnie was his campaign manager.

Bonnie said absolutely not. "I had weakened," Cox said. "Bonnie was the one who pounded the kitchen table and said 'No!.'" So, Cox told the committee it could keep its money.

"There was a lot of pressure on us," Bonnie says. "The message we got was that John really didn't want to win. They said he couldn't afford to be that idealistic."

Dumb luck struck when a sheriff's deputy caught Hallock speeding at 105 mph. Hallock refused to pay the ticket and was arrested. Some of the local newspapers made hay with the story.

"I didn't say a word about it," Cox says. His advisors wanted him to turn the arrest into a campaign issue, but he refused.

Hallock also blundered during a debate, according to Cox. When asked about abortion, Hallock hedged. On the other hand, Cox says, he stated his position clearly, saying that, although he personally opposes abortion, he believes women should be able to follow their own consciences. Pro-choice supporters rallied around Cox, and virtually no one from any side of the abortion debate helped Hallock.

Steadily, Cox's popularity grew. The House seat became his.

The first vote the newly-elected representative cast was a vote against the Persian Gulf War. It was late January of 1991, after Iraq invaded Kuwait. The war was popular among the public, but Cox said he chose to study the issue and reach an independent conclusion.

Within six weeks of starting his new job, he received a call from Ways and Means Chairman Dan Rostenkowski. "He said, 'Are you ready to chair the House?' I said, 'Uh, sure. What do you mean?'"

For four days Cox ran the House debate, sometimes having to call senior Congressmen out of order. He was afraid he would make an ass out of himself, but he apparently did just fine. A woman who watched the proceedings on CSPAN, called his office to find out if he was married.

Better yet, Cox says, he became known by the other members of Congress, which smoothed the way for working with them.

But those months proved to be difficult, too. Bonnie and the children had stayed in Galena. Although Cox called home every night and discussed the issues with Bonnie, things were not the same. John was busy with his new responsibilities, and the conversations were often rushed. He could no longer confer with Bonnie on everything the way he once had.

"I was in Congress, and there she was at home playing Scrabble with an 8-year old. When it became obvious that Bonnie was re-evaluating the whole nature of what she was about and the nature of our relationship, it was scary."

In the end, however, the marriage grew stronger, Cox believes. Both he and Bonnie became more independent.

Bonnie says it was the worst time of her life. In addition to being apart from her husband, she was seeing the dark side of politics. "I disliked the whole political culture, in terms of campaigning and being forced to choose issues that are not relevant, and in terms of politicians not facing and debating the issues with each other. People would tear down the other side and simplify the issues into 30-second sound bites. There were certain vested interests behind each party and not enough independent people to come up with creative solutions."

She also saw her husband fight to maintain his idealism while learning to work within the system. "It was very hard on us. It was very hard on me."

But Cox did all right. He helped pass some important legislation during the session. He co-sponsored the Campaign Spending Limit and Election Reform Act. He voted in favor of the Family and Medical Leave Act, the Emergency Unemployment Compensation Act, the Civil Rights Act, the Brady Handgun Prevention Act and the National Voter Registration Act.

He also voted in favor of a constitutional amendment requiring a balanced budget, but Pres. George H. Bush vetoed it. (The bill failed to meet the required two-thirds majority to override a veto.)

Usually Cox voted with what then was the Democratic majority in the House, but not always. He broke ranks when he voted in favor of the balanced-budget legislation and fast-track legislation involving trade agreements.

He vividly remembers one debate, when he spoke against an amendment to a tax bill, which allowed senior citizens to earn unlimited incomes without losing any Social Security benefits. "I basically said no senior citizen I know would want me to vote for this bill knowing that it would be paid for by their children and grandchildren."

Other lawmakers privately agreed with Cox but publicly catered to the large elderly constituency. During two voice votes, the House defeated the amendment. But when Rep. Dennis Hastert, R-Ill., called for a roll-call vote, only a handful of representatives voted against it. Cox was one of them.

Cox says he was more concerned about doing what he thought was right than about making political points. "I didn't want to be a member of Congress just so I could tell my grandchildren I was in Congress."

As far as he is concerned, Congress did a terrible job. "Just like they are doing today. Congress continues to spend money it doesn't have and continues to create massive deficits."

But the lawmaker felt he was poised to make a real difference if re-elected. He says many of his fellow representatives sought out his opinion—because of his independence—and that he was assured of being assigned to the powerful Ways and Means Committee, which has a lot to say about how money is spent.

But, in 1992, Cox lost his bid for re-election to Republican Don Manzullo. During the campaign, Manzullo said Cox tried to balance the budget on the backs of senior citizens.

"What he said was true in a way, but it was a distortion of the truth," Cox says.

However, he believes that reapportionment is what actually caused his defeat. District lines were redrawn, taking a Democratic-leaning county out of the district and replacing it with a county skewed heavily toward the Republican side. "I think I would have won the election if it hadn't been for reapportionment."

After his loss, Cox returned to Galena, where he resumed his law practice. He thought about running again in 1994, but decided not to. His law practice was taking off again, and he doubted he could win. Besides, Bonnie had had it with politics.

He probably will never run again. "I am 57 years old, and I am getting to the point where I recognize that my time isn't limitless. I need to think about how I want to spend the rest of my time. The next election for Congress will be in 2006 and, if I won, I would be almost 60 years old."

Cox sounds wistful, even sad, when he talks about politics. "I probably could have been a darn constructive member of Congress. And I really did like the job. I liked going to work and trying to work out solutions."

But he says he doesn't want the job. It would be too hard on his family. "And my family is very important to me."

If re-elected, he isn't so sure he would not succumb to political pressures. "I really do believe that, in the end, it is difficult not to be corrupted. People don't give you money without strings attached. Are they bribes? Hopefully not. But are you going to end up slipping away from your principles? I think I would end up slipping away, eventually.

"I think the sadness you see is really about the political process. It is painful and sad watching Congress not confronting the issues. Just take health care, for instance. How can you possibly defend doing nothing, when more and more people are not covered?"

Meanwhile, Congress is borrowing from the Social Security surplus to meet its operating budget. Because of that, the actual national debt is greater than $8 trillion, he says. "All that does is redistribute wealth from lower income people to higher income people. It is evil. Members of Congress understand exactly what they are doing, but they go ahead and do it anyway, because of the fear of not being re-elected."

And there is no way he would ever consider running for president. "Until I watched 'The West Wing' (a TV show) and 'The American President' (a movie), I never really thought through the fact that, as president, I could make a decision, and people would die."

Perhaps it is better to leave well enough alone anyway. Cox comforts himself in the fact that he won his first Congressional race by being honest, explaining the issues and then letting the people decide.

"I have always believed—and I still do—that, generally, if people know the truth, they will do the right thing."

"Public Servant's Lament" — ***Anonymous***

If I express myself on a subject, I'm trying to run things.
If I'm silent, I'm dumb or have lost interest.
If I'm always at my office, why don't I get out and learn what's going on.
If I'm out when they call, why am I not tending to business.
If I'm not at home at night, I'm out carousing.
If I'm home, I'm neglecting important outside contacts and activities.
If I don't agree with persons, I'm bullheaded.
If I do agree, I don't have any ideas of my own.
If I don't do what I'm requested, I'm a darn poor official.
If I do agree, well that's what I'm paid for.
If I give someone a short answer, I'm "too big for my britches."
If I attempt to explain the pros and cons of an issue, I'm a know-it-all and long winded.
If I'm well dressed, I think I'm a big shot.
If I'm not, I'm a poor representative of my office.
If I'm on the job a short time, I'm inexperienced.
If I've been there a long time, it's time for a change.

"Once in awhile, an issue just grows by itself." ***Ron Lawfer***

An affable, self-depreciating man with hefty shoulders and a hearty handshake, Ron Lawfer served in the Illinois House of Representatives from 1993 through 2002.

He said that some of his constituents probably considered him a "dumb farmer," and he admitted that keeping up with the issues presented a challenge. But I was impressed by his detailed knowledge of legislation. I called him often to get his thoughts about pending legislation for articles I wrote for the Telegraph Herald. Although I seldom agreed with his positions, I could understand how he arrived at them.

Most of his constituents liked him because he secured state money for several local projects, including refurbishing the Old Market House in Galena. In addition, he is a Republican and, like most of the voters in his district, he believes that state and federal government generally ought to keep out of local issues.

As most politicians, Lawfer had moments when things went his way and moments when they did not.

"Tell her about the camel jockey," his wife Pat said when I interviewed the Lawfers about Ron's years in the General Assembly.

One year Lawfer sponsored a bill that required new vehicles for large fleets to be powered by ethanol. The bill needed 60 votes to pass, but only 56 lawmakers were leaning toward a yes vote when it went to the House floor.

"After three hours of debate, emotions had become part of the discussion and, the way the discussion was going, I felt I needed a kicker to get it to pass," Lawfer said. As the bill's sponsor, he spoke last. "So I just said that it was a very simple bill that had been thoroughly discussed and that I felt the citizens of the state of Illinois should never be held hostage by a bunch of camel jockeys, as they were in 1974."

Soon the flak hit the fan. "Within two minutes a reporter from United Press International came to my side and said, 'Did you really say camel jockey?'" Yes, the lawmaker said.

The Freeport Journal Standard of Freeport, Ill. ran an editorial saying Lawfer should apologize. "They called it a 'racist slur,'" Lawfer said.

Several newspapers around the country picked up the story. "I got over 100 letters demanding an apology, from as far as Washington, D.C. and Arizona. I even got a letter from Jordan accusing me of being a spy for Israel."

But none of the letters came from his constituents, and Lawfer did not apologize. "I was just saying something I feel was common language in my district. I have yet to decide why Arabs were so upset with that."

More important to the assemblyman, the bill passed with 74 yes votes. "People who were sitting above me told me later that, as soon as I said 'camel jockeys,' heads began to nod."

Afterward, someone anonymously left a small stuffed toy camel on his desk. He still has it.

Lawfer said one of the most interesting pieces of legislation he sponsored was a bill regarding the tomb of President Ulysses S. Grant and his wife, Julia Dent Grant. "Once in awhile, an issue just grows by itself, and that was one of them."

In 1994, a New Yorker by the name of Frank Scaturro launched a campaign to restore the tomb, which is operated by the National Park Service and located in Riverside Park in Manhattan. Although the mausoleum was New York City's premier attraction before World War II, it had been sorely neglected. By the early 1990s, the exterior was deteriorating, the roof was leaking and the monument had been covered with graffiti and litter. It was so bad that people on tour would not get out of the bus to see it, said Terry Miller, who was a guide for Tri-State Tours in Galena.

Scaturro contacted Illinois lawmakers about the tomb's condition. Judy Baar Topinka, of North

Riverside, took up the cause in the Senate, and Lawfer championed it in the House. They introduced resolutions seeking permission to move the Grants' remains to Illinois, should the Park Service fail to clean up the site.

I covered the story for the TH and couldn't wait to use a lead-in with a new twist on the old Who-is-buried-in-Grant's-tomb joke. But I never got to use it.

Before long, several national publications, including People magazine and the Christian Science Monitor, came out with the story. It even made The London Times, according to Lawfer.

"The basic question the reporters all had was, 'Are you serious?'" Lawfer said. "Yes, we were serious."

Burying the Grants in Illinois might not have been what Scaturro had in mind, but the resolution apparently got the Park Service's attention. Under media scrutiny, it restored the tomb, and the Grants' bodies remain in New York. Miller, who recently visited the site, said it looks fabulous.

"Mission accomplished, I guess," Lawfer said with a shrug.

Lawfer tried to get legislation passed that would allow the University of Illinois to study the growing of hemp for industrial use. Lawfer believes hemp could become a viable alternative crop, helping to diversify the state's agricultural industry, but he had to fight the fact that hemp looks a lot like marijuana. (The plants are distantly related.) He collected reams of information about the topic and worked for nearly three years on his bill. Twice the bill passed both houses, but both times the governor vetoed it.

"The time will come yet," Lawfer said.

He chuckled as he showed me a picture of him standing on the Capitol lawn next to a homemade sign that said "Keep off the grass."

But there was another defeat that was much harder for Lawfer to take.

In 1995, the U.S. Department of Defense announced it would close the Savanna Army Depot Activity, a 13,000-acre military base in southern Jo Daviess County and northern Carroll County. The Army stored, tested and recycled ammunition there and provided training for people from other installations on ammo storage and maintenance. In 1995 it employed about 350 area civilians. Defense planned to shut it down in 2000.

The Jo/Carroll Local Redevelopment Authority, a committee of people from both coun-

Illinois Sen. Evelyn M. Bowles and Rep. Ron Lawfer (courtesy of Ron Lawfer)

ties, was appointed to find a new use for the property and to replace the jobs that would be lost. When, in 1997, the state publicized plans to build a new prison, the LRA and 21 other communities applied to provide a location for the new prison. Interest was high, because the facility would employ as many as 1,000 people and create new opportunities for local businesses.

With the competition so fierce, Lawfer lobbied hard on behalf of the Jo/Carroll LRA.

The following April, Gov. Jim Edgar flew to the Savanna Army Depot to announce that he had chosen a 140-acre site at the depot. School bands played, and people cheered. Lawfer was ecstatic.

But environmentalists were not. Biologists said construction might wipe out two plants on the

Illinois endangered species list and disturb a rare sand prairie, where dozens more endangered and threatened species exist. Other opposition came from people who said that a prison, with its bright lights and razor-wire fences, would be a blemish on Jo Daviess County's beautiful landscape. It would discourage tourism and other clean development at the depot, they said.

The prison question became the most hotly debated issue I covered during my seven years of reporting in the county. Local residents made impassioned pleas for creating employment by building the prison. They wanted their sons and daughters and grandchildren to be able to find decent-paying jobs close to home. Lawfer, who farms with his son, understood their desire. More than a few people cursed the protected species, especially one unfortunate enough to be called James Clammyweed. They accused opponents of caring more about weeds than people.

I became frustrated with both sides. A few of the strongest supporters seemed to want to hear nothing from environmentalists. Don Schaible, mayor of nearby Hanover and a depot employee, refused to talk to me for nearly two years after I wrote a story about the biological concerns. Local businessman and then-LRA Chairman John Sullivan gave me a major butt chewing.

On the other hand, some of the opponents seemed to exploit the environmental issue because they were more concerned about having a prison in their backyards than about the potential biological impact. Some said they did not want the "wrong element"—prisoners' family members and friends—coming into the county. Did their comments stem more from racism and classism than from genuine concerns about crime? I wondered.

Edgar rescinded his decision in July of 1998. It was a severe blow to Lawfer and many others.

Instead, the state built the prison about 20 miles south of the depot, near the small town of Thomson. The prison still could have helped the local economy but, before it opened, the state ran out of money. The prison remains empty, and the promise of many new jobs has faded. So far, only 125 jobs have been created at the depot, coming from a few small businesses that have located there.

Lawfer speaks bitterly about the situation and especially about the James Clammyweed. "I asked a biologist one time what a James Clammyweed looks like, and he said it's not even very good looking."

He said the plant is not native to the area and probably was introduced only after European settlers began shipping cattle across the plains. (Randy Nybor, program manager for the Illinois Endangered Species Protection Board disputes that notion.)

What further irks Lawfer is the fact that Harry Drucker, an activist who alerted state officials to the endangered species and headed a group called Friends of the Depot, did not live in or near Jo Daviess County.

Lawfer believes that, if the prison had been built at the depot, it would have been completed on schedule and the Department of Corrections would have had it operating before the budget crisis hit.

But Lawfer ended our talk on a high note.

He said one of his favorite moments at the state capitol occurred on his birthday on May 15, 2002. On that day House Republicans received an invitation from Gov. George Ryan for dinner at his mansion. That evening, much to Lawfer's surprise, the governor presented him with a birthday cake.

"Imagine, the governor sang 'Happy Birthday' to me. It doesn't get any better than that."

Lawfer retired from the House after serving 10 years and never missing a day in session. He was 69, had survived prostate cancer and thought it was time to move on.

Now he is writing a book about the prison situation. "I'm trying to figure out whether the James Clammyweed was the real issue, whether people didn't want a prison in Jo Daviess County or whether the opposition was just anti-prison."

Every so often he travels down to the state capitol in Springfield to testify before a legislative committee or to lobby for legislation on behalf of livestock farmers.

He still farms 160 acres and lives within a mile of where he grew up, about six miles southeast of Stockton.

Although he spent 10 years in the General Assembly, Lawfer jokes, "I never went very far."

A much sought-after job

One might wonder why anyone would want to run for Galena City Council, when the job pays so little and results in so many headaches.

But, in 2005, six people ran for mayor, and five competed for one alderman-at-large seat. Richard Clark, who has been writing about local politics for The Galena Gazette for many years, believes the interest arose from underlying tensions between two broad constituencies—native Galenians and relative newcomers.

Both groups were represented in each race. Tom Brusch, a transplant, became mayor, and Terry Murphy, a native, won the at-large seat. The mix did not surprise Clark. He said "old-timers versus transplants" has been an unspoken but underlying theme in Galena elections for at least two decades.

"Before then, the power resided in a particular group of people—-people you would consider 'first citizens,' whether they happened to be elected or not." Ordinary natives didn't see much hope of breaking into the power structure and effecting change, so they pretty much stayed out of politics. But the newcomers, who tended to be wealthier and more experienced in business management, believed they could make a difference.

"They challenged the old power structure and became part of the new power structure."

As the natives saw the transplants winning elections and becoming the new "first citizens," they began to demand a say in local politics, too. Now the old-timers and the transplants battle fairly evenly for power and influence.

The two groups tend to have different interests, Clark said. The newcomers tend to favor historic preservation, while the natives focus more on economic development and job creation.

That seems to have played out in the 2005 election. Brusch, the newcomer, campaigned on a promise to "preserve our rich heritage." Murphy, the old-timer, said Galena must stop "wasteful spending," cut the budget and promote new business growth.

"The whole thing depends on the clean-up."

Randy Nybor

The former Savanna Army Depot Activity seems vast and strange to me. Old brick office buildings, abandoned maintenance shops, ramshackle barracks and rusting warehouses stand in clusters on the southern end of the site.

Farther north, earth-covered ammunition storage bunkers, or igloos, poke through dry prairie grass and are scattered among stands of oak trees. The western side of the depot stretches along the Mississippi River, encompassing small islands in the river's backwaters.

The 13,000-acre area, which once teamed with activity, is eerily quiet.

In 1917, During World War I, Congress set aside $1.5 million to buy a long, narrow strip of land along the eastern shore of the

Igloo, Savanna Army Depot

Old warehouse, Savanna Army Depot

Mississippi River in Jo Daviess and Carroll counties. The site became a proving ground, where the Army fired ammunition from howitzers at the southern end of the depot toward the northern end. Its mission was to test the range and capability of the artillery and ammunition.

The depot's mission evolved from testing to manufacturing, storing, shipping and recycling ammunition. In 1950, the Army started a training school for ammunition maintenance and storage.

Over time, the Army built more than 1,000 structures, including 923 buildings, 28 warehouses, 156 above-ground ammunition-storage warehouses, or magazines, 437 igloos and 28 general-supply warehouses. It also constructed 138 miles of roads and 68 miles of railroad track.

The installation reached its height of activity during World War II, when it employed 7,195 people. The majority of workers were civilians, and many were the fathers, grandfathers, aunts and uncles of people who now live in Jo Daviess County.

After that, the employment level began to dwindle. In the fall of 1994, only 470 people worked there.

By that time, the Army had leased much of the prairie to area farmers for livestock grazing. I remember seeing weeds growing from the cracks in some of the roads.

The depot also had become a sort of nature preserve. An on-site natural resources manager, along with the Illinois Department of Natural Resources, looked after 22 native plant and animal species then known to be on the state's endangered and threatened species lists. (Now biologists have identified 47.)

In February of 1995 the Base Realignment and Closure Commission slated the Army depot for closure. The depot ended its Army career in 2000 when it was decommissioned.

Meanwhile, Congress placed the depot on a national priority list for clean-up, because it had become so contaminated. By 2005, a team of environmental remediation specialists had identified 233 hazardous sites. Many require years and millions of dollars to restore. Some of the worst problems include the possible existence of unexploded ordnance, or live ammunition, laying on or beneath the ground; two areas where TNT and other explosives washed into the soil; a site where mustard gas leaked; and several areas where the ground water is contaminated.

So far, the U.S. government has spent about $150 million to investigate and clean up the pollution.

John Clarke, environmental coordinator for the Base Realignment and Closure Commission, feels proud of the work that has been done, especially the removal of 860 tons of pesticide that was dumped there during the 1960s. "It would have been a serious threat to the environment and to human health if left there," he said.

In addition, scientists concluded that 3,000 acres of backwaters are free of unexploded ordnance.

However, work has progressed slowly. "Ten years ago, we thought we would be a lot further along than we are now," said Ed Britton, district manager of the Upper Mississippi River Wildlife Refuge for the U.S. Fish and Wildlife Service. "But that's how the process works."

Clarke said a few areas are so dirty that the Army might never be able to restore them. In other areas, the source of contamination has been removed but the ground water remains polluted. The Army has yet to decide how to handle the problem, which affects more than 200 acres. It might simply let time take its course, waiting for the natural process of attenuation to purify the water.

In some cases that could take as long as 100 years. No one knows for sure.

As clean-up has occurred, the Army has transferred property ownership to other agencies. The Jo/Carroll Local Redevelopment Authority (LRA), which is working to replace lost jobs, had received 800 acres by the end of 2005. Eventually it will own nearly 3,000 acres. The U.S. Fish and Wildlife Service has received 3,000 acres of backwaters and will get up to 7,000 more.

The Illinois Department of Natural Resources has taken possession of 187 acres, and the U.S. Army Corps of Engineers owns 143 acres, with 33 more to be added.

Job replacement has gone more slowly than expected, too. Not only did a state prison not materialize as hoped, an electronics recovery and recycling company that located at the former depot, called ERS, went out of business. And recently, the chairman and chief executive officer of the parent company of Stickler Warehousing (now Midwest Third Party Logistics), which set up an operation there, was found guilty of dumping contaminated wheat into the South China sea. Officials are not sure how that will affect the company.

As of May of 2005, 125 people worked at the site, including some at Riverport Railroad, which stores and maintains railroad cars. There has been talk of starting an ethanol production plant; food processing, packaging and shipping facilities; and a winery.

Meanwhile, outdoors men and women are enjoying the natural areas that are accessible. The U.S. Fish and Wildlife Service provides public access to part of a popular hunting and fishing area known as Crooked Slough. The agency looks forward to opening more land to the public, as soon as it becomes certifiably clean.

Many wildlife enthusiasts believe the former depot and surrounding natural areas offer significant potential for eco-tourism. It will take word of mouth and a cooperative marketing effort among nearby towns to make that a reality, according to Chuck Wemstrom, president of the Natural Area Guardians of Jo Daviess and Carroll counties.

Meanwhile, the Illinois Natural History Survey and Illinois DNR are restoring animal habitats by planting native seeds and removing unused railroad tracks and other infrastructure. That will encourage nesting by several state endangered and threatened birds that require large areas of continuous grassland in order to nest.

Mississippi River, Savanna Army Depot

Recently biologists discovered a species of moth that exists in only one other place, according to Randy Nybor, program manager for the Illinois Endangered Species Protection Board.

"We have made remarkable strides here the last two or three years," he said. "But the whole thing depends on the clean-up."

"I am going to make things hum about this place."

Angela Canfield

Jo Daviess County women have made their mark on local political history. Here are a few highlights:

March 1869

Sarah Coates Harris organized the Grand Woman Suffrage Convention at Davis Hall in Galena regarding the right women should have to vote. Susan B. Anthony and Elizabeth Cady Stanton spoke at the convention.

1870

Sarah Coates Harris collected 1,000 signatures on a petition asking the Galena City Council to enforce an Illinois law requiring establishments selling liquor to close on Sunday. With the help of 14 other women, she also petitioned the Jo Daviess County Board of Supervisors, asking that it grant no liquor licenses in the county. The board still issued licenses but set the fee at the high price of $300.

March 1871

Susan B. Anthony again visited Galena. Galena historian Steve Repp found this Galena Gazette report about her visit: "We confess that when Miss Anthony was in this city two or three years ago, she did not impress us favorably. We thought as did many others, that if she possessed a little more of Mrs. Stanton's sweetness of temper, and like her, would endeavor to lead the people, rather than to drive them, she would accomplish more for the cause which has long been so near to her heart. Last evening, however, Miss Anthony more than redeemed herself. Her subject was presented forcibly, in language fitly chosen, and without any appearance of bitterness. ... While we cannot agree with her, we cannot but admire her perseverance."

January 1891

The Galena City Council elected Sarah Coates Harris to the board of school directors. Harris, a homeopathic physician and second wife of steamboat captain Daniel Smith Harris, was the first woman elected to the position in Galena. She never referred to herself as "Mrs. Harris."

June 1913

The Illinois General Assembly passed the Illinois Municipal Voting Act, giving women the right to vote for presidential electors, some local officials (such as school superintendents) and local propositions. (The 19th amendment to the U.S. Constitution, which gave all women the right to vote, did not win approval until 1920.)

April 1914

Casting her vote on April 6 at 7:01 a.m., Mrs. A.L. (Annie) Avery was the first woman in East Galena Township and in Galena to vote in a city election. Miss Lula Gerholt, Mrs. Martin (Carolina) Blum and Mrs. Richard Bauer were the first in their precincts to vote.

"As early as seven o'clock women gathered near the polls and remained there during the entire day many bringing camp chairs," the Galena Gazette reported. "One of the most beautiful sights accompanying the right of women to vote was when Mrs. Harriett E. Lewis, who is ninety-four years of age, was brought to the polls in an auto by her friends. This privilege was what she had been praying for, for many years, and as she stepped from the auto her face was fairly aglow with radiance due to the honor she placed upon the fact that she was about to cast her first ballot."

Like voters in many cities throughout the state, Galenians then were considering whether to stay "wet," continuing to allow local liquor sales, or to go "dry." According to the Gazette, "the fate of three thousand saloons in Illinois depended today upon the votes of the women. Fifty thousand down-state women are eligible. Despite the generous rain many women accompanied their husbands to the polls early."

Women were required to use separate ballot boxes, and their votes were counted separately. In East Galena Township, 71 percent of women voted "dry," compared to 41 percent of men. The township went "dry."

Sarah Coates Harris (date unknown, courtesy of the Galena Public Library's History Room)

In West Galena, 45 percent of women voted "dry," compared to 38 percent of men. The township remained "wet."

April 1915

In one of Warren's "hardest fought village elections in several years," 75-year-old Mrs. A.R. (Angela) Canfield, of Warren, became the first woman to be elected mayor of an Illinois city. She received 221 votes, edging out her opponent, D.M. Staver, by four votes.

The Warren Sentinel Leader said she deserved to win because she was "ever ready to give up her own work to go out and campaign for something that was for the betterment of citizens, without even a thought of compensation" and that she would give Warren "a good, clean government administration." Canfield owned a hat shop, had lived in Warren 34 years, belonged to the Women's Christian Temperance Union and was active in the women's suffrage movement.

Canfield vowed to rid Warren of corruption. Upon her election, she said, "Officers who don't earn their money are just as wicked as any other kind of grafter, and I am going after them good and plenty. I am going to appoint a chief of police and a street commissioner who will make things hum about this place. Bowling alleys and pool rooms are sinful places and must go. Too many young men waste their time on those places when they might better be working on farms."

During her first village board meeting, she assumed her role as mayor "in a calm and dignified manner." The six village trustees, all men, agreed with her stance against pool rooms. They denied license renewals to two pool halls, as well as a shooting gallery. However, they turned down all but two of Canfield's appointments, saying she based them on sympathy rather than qualifications.

The appointment issue soon was resolved, and the council focused on typical city business--such as street construction, speeding cars and the local spitting ordinance.

January 1918

The Galena Unit of the Women's Committee, National Council of Defense formed with Mrs. H.L. (Myrtle) Heer, Miss Julia Jones, Mrs. P.T. Sheean, Mrs. J.T. (Elmira) Dawson, Miss Irene Bench, Miss Ethel Hughlett, Miss Antionette Beam and Mrs. W.L. Miller as its officers and directors. The committee's first task was to take a census of the women of Galena to find out how they could help the nation during World War I.

The Galena Gazette published several articles encouraging Galena women to register for the census. It wrote: "Today we must work to win the war: Some must go into factories, some must work on the farms or in gardens, some must help with Red Cross work, others must care for their families and save the food so badly needed across the ocean." It listed 154 occupations that women could take up to help on the home front, including several occupations normally held by men—such as, printer, dentist, engineer, physician and accountant.

In the same month, Mrs. H.M. (Bertha) Stryker attended the monthly board meeting of the Illinois Equal Suffrage Association in Chicago.

April 1926

Minnie D. Fitch became the Republican Party candidate for Jo Daviess County clerk, receiving 3,052 votes, compared to 822 votes for W.J. Shipton. On April 8, she ran a small ad in the Galena Gazette addressed to voters: "In seeking the nomination for the office of County Clerk of Jo Daviess County, I have not been able to personally see all the voters as this is a very busy time at the clerk's office. I therefore take this opportunity of earnestly soliciting your vote at the primary April 13, 1926. Having made my home in Galena for the best part of my life, I feel there is nothing I can say to you that you do not already know. I wish to call your attention, however, to the fact that I have been employed in the County Clerk's office for the last three years as Deputy County Clerk and am familiar with the work of that office. I can assure the public, if I am nominated and elected, of courteous and efficient service. Your vote means a great deal to me and my family."

With no opposition in the general election, Fitch became county clerk. In 1930, she sought and won a second term. She proved that "a woman can be efficient as well as gracious, affable and accommodating," according to a Republican political ad. She had no opposition.

Ruth Hanna McCormick, a Republican Congresswoman from Byron, Ill. and the first woman nominated by a major party for the U.S. Senate, received the majority of votes in Jo Daviess County in the primary election. Although she was "dry," she ran on the promise that she would act according to voter's wishes regarding prohibition, rather than on her own preferences. She lost in the November election to J. Hamilton Lewis. Voters in Jo Daviess County also favored Lewis in the general election, 2,419 to 1,934.

November 1930

Illinois voters approved a measure to allow women to serve on juries. The first women to be called to jury duty in Jo Daviess County were Myrtle Bader, Blanche Goldsworthy, Blanche Cramer, Anna Schilling, Vera Walter, Eula Klassy, Florence Bryson, Mary Lutter, Lena Evans, Ora Drane, Julia Durant, Clara O'Neil, Gertrude Bonnet, Rose Smith, Myrtle Meador and Cecelia Stevens. They sat on the petit jury. Not until 1939 did the county select women to sit on the grand jury.

April 1953

Running as a Citizens Party candidate, Alma Howe became the first woman to be elected to the Jo Daviess County Board of Supervisors and the first elected as a township supervisor. (People were elected to both positions simultaneously prior to the 1970s.) She garnered 215 votes, compared to 47 for her write-in opponent, John Gunn.

During her first year on the board, the county budget totaled $305,900, including $33,000 for the tuberculosis sanatorium, and the county levied $182,500 in taxes. In 1954, the county issued $500,000 in bonds for road improvements, and most of the county's business dealt with roads and bridges.

In 1964, Howe was one of 15 supervisors to vote in favor of "considering zoning in conjunction with cities in Jo Daviess County." Five board members voted no. But the board did not pass a zoning ordinance until 1993.

Howe continued to serve on the county board and as East Galena Township supervisor until 1975.

Carlene Stephenson, current East Galena Township supervisor, said she and her husband rented an apartment from Howe when they were first married. She described Howe as "a very nice lady" with "a nice sense of humor." She said Howe was a homemaker and that she and her husband, Max, had no children, but that she was like a mother to a young girl who grew up in Howe's apartment.

No other women served on the county board until 1974, when voters elected Vera Heller and Dorothy Miles to the board.

November 1954

Emma Grebner, an Independent, beat her Republican and Democratic opponents, Percy Hutchison and Mike Ricke, for Jo Daviess County Sheriff, becoming the first and only woman to hold that position and the first woman elected sheriff in Illinois. She had lost the Republican primary by a narrow margin to Hutchison, so she ran as an independent. Grebner promised voters she would appoint her husband, Lawrence Grebner, as chief deputy. Lawrence had been county sheriff before the election, and Emma was his chief deputy. Hutchison had been sheriff from 1938 to 1942 and from 1946 to 1950.

"It is important to keep gambling out of the county for the protection of families," she said before the election. "Having a woman in

Emma Grebner with smashed slot machines (1954 by Joe Willy from the Alfred Mueller Collection, Galena)

the sheriff's office helps in many family problems. We have had the co-operation of the supervisors and other law enforcement officials as well as the assistance of church leaders where religious help was needed."

The race was a cliff hanger, with the vote going back and forth between Grebner and Hutchinson throughout election night. She finally took the lead by only 38 votes, with a total of 3,336 votes compared to Hutchison's 3,298.

Grebner made good on her promise to fight illegal gambling. in October of 1956, she and 10 of her deputies led a raid on four establishments, one each run by the Elks, Moose, Eagles and American Legion. They arrested all the bartenders and confiscated 13 slot machines. "Mrs. Grebner herself led the raid on the American Legion home," the Galena Gazette reported. "Raiding parties were armed with guns and axes."

"People called her Two-Gun Emma," said Eldon Glick, a retired businessman and former Galena City Councilman. Glick believes Grebner beat him out of a $25 reward from the Chicago Motor Club. He said he gave information to the sheriff's department leading to the arrest of a young man who stole a car, for which the club offered a reward. However, he never received it. Instead, he received letters from the club addressing him as "Officer Glick," even though he was not with the sheriff's department, indicating that the money had gone to the department.

Lawrence Grebner ran again in the 1958 election but was defeated.

December 1994

Judith (Judy) Gratton became the first woman to chair the Jo Daviess County Board of Supervisors and served as chair for four years. She was elected to the board in 1984 and left in 2000, after deciding not to run for re-election. During her tenure, the board grappled with several controversial issues, including zoning, gambling, a proposal to build a prison at the former Savanna Army Depot Activity and the regulation of big livestock operations.

Helen Schamberger, who served on the board with Gratton during the 1980s and early 1990s, said she and Gratton worked together on a land-use plan but, when it came time to present it to the board, they asked the late Paul Kindig to do it. They agreed that the rest of the board would be more likely to listen to a man than a woman, Schamberger said.

But Gratton became a strong leader. She called it "ironic" that, although she adamantly opposed bringing the Silver Eagle Casino to the county, as board chairwoman she later had to testify to the Illinois Gaming Commission on behalf of the casino. The majority of the board favored the gambling operation, and she had to represent the board. "That was a sign of doing what my peers (fellow county board members) elected me to do, but putting aside my personal feelings," she said.

At the end of Gratton's term as chairwoman, eight of the 17 members of the board were women. They were: Gratton, Lynn Sisler, Hylene Anderson, Yerda Potter, Joanne Bielenda, Margie Montellius, Charlice Offenheiser and Merri Berlage. Berlage now chairs the board.

References

Biographical Directory of the United States Congress, www.bioguide.congress.gov.

Bush, George W., transcript of presidential debate, Oct. 8, 2004.

Clarke, John, interview, 2005.

Cox, Bonnie, interview, 2005.

Cox, John, interviews, 2005.

East Dubuque Register: "Tuesday's Primary Election Results," April 10, 1930; "Democrats Score Sweeping Victory," Nov. 6, 1930.

Elizabeth Weekly News: "Endorsed Ticket Wins," April 6, 1930; political advertisement, Oct. 29, 1930; "Women Will Serve on Juries in Illinois," Nov. 12, 1929; "Jo Daviess County Women Called for Jury Duty," Dec. 10, 1930.

Galena Gazette: "In Brief," Jan. 7, 1881; "Women Vote on Poll Tax," March 27, 1914; "Many Women Vote Today in Illinois," April 7, 1914; "Women's Votes Knock out 1,000 Saloons," April 8, 1914; "West Galena Is Wet, East Galena Goes Dry," April 8, 1914; "Woman Mayoress of Warren," April 21, 1915; "Warren's Woman Mayoress," April 22, 1915; "Rebuff for Warren Mayoress," May 3, 1915; "Women Organize for Patriotic Service," Jan. 2, 1918; "For Constitutional Convention," Jan. 22, 1918; "What You Can Do," Jan. 31, 1918; "Why Should You Register," Feb. 1, 1918; "Volunteer for War Service," Feb. 2, 1918; "All Women Should Register for War Service," 1918; ad placed by Minnie D. Fitch, April 8, 1926: "Results of the Primaries Here," April 15, 1926; "Lady Supervisor Wins in East Galena's Race," April 8, 1953; "Record Primary Vote Seen as Local Contests Generate Heat," April 9, 1954; "Sheriff's Race Is Top Local Contest," Oct. 29, 1954; "Grebner Bests Hutchison As Republicans Dominate County," Nov. 5, 1954; "Sheriff Hits Slots," Oct. 30, 1956; and "Alderman, Mayor Candidates Sound Off," March 30, 2005.

Glick, Eldon, interview, 2005.

Gratton, Judy, interview, 2005.

Lawfer, Ron, interview, 2005.

Lawfer, Pat, interview, 2005.

Miners' Journal: "Sarah Coates Harris: A Woman of History," Winter 1999.

Repp, Steve, "The City Among the Hills: Famous Visitors to Galena, Illinois," 1995.

"Savanna Army Depot Activity," booklet published by the U.S. Army (date unknown).

Schamberger, Helen, interview, 2005.

Schwerdtfeger, Carl "Skip," interview, 2005.

Supervisors Records, minutes from the meetings of the Jo Daviess County Board of Supervisors, Vols. 20, 21 and 26.

Telegraph Herald: "Hallock, Cox to square off for district seat," March 21, 1990; "Demo candidate from Galena: Use tax surcharge for bailout," July 20, 1990; "Cox trounces Hallock," Nov. 7, 1990; "Cox newsletter looks to future," Nov. 2, 1991; "Cox bucks advice, suggests debates," March 18, 1992; "Illinois debate no mud-slinger," Oct. 30, 1992; "Manzullo defeats incumbent Demo Cox," Nov. 4, 1992; "Panel to Edgar: Change site for prison at depot," June 9, 1998.

"U.S. Army Defense Ammunition Center," booklet published by the U.S. Army (date unknown).

Warren Sentinel Leader: "Village Board Meets," April 22, 1915; "Village Affairs," May 5, 1915; and "Village Affairs," May 12, 1915.

Scales Mound

Scales Mound

People don't have fences to separate their neighbors from them."

Rick Koehler

In 1990, most of Scales Mound became listed on the National Register of Historic Places.

The little town isn't fancy or quaint like Galena. Few buildings are made of brick or stone — although there are some — and not many boast of turrets, columns or gingerbread trim. The fact is, Scales Mound is fairly plain and hasn't changed much through the years. The main street, which runs next to the Illinois Central Railroad tracks, consists only of a house or two, a few stores and a couple of taverns.

For me, the most important element is the people.

Some towns are on the move, constantly trying to improve and keep pace with the times. Some are almost the opposite, sluggishly plodding toward eventual demise. Some seem contentious, with various factions fighting for different things and, in the end, either getting nothing done or accomplishing an amazing amount. Some even exude an air of superiority and closed mindedness.

Scales Mound strikes me as friendly and content. The people there want to preserve what they have, yet they don't resist change. They seem to like their town and, for the most part, they like each other.

The village grew up around the railroad — as several towns in Jo Daviess County did — after the Illinois Central laid tracks in 1854. As soon as the railroad was up and running, Sherman Eddy opened a supply station for nearby miners, farmers and railroad workers. Shortly thereafter, a few houses and a blacksmith shop sprang up. By 1856, the Methodists had built a church, and, the next year, The Brick School House of District 1 opened its doors. Two general stores and three hotels soon followed.

The first hotel, built for $6,000 in 1856, still stands. People today know it as Pop a Tops Again, a bar and restaurant. Residents say it once was a "house of ill repute." I honestly don't know if that's true, but locals get a kick out of the legend.

The village became incorporated July 14, 1877. It got its name from Samuel Scales, who built a public house nearby, at the base of a mound now called Scales Mound.

The first ordinance passed by the village board ordered grocery stores to close on Sundays and set a license fee of $100 for saloons. Two years later, it upped the fee to $500.

At different times throughout its history, there were livery stables, a doctor's office, a pharmacy, a lumber yard, car dealerships, a poultry business, a dance pavilion, a bulk-oil storage facility, a saw mill, a warehouse — complete with an opera house on the second floor — and other businesses. A man by the name of Dale Jewell opened the first "beauty shop" in 1929.

The village embraced the modern age in 1899, when it gave L.D. Pitcher permission to start a telephone system. In 1916, it started to replace its oil lamps with electric lights and its board walks with cement walks.

Residents loved competitive sports. In 1899, the town basketball team traveled as far as Freeport, Ill., Epworth, Iowa and Platteville, Wis. to play. It won the local championship in 1915, with members Earl Rummel, George Trevarthan, Edgar Johnson, Delbert Hicks and Milton Rittweger. Baseball got started in 1890, and the town team took the championship in 1930.

Melvin Dittmar, who grew up in the 1940s, remembers there being more businesses in town than there are today, including two or three grocery stores, a couple of restaurants, three farm implement dealers and a stockyard.

It was a good time to grow up, he said. He and his friends would run over the old railroad bridge, as the trains passed under it, through the white smoke of the steam engines. They roller skate at the township hall. In high school almost all the boys played basketball. There were only 17 boys in the school.

There was nothing like a practical joke. "Years ago, they had the desks all in a row. There was one girl, we thought she was a little dainty. Everything had to be so nice. Well, guess what I put in her desk — an old petrified cat. When she reached in there, boy, she let out a scream!"

Dittmar and his friends enjoyed pulling a good one on the mayor. "The mayor would be in town playing cards, and we'd jack up his wheel and put a block in. When he'd come out to leave, he couldn't go anywhere. That wheel would just spin."

In 1953, when Scales Mound turned 100 years old, things were going well, according to the authors of a history of the town. Just two years earlier, the school district had completed construction of a new school and gym. Three alumni of the old school — Tossie Edge Rummell, Mildred Berryman Horan and Dorothy Pooley Ople — raised money to buy a stage curtain.

Television was still new. "A home with a set installed is easily identified by the aerial on the roof, usually 20 feet high with prongs protruding from the mast. Many residents have not been to a movie since their sets have entered their homes," according to the history's authors.

World War II had ended, and the days of rationing and the unavailability of durable consumer goods had passed. People were buying new cars, farm machinery and modern appliances. Many property owners had spruced up their homes, and, in 1952, farmers enjoyed bumper harvests.

There was talk of the possible resurgence of the mining industry but, by 1978, all the local mining leases had been canceled.

The history ended on this note: "Early in 1953 finds new hope for peace in the world as the Korean Conflict dies down to almost a standstill. This is of great importance to us all as many of our young men are still on that battlefield.

"Continued high farm prices are another big question in 1953 with many farmers and businessmen alike watching the chances of peace and war. It is their great desire to prevent another depression like the one of the '20s and early '30s."

Today about 400 people live in the quiet village, and there are about 40 businesses, including a grocery store, an appliance store, plumbing and heating shop, a trucking company and several home-based businesses.

In March of 2004, Mike "Wulf" Clifton and his wife Tina Hollis bought the old Shipping Association warehouse — the building with the opera house on the second floor — where they hold auctions and host community events. They call it Dr. Woodchuck's Antique Emporium.

"Business is slowly coming along," Clifton said. "The building was a feed store so long, so it's just now getting into people's minds that it can be used for other things."

He said, although they knew they would have to do a lot clean-up work and repair, he and Hollis "fell in love" with the building. "About 90

Township Hall

percent is still original."

They were impressed with Scales Mound, too. "It seems to have a real community spirit. The town went together and built Rec Park. People seem genuinely to want to save the town."

Village President Jim Davis said the town has the second highest "pull factor" in Jo Daviess County. That means that it brings more sales dollars from outside than every town except Galena. "We receive 400 to 500 percent more money from sales-tax revenue than from property-tax revenue. We like to think that the residents of the Galena Territory and Apple Canyon Lake (two unincorporated resort communities) think of this as their home town."

During the mid-1980s, Ken and Sandy Frank organized a community effort to build a park. People sold food, had raffles and held fund raisers to pay for it. Almost every year since the park became a reality, the community has added something to it, such as lights, another ball diamond, and a concession stand.

Now big crowds turn out to watch town teams play ball. "You get all ages there," Joann Schultz said. "It's a Norman Rockwell painting, all right."

Among its more recent accomplishments, the village has nearly finished restoring the old township hall. That involved cutting the roof into four sections and pulling the sections away with a crane. "When they pulled the first section away, they found that the wires were still attached," Schultz said. "It tilted and went down into the town hall. That stopped a few hearts."

Dave Carscallen, who moved to town 8 or 9 years ago, did the plumbing, wiring, insulation and drywall. "Everybody will help, and everybody is friendly," he said.

He called the building "plain and simple" and its molding "Plain Jane," but said he enjoyed working on it. "It just does its thing here," he said.

The renovation is costing $160,000. Scales Mound Township contributed $30,000 to the project, and the community raised $100,000 through fund raisers and private contributions.

"You realize that maybe we really do have a special town here," Schultz said.

Scales Mound is just a nice place to be, Davis said. "Really, it's the ultimate small town. It's friendly. It's quiet. It's safe. It's very traditional in values. If a child does something wrong, that child gets scolded — and not from just the parents. People care. They genuinely care. To me, it's the perfect place to be."

"People don't have fences to separate their neighbors from them," Rick Koehler said. "It's our town. We love it. It's the closeness I like. If I was in a bind, I would be able to call that guy over here, one over there or her over there."

Even though I don't live there, I bet I could do the same.

"You never get bored in Scales Mound."

Joshua Winter

Joshua (Josh) Winter loves his home town and the people in it.

At age 12, he cannot think of a thing he would change. "I like how big it is. It's peaceful, quiet and friendly."

"If I ever fell off my bike and scraped my knee, I could go to any one of these houses for help," he says, as he sweeps his hand across the village scape.

Many of the people who live in those homes helped take up a collection for Josh when he was diagnosed with leukemia. He was in the first grade and now is doing fine.

Josh lives in a big white house on the edge of town with his mother Sharon, his brother Zach and his sister Nicole. Farm fields surround his home on three sides, and the village lies southwest.

His favorite place in town is the fire station,

Joshua Winter

where he helps volunteer fire fighters wash their trucks or do other odd jobs. "I can't wait to get on the department," he says.

"John Duerr — he's a guy I really respect — and Leo Werner took me to the Monroe fire school one day. We walked around and looked at trucks and saw demonstrations."

One day in 2004, Josh gave me a tour of Jo Daviess County's new smoke house. He pointed out its features as proudly as though he had built or paid for it himself. "One guy sits in the control room and he can see everyone on a camera."

Josh doesn't register the typical complaints that kids who grow up in small towns normally do. "You never get bored in Scales Mound."

When he isn't at the fire station, Josh is helping his great uncle, Cletus Winter, on his farm ("He is a good guy"), playing sports, attending a ball game, working on his friends' bicycles ("Mom doesn't like it because, usually, I take the bikes apart and don't have time to put them back together") stopping at Country House Grocery to talk with co-owner Sheila Ohms, meeting up with his friends or golfing, hunting or going for a ride with his dad, Don Winter.

"The whole town gets together on Wednesday or Thursday night, usually for the men's softball games. It's amazing how the balls fly. The nice part is, they don't hire refs. The team before does the reffing. Usually you get honesty out of them. People usually call it straight. Everybody has a good time."

Afterward, many townsfolk stop at Pop a Tops Again or Jake's Place. "You go to most towns, and they don't let little kids go in the bars. You go to Scales Mound, and it's like the bars are family restaurants."

Most of Josh's relatives live in or around town. "In a day in Scales Mound, I do not go without seeing at least three relatives."

Josh likes and admires his relatives, starting with his mother and father, who are divorced. "Mom's a pretty easy-going person. As long as Mom knows where I am, there's no problem."

"My dad and I hang out a lot. We have a lot in common. He takes us out hunting — Leo Werner and I and Leo's brother Dennis. We go to the bottom of Kording Road. We just shoot raccoons, but we have a blast."

"My mom and dad tie in together. Both of them are really fantastic."

Josh's enthusiasm extends to his home and his possessions. One day he gave me a tour of his sunny, neatly decorated home. I had to tell him that, no, I didn't really need to see the basement. Perhaps his favorite possession is his .22 single-shot, long rifle. "It's Dad's old one. I cherish that thing like a baby. It kicks the shell right out and everything."

Josh used to dislike school, but even that has changed, "I talk to my friends and have gotten more active."

He thinks his reading teacher, Mrs. Werner, is the greatest. "I grew up with her, I guess. When I would go out to the farm, she would be there. We'd swing on the tire out there and pick up berries. She helps me out."

"Mabye I do it because it looks nice and because of my faith."

Ron Webster

If you need to go anywhere in northern Jo Daviess County, you had better know where the "Jesus Saves" rock is. It is the local landmark that nearly everyone recognizes and refers to when giving directions.

Looking for Council Hill Road? "It's just before you get to the 'Jesus Saves' rock."

Need to get to Apple Canyon Lake? "Do you know where the 'Jesus Saves' rock is?" county residents ask without expecting an answer. "Go three miles east and turn right onto Pea Ridge Road." You can't see the "Jesus Saves" rock while heading east, unless you look through your rear-view mirror.

The big, flat rock faces east on Stagecoach Trail and overlooks the land where, in 1830, Samuel H. Scales built a tavern. The tavern served the miners who traveled the "Sucker Trail" to the lead mines in northwest Illinois and later was on the Chicago & Galena stage line. Today the stone mass overlooks a pasture — the tavern having disappeared long ago — and lies a mile or so southwest of the village of Scales Mound.

The "Jesus Saves" rock outside of Scales Mound

No one seems to know just when people started painting "Jesus Saves" on the rock. Ron Webster remembers seeing a Potosi Beer ad on it when he was a kid. "There was a clothing store in Galena that was there, too," he says. Sometime since then it became the "Jesus Saves" rock, featuring large, simple letters.

About 1990, Webster took on the responsibility for the rock and its message. "The letters are seven feet tall. It takes pretty close to a day, with two or three people painting, to get it done.

"I get the best paint that Davis Farm Supply has and have the Barry Altfillisch family in Scales Mound paint it."

Webster's reasons for taking on the task seem to be tied to family, church and community. He also likes things looking neat. "Maybe I do it because it looks nice and because of my faith."

The Webster family goes back seven generations in rural Scales Mound. "The Websters go to the United Methodist Church in town. All my grandparents were members of United Methodist."

Webster has been a Church trustee since 1968, and his two children were married in the Church.

The family has stayed close to the old farmstead. "I was born 2 miles from the rock in a rock house," Webster says. "I've been a farmer all my life. I started right out of high school."

Webster now owns the farm that his great, great grandfather owned. His son Tom, Tom's wife Heather and the couple's daughters Alexandra and Bailey live on the farm. "All the original buildings are there. It's a mile-and-a-half from the 'Jesus Saves" rock on West Council Hill Road."

In 2004, Webster had a light installed at the rock in memory of his granddaughter, Eleanor Grace Downs, who died in July of 2004 at only 15 days old. "When the light is on, it really looks nice. Every time I go by, I think of my granddaughter."

Often around Halloween, a prankster climbs up the mound and, with spray can in hand, adds a line to the message. "Green stamps" or "at First National" are favorites.

It gives the unholy a good laugh, but Webster doesn't think it's so funny. He paints over the words as soon as he can. "I just think it shows lack of respect for what the sign reads," he says.

"As long as we're talking about street lights ..." *Jim Davis*

The Scales Mound Village Board meets the fourth Monday of every month in an old stone house in the center of town.

As the six board trustees, Village President Jim Davis, Village Clerk Margaret Townsend, Village Treasurer Karen Hesselbacher and Zoning Administrator Joe Lee assemble around a large oblong table, they tease each other and talk about the latest news. A few townsfolk and city employees take places in chairs around the edge of the room.

Village officials started a recent meeting with a report from Dennis Enright, an emergency-service technician who represents the local ambulance district. Wearing a T-shirt that said "5 Alarm Dennis," he said the EMTs had lined up entertainment for the following year's appreciation event.

Next, Steve Stadel talked about the upcoming fireman's dance, and the board approved a street dance on behalf of Jake's Place, pending approval from the Catholic Church next door. "I don't think they will have any objections, but it's just the neighborly thing to do," Trustee Ruth Foley said.

"If you're nice, they might advertise it in their bulletin," Trustee Dave Winter added.

The board then talked about safety concerns. Perhaps the village should ask for a 45 mph. speed limit on Stagecoach Trail, where it intersects with the Elizabeth-Scales Mound Road. A bad accident occurred there the day before. And maybe it ought to require a wider set-back for quarries.

Before long, the discussion broke up into twos and threes, but not by design. Davis said something to Townsend, while Trustee Carrie Stier

Jim Davis and Karen Hesselbacher

exchanged quips with a resident. Trustee David Hesselbacher asked Foley a question, and someone on the side made a comment to no one in particular.

"We're pretty informal around here," Stier

Joe Lee and Ruth Foley

said later.

Finally, the group got back to business. Davis said the village needs to do something about

David Hesselbacher and Chris Schultz

sewer, water and garbage rates. He suggested conducting an audit to make sure everyone is billed the right amount.

"If you look at the $25.50 you pay for water and sewer every month, even for a little old lady, that's a damn good deal," Winter said.

"We don't need more money, and we don't need more water. What we need to do is simplify our rates. We have 15 different ways of billing."

The board's Finance Committee set up a time to work on the problem.

Next, Lee reported that someone wanted to put up another Internet tower. He also said the board should "think about annexation."

The conversation meandered on to street lights. "As long as we're talking about street lights ..." Davis said.

He and board members peppered their discussion with "As long as we're talking about ..." and "Oh, speaking of ..."

After analyzing several ideas related to utility rates, street lights and other topics, Karen Hesselbacher said, "I think we have brain stormed enough already."

"Yeah, my brain hurts," Davis said, as he leaned back in his chair.

It was time to swear in Chris Schultz as a board member. Schultz is filling an unexpired term. He solemnly took the oath of office, then proceeded to sit down but missed the chair and fell on the floor. Everybody laughed, including Schultz.

Finally, the board approved appropriations of $361,000 for the next fiscal year. "We might not spend all that," Davis said. "There are no major, big

Dave Winter and Carrie Stier

plans on the table."

The budget consisted of 22 items and fit on two-thirds of one page. The biggest items were $70,000 each for the water and sewage funds, $50,000 for the public works department, $30,000 for buying property, $25,000 for emergency services and $18,000 for garbage collection. The board also approved $14,000 for the city park and $9,000 in salaries for city officers.

Afterward, Davis talked with me about being village president and about the town. He was president from 1987 to 1996, from 1998 to 2000 and from 2003 to the present.

"I'll probably stay until they throw me out now. When you live here, you become passionate about serving.

"Every person who sits here at the table is here for some reason. Everybody wants to do what is right for the town."

Sure, there have been disagreements and controversies, he said. "But, when the motion is made and the vote is taken, there is no reason to hate each other."

The biggest challenge the village faces is adding more homes and finding more spots for businesses. "We need more heads in our school. We have businesses looking for places. We already have 40-some businesses in town."

"We're not looking for things to explode," he added. "I've seen some towns do some crazy things when they are looking to explode. I think cities ought to leave development to developers. Maybe we can aid them, but we should not become developers."

"This is where we're at and what we do."

Sheila Ohms

In 1979, a few years after they were married, Pat and Sheila Ohms bought the Country House Grocery from Pat's uncle, Bill Brickner. Pat had worked for Bill for several years.

"Now it's just like a blur, having three kids and buying the store," Pat said. "We had our oldest and then, 26 months later, we had twins."

Country House harkens back to an earlier time: It is one of just a few mom and pop grocery stores remaining in Jo Daviess County.

Built in 1859 by George Allan, the building in which the store is located is one of the oldest in town. Except for a few years during the late 1930s when it was empty, the building has always housed a store. At first it was a general store with the local post office in back, but it became a grocery store, as well as a general store, during the 1940s when Mr. and Mrs. Ernest Grebner bought it.

I can hardly imagine it having room for shoes, boots, overalls and other items that typically were sold in general stores. "We even sold a little jewelry," said Pat's aunt, Mary Saam. Mary worked there for 37 years and now is retired. "You could buy almost anything you needed there."

Sheila and Pat Ohms

Today its shelves are crammed with boxes, bags, bottles and cans. The dairy case and produce section are fairly small, in order to leave room for the meat counter.

The store has carried some of the same products for years — Sheila can remember the

Sheila Ohms and Joshua Winter

Creamette macaroni boxes from when she was a child — but some items have changed. "The water thing is so amazing," she said. "Who would have thought years ago that we would sell so much bottled water!"

Keeping up with customer tastes presents a challenge. "When new stuff comes out, we have to find room for it," Sheila said. "The hard part is keeping a variety of things."

The store itself doesn't look much different from the days when the Allan family ran it. It has the same wooden floors and narrow aisles.

A few grocery carts are pushed together in the corner of the store between the entrance and the meat counter, but few customers use them. Instead, they carry their items to the counter, sometimes making several trips.

"We have a lot of loyal local people," Sheila said. "But we also get a lot of trade from the lakes (the Galena Territory and Apple Canyon Lake). "If it weren't for the lake people, I wonder how long we would have been here."

The meat counter draws in a lot of people. Pat butchers some of his own meat — he learned the trade from Mary — and makes sausage. "We buy all our meat from Pat," said Bonnie Lopp, who co-owns Pop a Tops Again, across the street. "We have never gotten any bad meat from him."

During school lunch hour or after school, a lot of students stop in for sandwiches, pizza or candy. "It's like a whirlwind then," Pat said.

Sheila and Pat work hard. They open the store seven days each week and are open until 8 p.m. on Fridays. "I stay down here until 9 or 9:30," Pat said. "It depends on what's going on." Delivery trucks come in every Monday and Thursday.

"I'm here full time," Sheila said. "I compare it to dairy farming. You've always got to be there."

Sheila said she and Pat work well together. "I think that's because we started so young. We either get along, or it doesn't work."

The couple lives above the store in a nice home. "Living upstairs makes it easier," Sheila said.

When Pat was in high school, he dreamed of becoming a basketball player. Sheila thought she would go into nursing. But, obviously, their careers went a different direction. Yes, there have been ups and downs, Sheila said. "But this is where we're at and what we do."

"Everything here is home cooked."

Bonnie Lopp

Usually quite a few people who work in town or on the Illinois Central Railroad stop at Pop a Tops Again for lunch. Some park perpendicular to the building, while others park at an angle, which can happen only in a town where people have room to maneuver. They sit at the bar or grab a table near the wall of the long, narrow tavern.

Dollar bills hang by yellowed tape from above a mirror, and various trophies are lined up along the old wooden back bar, which is original. Beer lights hang from the ceiling, and people shoot pool in the back room. An antique ice box stands in for a cooler. The old outhouse, with ladies on one side and men on the other, still sits out back. The building, built in 1856 as a hotel, is brick but has been covered over with white siding.

A green plastic ape hangs in a corner with a sign on it that says, “Jerry on a good day.” Jerry is Jerry Lopp, who owns the place with his wife Bonnie. They have lived in Scales Mound since they were born.

“We’re both retired from other jobs, but we wanted something to do,” Bonnie said. “We love the people.” At one time their daughter, Becky Reitz, and Becky’s ex-husband owned the bar. Now Becky, a slender blonde, works there as a bartender/waitress and lives in the apartment on the east side of the building. Cindy Koester, who also owned the bar at one time, works there, too. “She gave Becky her first job,” Bonnie said.

Recently, when I stopped in for a bite to eat, an old “Leave It to Beaver” episode was winding down on the TV and was followed by “Family Feud.” I tried to guess the last names of “famous Jerry’s” with a man sitting a couple of bar stools down from me, whose name I didn’t catch.

Usually there is a lunch special. That day it featured ham, cabbage, potatoes, carrots and homemade bread. “Everything here is home cooked,” Bonnie said. “I don’t like stuff that comes out of a bag.”

Every Tuesday night is “euchre night” at Pop a Tops. Euchre, a card game commonly played in northwest Illinois, northeast Iowa and southwest Wisconsin, draws four to eight tables of four players virtually every time.

Many townsfolk play cards at other times too. “You can tell from the tables,” Bonnie said. The red, 1940s-era tables are worn down to a light pink in spots where customers hold their cards.

“We’ve thought about redoing the place, but people say, ‘Oh no, keep it like it is.’”

Once a month Pop a Tops entertains with keroke. “Sometimes we get really good singers,” Bonnie said. “Right now keroke is more popular than live bands.”

Dick Bauer is one of the locals who can “really sing,” Becky said. “When he comes up here, he is very quiet and reserved. But one time we got him to dress like Alice Cooper. He had a big rubber snake around his neck.”

Bonnie Lopp and Fred Winter

The tavern attracts people of all ages and walks of life, Bonnie said. One of the oldest customers is Fred Winter. At 92, he was still mowing lawn and, until just a few weeks before I met him, was cooking his own meals. “He comes in to play cards. He brings one cigarette with him and keeps one in the truck,” Bonnie said. “He never smokes in his house.”

During the summer, a lot of motorcycle riders stop in and, during the winter, the snowmobile crowd comes around. “Jerry started keeping a couple of cans of gas in the garage. He won’t take anything for it.”

“All of ‘em get along pretty good,” Bonnie said. “The people around here are like family.”

"We went through three hogs."

Floyd Molitor

The 2003 Stagecoach Trail Festival was over. The annual event ranked as one of the biggest, because Scales Mound was celebrating its sesquicentennial.

A group of people who planned it sat on Pat and Sheila Ohms' porch talking about what went right and what needed to be changed for the next year's festival. They had eaten a potluck dinner and were enjoying a warm summer breeze.

Craig, Teresa and Raechel Raymon at the Stagecoach Trail Festival

"The play was cool," Mary Ellen Lyne said. An anonymous writer with the pen name "Ima Goestriter" had written a short play called "The Town that Didn't Disappear," and local residents performed it at the Scales Mound High School.

The play included a scene in which one of the actors was to put a cage containing two chickens on a train, but a prankster backstage let the chickens loose. One waddled on the stage and gave the cast a surprise. Audience members got a good chortle.

Some of the acting was pretty good, Susie Davis said. Bill Brickner, who played the old man who used to drive his tractor to town and get drunk, made the old man "come alive."

"I thought there was an inappropriate line or two," someone said.

"There were a lot of inappropriate lines," Joann Schultz added with a laugh.

In addition, the raffle went well. Sixty teachers showed up for the reception for current and former teachers. And the public was pleased with the crafters who sold their wares.

"I heard nothing but good about the parade," Village President Jim Davis added. "The music at the bandstand went extremely well this year, and the obstacle course went better than expected. Joann's history tour went well, but a lot of people waited until the last tour."

Joe Lee said he got compliments from runners and walkers about how smoothly the race went.

"It looked a lot smoother from the outside than the inside," Joann said.

Floyd Molitor noted that the guy who won the cake-eating contest, "sat at the beer tent chugging beers afterward."

But there were a few glitches. The weekend was too windy to offer tethered balloon rides, as scheduled.

"I should have hammered the pre-sale of tickets for the kids' rides," Jim said. "People didn't understand their value."

Only two groups entered the bed race. And, although the street dance was a hit, festival planners ran out of food. "We went through three hogs," Floyd said.

"We should have had the dance up in the park, because the vendors lost part of their crowd," Jim said.

There was one other problem, as far as Jim was concerned. "This is the first year I didn't win anything, and this year we had more prizes than ever."

The festival entailed a lot of work, according to Joann, who has helped organize the event for many years. "But I'm just stupid enough to do it again."

The others agreed. They set a date for the following year before saying good night.

I wasn't able to get to the 2003 festival, but I made a point of going in 2004.

The weekend floated lazily by under a bright, warm sun. People sat on bales and watched Matthew Krug, Vance Koehler and Rob Forsyth perform a skit written by Chris Schultz. It involved a calf by the name of Buttercup. Many stuck around for the "Little Cowpoke Contest," in which about 20 little kids paraded on an outdoor stage in cowboy and cowgirl outfits. One shy youngster ran off the stage.

Meanwhile, Jeff Bader gave horse-and-wagon rides, while Joann told riders about some of the town's history. She said the Harlem Globe Trotters came to town in 1933 to play Scales Mound's own Rainbow Oilers at the township hall. Jake's Place used to be a barbershop and, at one time, housed a men's clothing store. Kids used to stand on the railroad bridge — which was torn down during the mid-1950s — and throw rocks onto the trains. "One hit the lantern man on the head and knocked him out cold," she said.

Joann said Samuel Scales, after whom the town is named, and a man by the name of Huling (there is no record of his first name) bet everything they had on a horse race. "Scales won. Huling left town, and no one knows where he went."

The village also held an auction to raise money to refurbish the township hall. The old roller skates from the hall went up for bid, and the first skate key sold for $20. Dinnah Dittmar bought a pair of skates for her dad, Melvin Dittmar, who remembers skating there back in the late '40s.

"I put them on," Melvin said later, "but they didn't work as good. It seems those wheels go around quicker as the legs get stiffer."

Carrie and Kevin Stier put their covered wagon in the auction. It was genuine. They had sold French fries and lemonade from it at previous Stagecoach Festivals. It brought nearly $1,000.

Leslie Koehler bought a huge crock, a quilt, a balloon ride, a savings bond, a couple of gift certificates, a day at the spa for a dog, a T-shirt and a table. "I simply wanted to help the township hall," she said afterward. "I consider Scales Mound my home."

Scales Mound Trivia

Written by Carrie Stier for the Stagecoach Festival

What do Betty Schoenhard, Ida Travis, Marge Knuckey, Barb Hoppe and Wayne Ollerich have in common?
They spent time together in the vault of the Scales Mound Bank when it was robbed in 1973 and were "saved" by Mildred Horn.

Olive Finkenbinder was the village's only woman what?
Water operator.

How many days was Col. Leland Holland (who grew up in Scales Mound) held hostage in Iran?
444 days.

Clint Youle (a Scales Mound native) was the first TV weatherman for what major network?
NBC.

What names appeared on the village ballot for the 1971 village election?
None. No one filed for office that year. Through write-in votes, Charles Davis was elected president and Charles Koester, Ralph Schoenhard and Joe Lee were elected village trustees.

Who wrote "Farm Boy" and who was it about?
Photographer Archie Lieberman wrote the book about Bill Hammer, Jr.

Who was the first woman mayor?
Helen Phelps

At what dance hall were dances once held?
The Arcadian Dance Palace (during the late 1920s and '30s).

Livingston Beebe trained many young men in what profession?
Barbering (during the early and mid-1900s).

In 1907 the Curtiss family opened a factory in the Scales Mound area to be near a good supply of hickory trees. What did they make?
Ax handles. The Curtisses stayed only 3 or 4 years, then moved back to Wisconsin.

Vance Koehler

What color was the star in the White Star Cheese Factory logo?
Black

Besides having been a steadfast Democrat, a village historian and a helluva nice guy, "Old Ern," the late Ernie Schoenhard, was a fan of what baseball team?
The Brooklyn Dodgers.

What did the local boys do in May Perry's bottom?
Fish.

In 1879 what new law started a riot?
A law requiring hogs to be penned.

When was the last time LaVerne Ehrler got lucky?
In 1985, when he won $100,000 in the Illinois State Lottery.

True or false: You can lead a cow up a flight of stairs, but not down.
True. They had to lay plywood over the stairs to get the cow off the second floor of the school, after a group of pranksters put the cow there one Halloween.

Where was the Allen Opera House located?
Upstairs at the Countryside Feed Store. James Allen built the store in 1864 and added the opera house a few years later.

How many teenage boys does it take to put an outhouse on top of the school?
At least five (from Jim Davis's class).

What is the elevation of Charles Mound?
1,241 feet, the highest point in Illinois.

The first village liquor license was issued in 1877. How much did a liquor license cost in 1879?
$500, the same as today.

Which of the following slogans did not appear on the "Jesus Saves" rock - "Potosi Beer," "Obermiller Clothing" or "Got Milk?"
"Got milk?"

What time does Steve Winter lock the gate to the village dump?
5 p.m.

True or false: In order to be known as a "local," a man has to be a pall bearer at two funerals.
True. Being invited to a wedding or graduation, or being called at the grocery store, also qualifies you.

What is the top speed a car can reach when driven backward around town?
40 m.p.h. (Jim Davis might have had something to do with that one, too.)

Cletus Winter and Leslie Koehler

Cassy Lopp, Brittany Benson, Courtney Busch and Paige Trebian

Matthew Krug, Vance Koehler and Rob Forsyth

Nickolas Davis and Matthew Davis

Dinnah Dittmar

References

Carscallen, Dave, interview, 2004.
Clifton, Mike "Wulf," interview, 2005.
Davis, Jim, interview, 2004.
Dittmar, Melvin, interview, 2004.
"History of Jo Daviess County: 1887," pp. 555-557.
Koehler, Rick, interview, 2004.
Koehler, Leslie, interview, 2004.
Lopp, Bonnie, interview, 2004.
Ohms, Pat, interview, 2003.
Ohms, Sheila, interview, 2003.
Reitz, Becky, interview, 2004.
Saam, Mary, interview, 2004.
"Scales Mound: 125 Years of Progress; 1858 - 1978."
Scales Mound Village Board meeting, 2005.
Schultz, Joann, interviews, 2003-5.
Stagecoach Festival, 2004.
Stagecoach Festival Committee meeting, 2003.
Webster, Ron, interview, 2004.
Winter, Joshua, interview, 2004.

Graveyards

Evergreen Cemetery, Hanover

"I would hate to have everyone forget the people who came before us." ***Joann Schultz***

The project began with a short e-mail on a genealogy Web site. A woman from Colorado was looking for information about the wife of Ira Mann, who she said was buried three miles east of Scales Mound. Joann Schultz stumbled across her e-mail one winter day in 1999.

Even though dozens of small, well maintained cemeteries dot the Jo Daviess County countryside, Joann had never heard of one three miles east of Scales Mound. The e-mail got her attention.

Joann, who had recently become interested in history, recruited one of her friends, Susan Ertmer, to help look for the site. Susan's aunt, Carolyn Case, wondered if the cemetery in question was the one she rode past on horseback as a young girl. Carolyn knew exactly where it was and took Susan and Joann east on Stagecoach road to the top of a hill. She turned into the entrance to a field.

It was bitter cold, with the wind sweeping across the field. Joann and Susan shivered as they made their way through dry brush and fallen limbs to see what they could find.

At first glance, they didn't find anything. "I was horrified. I even remembered it being there in the 1960s," Susan said. Someone had bulldozed the graveyard years before, and it had become overgrown with weeds and bushes.

After a few minutes, however, they spotted a tombstone. Within half an hour, they found two more. They knew they had come to the right place.

"It was exciting to find exactly what we were looking for," Joann said.

They decided they would wait until spring to look for more stones. As soon as the weather warmed up, the graveyard became a nearly all-consuming project for Joann and Susan. Enlisting the help of family members and friends, they chopped and yanked away gooseberry bushes and bramble. The vegetation was stubborn and scratchy.

"We used everything we could get our hands on. We even used chain saws to clear the area," Susan said.

Susan then devised dousing sticks from metal coat hangers in order to find grave sites. She slowly walked the area with a stick in each hand. Wherever the sticks crossed, she believed, there was a body, and, where there was a body, there likely was a grave marker. The sticks crossed about 40 times.

The group then began the backbreaking task of unearthing the markers. "Whenever somebody found something, everybody would run over and start digging," Joann said. "We would start with a shovel and dig until we got close. Then we would use our hands. When we could get a crowbar underneath one side, we would pull it up."

The group had to work carefully as well as hard. The stones were large and made of marble. "Marble is delicate and easy to scratch," Joann said.

They spent most of their weekends that spring, summer and fall and the following year in the old graveyard.

One of the first stones they uncovered was etched with the words: "wife of Ira Mann." But the stone had broken off, and the group does not know the woman's first name.

Mann had been married twice, Joann later learned. He had a baby with one wife who died shortly thereafter, and the baby was sent elsewhere to be raised. The woman from Colorado descended from the baby.

Excited, Joann sent an e-mail to the Colorado woman. She had hoped to trade more information with her. "But, after all that, I never got a reply."

So far, the group has found 18 to 20 stones.

"Most of these are awfully fancy and are

awfully big stones," Joann said one day as she gave me a tour of the cemetery. The stones were laid carefully on their sides and reflected the dappled sunlight. Although the cemetery is close to busy Stage-coach Trail, it seemed miles from civilization.

Joann Schultz

Many markers are decorated with engravings of flowers or other images. Several include verses, such as the one on Harriet A. Thompson's stone: "Her toils are past, her work is done, and she is fully blest. She fought the fight, the victory won, and entered into rest."

Mary Torrence's stone hints at a heartbreaking story: "Weep not for me, my children. I am not dead but sleeping here." With engravings like that, Joann wanted to know who these people were. She began to ask around and search through old newspapers. Although she has spent countless hours on the project, she is missing many pieces of the puzzle. No descendants live in the immediate area. Except for finding the names in some old U.S. Census records, Joann has seen few references to them elsewhere.

However, she learned that some of the relatives of the deceased moved to Warren, including the wife of the Rev. S.E. Phelps. Phelps died in 1863 at age 38. The couple's two children, Carolyn and Jonathan, died at ages 1 and 3. She became a postmaster in Warren and was one of the first women postmasters around.

Joann believes many of the people were either itinerant preachers or members of the preachers' families. All died between 1854 and 1887.

"I am getting a whole lot more than I ever thought I would. I think it's pretty neat."

Besides doing the research, Joann has been trimming the weeds at the cemetery, together with her 81-year-old mother, Helen Walter. A few years ago, a group of 4-H kids and their parents built a fence around the cemetery, filled the holes where the tombstones were and helped look for more.

Why put so much effort into the grave sites of long-forgotten people?

"I can't imagine bulldozing a graveyard. You can't do that to people. That's their home," Susan said. "We felt this has got to be put right. We wanted to restore these people's dignity."

"This is where we came from," Joann said. "I would hate to have everyone forget the people who came before us, what they were like and how they lived. Besides, it interests the heck out of me. I have 'knows' trouble: I have to know everything."

"I feel pretty good about what we have done," she added, "except that I don't get out there as often as I would like to."

Joann believes that more gravestones lie hidden beneath the soil and hopes to organize a group again to look for them.

"I started to think, 'What about the blacks who lived in the North?'"

Scott Wolfe

Look around Galena and the rest of Jo Daviess County. If you are white, you will see lots of people who look like you. If you are Latin American, you will see a few others such as yourself, especially if you walk along Bench Street, just one block up the hill from downtown Galena. Many Latinos live in crowded apartments above restaurants and gift shops.

If you are black, you won't see hardly a soul who looks like you. As of the 2000 U.S. Census, only three blacks were living in Galena, a town with about 3,500 residents, and only 44 in Jo Daviess County, a county with about 22,000 people.

That wasn't true back in the mid-1800s. According to Scott Wolfe, historical librarian at the Galena Public Library, more than 200 blacks lived in Galena in its heyday before the Civil War. Wolfe has traced many of their stories and has found some of their gravestones at Galena's Greenwood Cemetery.

Wolfe, who is white, became interested in Galena's African-American people as he studied such historical icons as abolitionist John Brown. During his research, he often encountered the names of people who were identified as Negro or black.

"I started to think, 'What about the blacks who lived in the North?' When people think of the history of blacks, they tend to think of slaves and of the South."

Wolfe looked at 19th Century U.S. Census records, which categorized people as black, white or mulatto and listed their occupations.

He noticed that many blacks worked in jobs related to mining, the steamboat trade or the hotel business. There were miners, porters, cabin boys, chamber maids, cooks, waiters, wood choppers, laborers, barbers, grocers and brick masons. Some were slaves. In fact, 75 to 100 slaves came to Galena with the first wave of white settlers who mined for lead during the 1820s. Whites called them "indentured servants."

A few African-Americans worked in prestigious or highly skilled professions. For instance, Clayborne Stamps was a master brick mason, and Albert Richardson owned a blacksmith shop.

Scott Wolfe

Wolfe didn't stop with the Census data. He familiarized himself with the people's names and watched for them as he sifted through old newspapers. He hunted down property deeds, death certificates and other original documents for more clues about their lives. He has spent most of his vacations traveling to other parts of the country, digging through records to see what happened to those who left Galena.

He said he has always been interested in history and remembers his first trip as a boy in 1957 to Gettysburg. In college he studied biology and now uses his scientific research skills to piece together historic events. "History has always been satisfying to me. It's fun."

Wolfe has learned that most of Galena's blacks lived on both sides of the Galena River, in most cases with working class Germans or Irishmen. Some of their homes still stand.

He found records of two black churches, the African Methodist Episcopal Church and the Colored Union Baptist Church, neither of which remains today. "The church was the center of the black community—religiously, socially and politically." The black community also formed a brass band and several singing groups.

An active debating society contributed to the community's intellectual life, he said. The topic of its first debate, which took place in 1879, was, "Resolved, that the colored exodus from the South is justified."

The Order of the 12, a black fraternal organization, promoted Christianity and temperance.

The black community observed special holidays, too, Wolfe discovered. On Aug. 1, they celebrated the end of slavery in the West Indies and, on Jan. 1, the anniversary of the date when Pres. Abraham Lincoln declared in his Emancipation Proclamation that all slaves in the Confederacy would be freed.

In addition, there were several schools, but the schools were segregated, and most of the teachers were young white women from prominent families, he said.

Eventually, the black population dwindled, just as the overall population of Galena fell. The drop in population coincided with the decline in the steamboat trade. Most blacks moved away to find work. By 1900, only 24 African-Americans lived in Galena.

Those who remained until the end of their lives are buried in Greenwood Cemetery in one of two separate sections that were reserved for people of color.

One such individual was Swansey Adams. "He came to Galena as a slave very early, and lived his entire life here," Wolfe said. "He became the Galena Water Department. He would go to the town pump, fill his barrels and sell buckets of water to merchants on Main Street."

John Hall, who lived from 1842 to 1913, was, as his tombstone states, "born and raised in slavery." A free man after the Civil War, he moved to Galena, where he worked for 35 years for the Corwith family. Although he held a fairly menial position as a coachman, he was popular on the lecture circuit in the South. "He would disappear a year at a time to lecture."

Moses Lester, who was employed as a servant to Dr. Edward D. Kittoe, of Galena, during the Civil War, went to Galena after the war. He worked in a variety of occupations — carpenter, miner, church sexton and boarding-house operator—but people knew him best as the "weather prophet." Apparently, he could predict the weather better than the weather bureau. Townsfolk also remarked about his orchards, where he planted many trees native to the South and helped them survive the winter by building sheds over them.

Among those who moved on, but not very far, was Henry Christopher, who worked as a paper hanger and white washer. During the Civil War, he served as a bugle instructor and later became a member of the GAR, the main Union veterans organization. He also gave vocal lessons, organized the brass band, the Galena Glee Club, the Jubilee Singers and the Colored Literary and Debating Society. "To me, he is the most accomplished Galena black who stayed in this area," Wolfe said. He later moved 15 miles west to Dubuque, Iowa.

Then there was Henry Smith. "Henry Smith was a preacher. He also ran a junkyard on Spring Street. In 1860, when a youth stole some copper from the steamboat levy, he sold it to Smith. The police nabbed Smith for receiving stolen property. He, his family and some other blacks then moved to Rush Township, which is on the eastern side of Jo Daviess County between Stockton and Warren. They started a black community there called Equal Rights. Folks around there still called it that long after the blacks had gone.

"They farmed and burned limestone in kilns to make lime. There still is lime laying on the surface of the ground out there, and there are remnants of the kilns in the woods."

Greenwood Cemetery

In 2000, I briefly interviewed LaMetta Wynn, an African-American woman who grew up in Galena. Born in 1935, she was not only the youngest of nine children but also the youngest of Galena's black residents. She told me that, although hers was the only black family living in town and that she was the only black person in her class, she did not feel different from her classmates.

"We were just another family, and I was just another person in my class and in my neighborhood." Her dad worked at the Savanna Army Depot Activity, which then was the largest employer in Jo Daviess County.

After graduating from high school, Wynn attended St. Luke's School of Nursing in Cedar Rapids, Iowa and became a registered nurse. She moved to Clinton, Iowa in 1955, where she raised 10 children.

In 1995, Clinton residents, 94 percent of whom are white, elected Wynn as mayor. Now she is serving her third term. "People have seen me around; they know what race I am," she told the Des Moines Register in 2004. "I think it just has not been an issue with people."

Several of the people who lived in Galena for awhile later became renowned leaders in other parts of the country. While living in Galena, Richard Cain worked as a barber and was involved in the African Methodist Episcopal Church. Later he left town and joined the ministry. In 1865, he moved to South Carolina and, three years later, voters there elected him to the state Senate.

In 1872, he won an at-large seat in the U.S. House of Representatives. Later he became a bishop in the A.M.E. Church and helped start the Paul Quinn College in Waco, Texas.

In addition, Garrett Johnson started a newspaper in Jackson, Mississippi, and James Lynch became the secretary of state of Mississippi.

Attitudes among Galena's white majority toward blacks varied, and whites often sent mixed messages, as they do today. "There was such an ambivalence," Wolfe said. "I noticed in my search through the newspapers that black people could be praised in one paragraph and, in the next, deprecated." Whites often referred to blacks as "niggers," "darkies," members of the "lime kiln club" and "sons and daughters of Ham."

Scott said he sees an underlying antipathy toward African-Americans in many obituaries. For instance, Adams' obituary said, "He was a quiet, inoffensive citizen and, although encased in a black skin, has commanded the respect of all classes and ages." Likewise, Jack Barton, a drayman on the steamboat levee, was described as "a black man with a white heart."

Wolfe said local whites likely were not involved in the underground railroad, as many whites today would like to believe. "Galena had a significant black population, so escaped slaves didn't need to hide in some white guy's basement."

Wolfe said he will continue to research Galena's black history. "There is always something being added or some new line to follow. I am drawn to a good story and to aspects of history that no one has looked into before."

He said he has gained personal satisfaction from having shed light on an important part of Galena's history. "I just want more outlets for sharing it with people," he said.

"The year 1854 was the saddest one in the history of Warren."

History of Warren, Illinois

People felt differently about death during the 19th Century than they do now. "Today we think of getting older and dying as something we don't want to do," said Susan Gordy, site manager for the Apple River Fort Historic Site in Elizabeth. "Back then, it was a reward for working so hard. It actually was a good thing. Death was something to be embraced."

As long as someone died peacefully and on seemingly good terms with their Maker, or their conscience, loved ones could accept the person's passing as fate or as God's will, she said.

An 1887 obituary for Alice Powell, who lived near Warren and died at age 16, illustrates this point: "She gave her heart to God when quite young, but the amusements of this world and the associations of life led in measure from Christ, but during her sickness she came back to her Savior, and it was a privilege to be by her bedside the last few hours of her life."

Another obituary from about 1887 described the final moments of William Whitham's life: "Near his last moments he requested his children to sing his favorite hymn, "Rock of Ages." And while they were singing the lines, 'While I draw this fleeting breath When my eyelids close in death,' his spirit passed to the brighter world beyond, to take up the song of Moses and the Lamb, a fitting close of an earnest Christian life."

Today we shy away from talking about death, but that wasn't true before. "There was more respect for the natural process. People wanted to know as many details as they could get," Gordy said.

Obituaries supplied many of the details. For instance: "Mr. Whitham suffered terribly during his last hours on account of the filling up of his lungs, not having strength sufficient to free them of their accumulation."

The obituary for James Barningham, who died in 1883 at age 65, talks not only about his death but of earlier health problems: "A severe accident in his youth resulted in lameness, which followed him through life. In later years another accident almost entirely deprived him of sight. Yet, notwithstanding these disadvantages, he was eminently successful in all his business relations, and ever maintained a quiet resignation and Christian cheerfulness. A few months since, having been conscious for some time of a singular sensation in the mouth, he consulted a physician who pronounced it an incurable cancer. This opinion was concurred in by all the physicians that examined it, which brought him face to face with death in its most painful form; but he never faltered or murmured."

The illnesses that can lead to death have changed significantly over the past 100 years. In 1900, tuberculosis caused the most people to die, accounting for 10 percent of all deaths, and pneumonia came in as a close second. Today, heart disease, cancer and stroke claim two-thirds of all lives lost. Tuberculosis, a highly contagious disease caused by a bacterial attack on the lungs, has all but disappeared. Likewise, influenza and pneumonia together rank as only the seventh most common cause of death.

Occasionally an epidemic of some sort swept through the area, killing a large number of people. Cholera, an intestinal disease caused mostly by contaminated drinking water, took the lives of many

Warren residents in 1854.

"The year 1854 was the saddest one in the history of Warren," according to "History of Warren, Illinois." "More than fifty of the pioneers died of cholera, among them George A. Smith, son-in-law of Mr. Tisdel, Mr. Ballard, Mrs. Chas. Cole and Mr. Lewis Cann. Sixteen victims were buried in the grave near the rock cut on Mineral Point Railroad, most of them railroad men. Mr. Burnett found three dead near a spring just below the DeHaven home. No one would help him so he loaded them on a sled and buried them in the old cemetery.

"In a school building on the David Hicks farm the teacher told her pupils there would be no school the next day as she had cholera. She died at midnight. There were seventy deaths from June to October, 1854."

Because fewer treatments for leading diseases were available, people died more quickly of their diseases than they do today. Now many people live several years with the illnesses that eventually take their lives, according to Mercedes Bern-Klug, of the Center on Aging at the University of Kansas Medical Center.

Suicides have always occurred to some extent and took place about as frequently in 1890 as they do today, In 2002, 31,855 people, or 10.1 out of every 100,000 people living in the U.S., took their own lives. In 1900, 10.2 did so, according to the National Center for Health Statistics. But the rate fluctuates somewhat. In 1908, 16.8 people per 100,000 committed suicide.

In the 19th Century, people tended to believe that genetics played a major role in suicide — now scientists know that a family history of suicide is only one of several risk factors involved — so family members were severely stigmatized. Often they covered up the fact that their loved ones killed themselves. They also kept the truth from the victims' children, if possible.

However, when the cause of death was known, the media made no attempt to cover up the tragedy. As late as the 1930s, headlines screamed with the news that a suicide had occurred. "William Bauer Ends Own Life: Commits Suicide with Shot Gun: Believed Despondent Over Ill Health," says a front-page headline of the Sept., 4, 1930 edition of the East Dubuque Register.

The media did not spare the reader of any of the details, nor did they hesitate to speculate about why people killed themselves.

The story about Bauer goes on to say, "His lifeless body with a gaping wound in his chest was found by his wife after she had returned from the store where she had gone to purchase groceries. ... Bauer was taken ill about four months ago, when he was obliged to sever his connection with the Dubuque Roofing Company. He was on the verge of a nervous breakdown. He went to the Mayo hospital at Rochester, Minn., but there was no improvement in his health and he was despondent upon his return."

A story about Emma Dalen, who was 17, provides a history of Dalen's previous suicide attempts. "The suicide which was successful on May 11th, was the third effort of Mrs. Dalen to end her life. One was from the local bridge last February, the other at Beloit, Wis."

Today newspapers seldom report suicides unless they occur in a public place or involve a well-known victim.

"I think newspapers are a lot tamer today," said P. Carter Newton, publisher of the Galena Gazette. "As editors and reporters, we are more sensitive today than our brethren from years ago."

Now people live much longer than they did 100 years ago. In 1900, about 25 percent of all babies born died before age 5. Americans lived an average of 49 years. Now only about 1 percent of babies fail to reach age 5, and the average life expectancy is 77 years. Fifty-three percent of deaths occur among people over 75.

Furthermore, most people formerly died at home. Now 60 percent of deaths occur in hospitals, and 17 percent take place in nursing homes.

Because death occurred closer to home, it seemed a more natural part of life, Gordy said.

Also, it was common to "wake" people in their homes, and it was not uncommon for families to have portraits painted of the deceased. "An artist would be called to the house and would sketch the person. Later, the artist would paint a portrait. Some even had the bottom half of the portrait done and just put a face in."

When James E. Furlong went into the funeral business in 1896 in Galena, he embalmed bodies in his home, according to his nephew, James T. Furlong. Then he took the bodies to the homes of the deceased to be waked. The funeral service also took place in the home.

Sometime during the early 1900s, he built a funeral chapel and began to embalm and wake the deceased there. "It was one of the first funeral homes in the area," James T. said. "At first, people didn't take too kindly to having visitations there, I understand." Now nearly all visitations occur in funeral homes.

Previously, virtually everyone received a burial in a town or township cemetery, a church yard or a family plot on privately owned property. In Jo Daviess County there are at least 80 graveyards. They range in size from small family plots to Greenwood Cemetery in Galena, which has thousands. As far as anyone knows, the Veta Grande Cemetery in Scales Mound Township is the smallest. It contains the bodies of only three people—a mother and her two baby daughters.

Evergreen Cemetery, Hanover

Many grave sites tell a story, and some of them a tragic one. Take the story told at Veta Grande. The 2-year old daughter of Emily A. Mourse died Nov. 28, 1845. Emily died only a few months later, on Feb. 11, 1846, when she was only 20. Another daughter, Mary, died four days after Emily at age 3. (There is no gravestone for Emily's husband, J.R. Mourse.)

In 1954, James T. Furlong took the funeral home over from his uncle. At age 80, he still works more than full time, usually putting in 15-hour days. Like his uncle, he made changes in anticipation of upcoming trends. During the 1990s, he built a crematorium, the first within about a 70-mile radius of Galena. Now he calls the business Furlong Funeral Chapel and Crematorium.

He said that, nationwide, about 27 percent of bodies are cremated. By contrast, less than 10 percent of the families with whom he works request a cremation. But the percentage will increase for his son, Thomas J., who is preparing to take over the business, he predicted. "When I started, people didn't even want to talk about cremation. Now there is a different category of people. A lot have no qualms about it."

Recently James T. built a new funeral home, too. He called it the most modern one around and said he does his work electronically.

Despite the changes, however, one thing remains the same: "In treating and meeting people, you have to be able to work with everyone, rich and poor alike. You still have to be cut out for the business."

References

The African American Registry, "Richard Cain, Politician with Conviction," www.aaregistry.com.

Bern-Klug, Mercedes, "Death at the Beginning and End of the 20th Century," www2.kumc.edu.

Carson, May Hawley, and Zoe Lenore Gray, "History of Warren Illinois: Its People, Industries, Achievements and Growth," 1928.

Cemetery records, History Room, Galena Public Library.

Des Moines Register, "River City's Allure Reflects Many Shades," July 18, 2004, www.dmregister.com.

East Dubuque Register: "Recover Body of Suicide," May 22, 1930; and "William Bauer Ends Own Life," Sept. 4, 1930.

Gordy, Susan, interview, 2004.

Furlong, James T., interview, 2005.

National Center for Chronic Disease Prevention and Health Promotion, "The Burden of Chronic Diseases as Causes of Death, United States," www.cdc.gov.

National Center for Injury Prevention and Control, "Suicide: Fact Sheet," www.cdc.gov.

National Center for Vital Statistics: "Crude Death Rates for Each Cause: Death Registration States 1900 - 1940"; "Life Expectancy by Age Race, and Sex: Death-registration States, 1900-1902 to 1919-21, and United States, 1929-31 to 2002," Vol. 53, No. 6, Nov. 10, 2004; and "Deaths and Percentage of Total Deaths for the 10 Leading Causes of Death, by Race: United States, 2002," Vol. 53, No. 17, March 7, 2005.

Newton, P. Carter, interview 2005.

"Scrapbook Gleanings - Part 1": "Obituary: William Whitman" and "Obituary: Alice Powell," www.rootsweb.com.

U.S. Census, 2000.

Wolfe, Scott, interviews, 2005.

Wynn, LaMetta, interview, 2000.

Crime

Courtroom, Jo Daviess County Court House

"Either this bootlegging and drunkenness must cease or this place will be closed."

A.L. Hathaway

The nation's mood turned against alcohol long before the passage of the 18th Amendment in 1919. Many early immigrants brought a bias against booze with them, especially against hard liquor. They believed, and probably rightly so, that heavy drinking brings out the worst in people.

(On the other hand, the Puritans brought 42 tons of beer and 10,000 gallons of wine along to the "new world.")

The American Temperance Society organized in 1826 and, by the end of the Civil War, temperance became a hot issue. In 1874, the feminist movement merged with the temperance movement, in the form of the Women's Christian Temperance Union. The WCTU took on many reform causes and believed that alcoholism led to poverty and domestic violence.

Ten years later, the Prohibition Party formed, and prohibition became a platform in many political campaigns. Even the Socialist Party, which carried more weight then than it does today, said over-indulgence in alcohol could set the working class back. Over time, Congress and the states passed a variety of laws to curb its use.

World War I brought another reason to rail against alcohol: It would rob the country of its ability to adequately defend itself and to use its grains wisely. Thus, drinking became unpatriotic.

In 1917, Congress passed a resolution to prohibit the manufacture, sale, transportation and importation of alcohol. Within about a year, the states ratified the resolution, and it became the 18th Amendment. On Oct. 28, 1919, Congress passed the Volstead Act in order to put the amendment into effect. Prohibition officially began Jan. 17, 1920.

The outlawing of alcohol led to new brands of outlaws. Suddenly, nearly everyone, from casual drinkers to bootleggers, became public enemies.

Jim Slaats was a young boy during the prohibition years. After school, he worked at Budden's Garage in downtown East Dubuque. "Guys would bring their cars in and say they had to have new springs put in. We'd put the cars back in the corner of the garage and put in overloaded springs. We weren't supposed to know why."

But Slaats knew what the "rum runners" were up to. "They would take the back seats out, put gallon cans of alcohol in and cover them up with an outfit that looked like a seat. Quite a few local boys were in on that."

Slaats kept his mouth shut. "Whenever you met a stranger and they started asking you questions about someone, you would say you didn't know anybody. You probably knew his name as well as your own."

Many law-enforcement officials looked the other way.

"East Dubuque has been for some time past noted for its open defiance of the prohibition law and none of the local officers seemed to make any effort to curb the violation," the Elizabeth Weekly News reported in 1926.

That soon changed, when a group of officers visited several establishments purported to be soft-drink parlors. Leslie White, Otis Henning, Lee O'Neil and Dave Petry were cited for violating the prohibition law.

Later, there were plenty of arrests. State's Attorney Harry C. Tear would send sheriff's deputies on raids without notifying the deputies in advance. That kept law-enforcement officials who were sympathetic to the "wet" cause from tipping off lawbreakers.

Although many people associate bootlegging with East Dubuque and its strip of downtown saloons, illegal activity ran rampant throughout the county. Bar owners, their patrons and farmers alike were hauled into court for the role they played in the alcohol industry.

For instance, in 1930 sheriff's deputies raided homes in Elizabeth and Stockton. Armed with search warrants, they found 100 bottles of beer and 10 gallons of mash in the home of Lilly Cook. They also found "considerable beer" at the home of George Casper and arrested George Schumacher for selling liquor.

Recently, Chuck Woodford, who owns property near Hanover, showed me a still that someone had set up in the woods on his property. He said there were lots of illegal stills in the county.

Slaats said there also were many stills on the islands in the backwaters of the Mississippi River.

In 1929, Sheriff A.L. Hathaway and his deputies strode into a Warren dance hall and arrested a Wisconsin man for bootlegging. Hathaway confiscated the bootlegger's car, as well as his jugs of wine. Then he stopped the dance and gave the owner of the establishment and his patrons a piece of his mind.

"One of two things must happen immediately," he said. "Either this bootlegging and drunkenness must cease or this place will be closed immediately."

Old still on Chuck Woodford's property

That same year, Deputy Sheriff Jack Ehrler raided several liquor joints in Hanover. As a result, Howard Berryman, E.M. Murphy and William Major were taken before a judge, fined $600 apiece and sentenced to 60 days in jail.

Many arrests focused on small-time, home-based operations, but some involved big-time alcohol production.

In 1930, federal agents found a large brewing operation in the garage of John Gilles, of Galena. Gilles had been pumping water from a block away into a concrete room beneath the garage for his operation. Agents seized kegs, vats, a 2,300-gallon tank, 630 gallons of beer and other materials used in brewing. Gilles sold beer only by the keg.

Perhaps the biggest booze bust occurred in May of 1929, two years after federal agents started watching a large warehouse in East Dubuque. They found "one of the largest and most up-to-date (distilling) outfits that has yet been found anywhere hereabout," the East Dubuque Register reported.

"The copper boilers were so large they were set in the elevator shaft, the big boilers filled with mash, with an estimated capacity of over 5,000 gallons each. They were approximately 14 feet in diameter and 12 feet high."

I don't know whatever happened to the distillery or who owned it, because the newspaper printed only one brief follow-up. Perhaps agents lost interest as the will to prosecute offenders diminished.

Many local people believe that Al Capone, Chicago's foremost bootlegger and crime boss, had direct ties to Jo Daviess County. They say East Dubuque became his playground when things got too hot for him in the Windy City.

"He had a cottage at Frentress Lake (near East Dubuque)," Slaats said. "My dad had a mail route there and took mail down to his house."

Prohibition ended in 1933 with the passage of the 21st Amendment. The government had underestimated how tough the law would be to enforce. A commission established by

Pres. Herbert Hoover found that the general public opposed prohibition.

The repeal was cause for celebration in East Dubuque, Slaats said. "When the first load of beer came down from the Potosi Brewing Company (in Potosi, Wisconsin), they didn't even get the truck unloaded. People just started grabbing cases of beer."

"Tell them to shoot, and shoot to kill."

Illinois Bankers Association

White settlers came to Jo Daviess County several years before 1828, but there was no court system until then. Unruliness and lawlessness prevailed.

In 1828 the county become part of Illinois' First Judicial Circuit Court (and now is part of the 15th Circuit Court). But that did not completely stop murder and mayhem. It also did not prevent local residents from sometimes taking the law into their own hands.

Here are some criminal cases that have gone to court over the years.

The first criminal case, 1828: Michael Dee earned the distinction of becoming the first citizen indicted in the new court on felony charges. After a trial that lasted less than a day, a jury found him guilty of assault and battery, with intent to commit murder.

The fate of a family, 1837: A large family of "rough characters named Davis," had settled near Apple River two years before and had become embroiled in a dispute with Alexander McKillips. One night they ambushed McKillips, tied him to a stump and "whipped him until almost dead."

Apparently, they either were not tried for the assault or were not severely punished. However, they eventually paid their dues.

"A just retribution overtook these brothers," according to an 1887 history of Jo Daviess County. "Several of them were hung, one killed by a falling mineral tub, and another chopped to pieces with an ax."

A possible miscarriage of justice, 1854: A 12-man jury found John I. Taylor guilty of murdering his wife. He had come home drunk one night and began beating her. A man by the name of Rosenburg, who lived downstairs and whom Taylor suspected of having an affair with his wife, tried to stop the fight. Taylor grabbed a gun and swung it at Rosenburg, but his wife stepped between the two men and received the blow—or did Taylor wield the gun?

Judge Ben R. Sheldon sentenced Taylor to death by hanging. Taylor was executed Jan. 19, 1855, and as many as 5,000 people watched.

However, Rosenburg supposedly admitted on his deathbed that he, not Taylor, killed Mrs. Taylor.

No time for a honeymoon, 1855: A man by the name of McCarty had just been married and was heading back to Galena with the priest who performed the wedding ceremony, when a blacksmith by the name of Bat Howe caught up with him. Howe accused McCarty of saying he was a better man, and the two began to fight.

McCarty shot at Howe twice, hitting him in the shoulder. Howe then jammed a knife into McCarty's thigh, and the latter died within minutes. He never made it back home to his new wife.

Howe was convicted of manslaughter and sentenced to seven years in prison.

A drowning in jail, 1859: A woman by the name of Mary Ann Miller moved to Galena. She was a rowdy alcoholic, and people believed she was living "in sin" with the man who came to town with her. Within a few days, she was arrested three times—the third for drunkenness and disturbing the peace—according to local historian Daryl Watson.

At the time, the Galena River had been rising, and the city jail, which was located in the basement of the Old Market House on Commerce Street, was prone to flooding. During Miller's second stay, the jail began to flood, and

Old Jo Daviess County Jail

was rescued. Later, a jury acquitted him of the murder.

A reaction to a house of ill repute, 1872: The Galena Evening Gazette reported: "There is a house at the upper end of town, on the edge of the school section, which is understood to have been occupied of late by several women of easy virtue. We learn that some of the wives and mothers of that neighborhood surrounded the house last night, and pelted it with stones, breaking the glass and making the 'shebang' too hot to hold its inmates. The soiled doves made themselves scarce in those quarters, but were seen walking the streets today. They have evidently learned that that neighborhood is not a healthy place for their occupation. The ladies up there declare they would as soon have the spotted fever in their midst, as this nuisance."

Historian Scott Wolfe said Jo Daviess County had its share of houses of prostitution, as well as people who wanted to get rid of them. "People would tie ropes or chains around the shacks and attach a team of horses and literally pull them down," he said.

A string of mysterious deaths, 1877: The court heard a murder case that Jo Daviess County residents still talk about, even though it occurred more than a century ago. The circumstances that led up to the murder were complicated and spanned many years.

The story began at a farm near Council Hill Station, a tiny settlement about 5 miles northeast of Galena. The wife of a farmer named Hiram Byers died suddenly, and her body was quickly buried. Soon, Byers married his servant, a young woman who had been living in the Byers home. Six months later, Byers's daughter (from his previous marriage) also died unexpectedly. Her body, too, was buried quickly.

Before long, Byers hired Jacob Ably to help him on his farm. Ably and Byers's second wife began to have an affair and, it was rumored, she gave birth to his child.

Soon Byers died mysteriously. He went to bed one night feeling fine but never got up the next morning.

lawmen safely moved her and other prisoners to the county jail.

During her third stay, however, Miller's cell filled with 18 to 24 inches of water. Drunk, she fell into the water and drowned before she could be rescued.

Although townsfolk didn't have much love for Miller, they were furious that she was allowed to die in their own jail. After being pressured to move its calaboose to a new location, the city began to use the county facility. Later, the jail moved several times and, today, the city again takes its prisoners to the county jail.

A surprising acquittal, 1867: Police found plenty of circumstantial evidence, but apparently not enough to convict murder suspect Samuel Stambrough.

Stambrough worked on the farm of Peter Stephens near where Apple River Canyon State Park now is located. In July, the body of Stephens's daughter, Sarah Ellen, was found. Next to her body lay Stambrough's buggy whip. Tracks around the body matched his boots.

Stambrough was taken to the jail in Warren. That night, a group of vigilantes captured him and strung him up from a willow tree. As he hung there, the mob yanked on the rope to try to get him to confess to the crime.

But the suspect did not confess, and he

Meanwhile, Byers had secretly willed his property to his son from his first marriage. After Byers's passing, however, the son transferred the property to his two half-sisters (the daughters of Byers and his second wife) and disappeared.

Later, the second Mrs. Byers married Ably and, within a short span, the two half-sisters died. Their deaths also were unexplained. At that point, Mrs. Byers Ably became owner of the property. She and Ably had three sons.

Ably wanted his wife to sell the farm and to move to Nebraska. She refused, and Ably began to beat her, their sons said later. One morning, Ably found his wife's body hanging from a tree in the back yard. An inquest panel deemed her death a suicide, but people always wondered whether Jacob Ably killed her.

On the evening of Sept. 16, 1877, Jacob Ably was shot and killed at his home, becoming the seventh casualty of possible wrong-doing. His three adolescent sons — Joseph, Henry and Jacob — and a neighbor, Peter Miller, Jr., were tried for the murder. Miller testified that he and Joseph Ably, who worked on a farm 18 miles away, walked to the Ably place to steal grapes. He said Joseph carried a musket, revolver and box of cartridges with him and went into the yard "to see what his old man was up to." Soon he heard a shot, and Miller saw Joseph flee.

A jury comprised of Albert Stevenson, Joseph Gothard, John McFadden, D. Maloney, G. Engles, W. Whippo, T.E. Reynolds, L. Weisegarber, R.S. Bostwick, E.A. Wilson, Conrad Bahwell and W.I. Bond found Joseph guilty and acquitted the rest. Later, while in jail, Joseph confessed to the murder.

The Ably house, which sits at the end of a long, narrow lane, still stands. To this day, teenagers find their way to the scene of the crime and dare each other to peek inside. Some have claimed to have seen blood on the kitchen floor.

A murder, and later a pardon, 1889: Jonathan Skene was only 16 years old the day he shot Prof. H.T. Matchett, a highly respected teacher and minister.

Matchett, who founded Hanover High School, was its superintendent and its only teacher. He also held Sunday services at Bethel School, south of Woodbine. He and Wesley Prisk were walking to Prisk's home after the service on May 5, when they saw Skene walking near the home of John Rankin. They greeted Skene, whom they knew, and invited the 16-year-old to walk with them.

They went only about 100 feet, when Skene stepped back and shot Matchett. The preacher died instantly. Skene then took after Prisk, who had started to run, and hit Prisk with three bullets before Prisk reached safety.

At first Skene coolly denied that he had murdered Matchett, but later he confessed.

The community was stunned. Matchett was "of grand physical proportions, with a countenance which bespoke the heart within, he was as noble mentally and morally as he was physically," according to the Galena Gazette.

The shooter's father was well known in the community. "Jonathan Skene is the son of Supervisor William Skene of Derinda, a very excellent, upright man and a well-to-do farmer and stock raiser. He was in Galena today, a

The Ably House

picture of despair."

Some people believed that Skene shot the men because they had seen him near the Rankin home, which he had burglarized. However, he did not take any valuables, other than the revolver he used in the shootings. Some said he read too many "blood and thunder stories and Jesse James literature." The shootings occurred in "true Jesse James style."

Skene refused to say why he shot the two men. Later, the community learned that he committed the murder "while he was under the maddening influence of a copious drink of powerful wine given him by an incautious neighbor."

Skene was sentenced to life in prison, but later Illinois Gov. John Altgeld reduced his sentence to 15 years. Still later, Gov. John Tanner pardoned him. Skene served 8 years and 9 months in prison.

Apparently Skene had been an exemplary prisoner, and many people felt sympathetic toward him because he had been "under the influence." Others were deeply opposed to his release.

While in prison, he studied electricity and was put in charge of the prison's light and power plant.

Prisk recovered from his wounds.

A shoot-to-kill order, 1925: After a series of bank robberies swept the country—with 40 percent occurring in Illinois alone—the Jo Daviess County chapter of the Illinois Bankers Association appointed armed vigilance committees in local communities to help capture or kill robbers.

"The banks of the county have signified their desire to make up a purse of $1,000 for every bank bandit taken in this county, dead or alive, and it is understood they prefer them dead," the Elizabeth Weekly News reported.

The association's effort began in 1921, when it issued a warning that criminals who formerly looted mail trains would turn to robbing banks, because armed Marines were beginning to guard the trains.

The warning said: "Arm your employees, the neighboring storekeepers and citizens, and have your public officials on the alert to respond with force when notified of an attack. ... Tell them to shoot, and shoot to kill, and to get the driver of the bandits' car first. ... If you should kill one of these fellows, there is no judge in your county who would condemn you, and you would be proclaimed a hero."

The county kept the names of its armed citizens secret. As far as anyone at the bankers association knows, they never shot anyone.

By the end of 1928, the bankers association had become less concerned about bank robberies and more concerned about speculation in the stock market, according to the IBA. The vigilance committees quickly faded away.

Two polite thieves, 1929: Two men who had stolen a car were apprehended in Alabama and were being returned to Illinois by Jo Daviess County Sheriff A.L. Hathaway and Galena resident Darius Hunkins. While at a gas station near Freeport, the thieves, Irvin Coolidge and Ray Walter, said they needed to use the rest room. Hathaway gave the fugitives, who were handcuffed together, permission to use the facility unsupervised. Instead of using the rest room, the men fled on foot through a field, stole another car and high-tailed out of town.

Later, they were arrested in Missouri and sent to Iowa, where they stood trial for an earlier offense. They were sentenced to prison and, while in prison, wrote Hathaway a letter. The thieves thanked the sheriff for being courteous to them during the trip from Alabama and apologized for rushing off without saying goodbye.

The snowball hazard, 1929: Some crimes were not as serious as others. In January of 1929, Andrew Gassman hauled four boys into court for throwing snowballs. He said he was turning from Montgomery Street onto Sinsinawa Avenue in East Dubuque, when his car was pelted with "a hail of snowballs." He claimed the snowballs distracted him, causing him to run into a car owned by J.D. Liddle.

The boys pleaded not guilty, and Gassman did not have other witnesses, so he withdrew his complaint.

"In this case, our sympathies are with the driver," said the East Dubuque Register. "It is a fact that prior to the accident pedestrians and motorists were targets for numerous snowballs thrown from the vicinity of this same intersection. ... Anyhow, letting bygones be bygones, there has been no snowballing on

Main Street since."

An abortion gone awry, 1930: A Jo Daviess County grand jury indicated Dr. James M. Stilson, 57, of Warren, on a charge of murder. He was accused of causing 20-year-old Anna Lou Garner, of Stockton, to die. Apparently, he had wounded her while aborting her month-old fetus.

Stilson claimed that Garner had asked him to perform an abortion but that he had refused. He testified at his trial that, instead, he told her he didn't think she was pregnant and that, if she was, the fetus would abort naturally because she was afflicted with gonorrhea.

The following day, Garner had severe pain, and her boyfriend, Charles Raab, summoned Stilson to her home. Stilson cleaned her womb with a glass instrument. Garner's mother said the instrument had fallen to the floor and had broken but that Stilson used it anyway.

Later, a second doctor also performed a cleansing procedure, but Garner was taken to the hospital, where she died. An autopsy report indicated that she sustained a puncture to the uterus and died of blood poisoning.

Stilson was not charged with malpractice, criminal neglect, negligence or involuntary manslaughter. However, because Garner's death occurred as a result of an illegal act, he was charged with murder.

Illinois law allowed abortions when they were necessary to save a pregnant woman's life, but the jury saw no evidence that the abortion was part of a life-saving strategy. A 12-man jury consisting of John Cousins, Henry Zahrndt, Charles Spittler, John Reed, Frank Bonjour, Dan Walder, James Holland, Anton Wurster, Henry Borsch, Joseph Wand, Neil Housnell and Woller Laird found Stilson guilty. They recommended that he serve 20 years in prison.

Stilson's attorneys, Frank Sheean and Louis Nack, filed an appeal with the Illinois Supreme Court. (Nack was the grandfather of Galena attorneys Joe and Tom Nack.) But the Supreme Court upheld the lower court's decision, as well as the 20-year sentence.

The Elizabeth Weekly News reported that Stilson had been tried on a similar charge several years earlier in Stephenson County. The newspaper said he was married and had two children.

A woman charged, 1969: Mary Zink, 48, of Nora, was charged with murder and voluntary manslaughter after killing Kenneth J. Vance, 22, of Warren. Witnesses said Vance and her son, Harry Phillips, were arguing outside George and Mary's tavern in Nora, when Zink intervened. They said she struck Vance over the head with a blunt object, possibly a baseball bat.

Zink initially pleaded guilty to the charges, but a jury acquitted her after a six-day trial. She testified that she didn't mean to kill Vance.

A case that caused outrage, 1984: It was just four days before Christmas, and 26-year-old Carol Lutgen, of East Dubuque, began divorce proceedings against her husband James. James was to be served with papers the following morning. He knew Carol wanted the divorce and planned to move out of the family home Dec. 26.

That afternoon, James saw Carol kissing another man while parked in front of a tavern. He hoped to use that information later in court, in order to get custody of their two children, ages 6 and 8, during the divorce proceedings.

After he arrived home, he and Carol began to fight about their evening plans. "She grabbed me and started choking me and then I grabbed her and pushed her back and she came at me again and I choked her again. Then I threw her down," Lutgen later told Sheriff Marlo Specht.

Carol stopped breathing. James called 911, but it was too late. When Carol was rushed to the hospital, she was pronounced dead upon arrival.

The couple's children witnessed the strangulation.

Lutgen was charged with murder. However, his defense attorney filed motions to bar testimony from the children, who he said were "not reliable as witnesses" because they "have been held 'hostage' by the victim's family;" to disallow the autopsy report, because Carol's body had been embalmed before the autopsy; and to bar testimony about alleged previous abuse on Lutgen's part.

Although there was no ruling on the motions, "the presiding judge actively discouraged a charge of murder," said J. Christopher Moore, who was the Jo Daviess County State's ence. He never meant to kill

a circuit
d a court-
spectators
his wife,
tting each
an argu-
at their
nee home.
actually
said, but
east two

Lutgen

n's testi-
otional statements from his

From the Telegraph Herald, July 16, 1985 (courtesy of the Telegraph Herald)

Attorney at the time. "He indicated that, because this was a domestic dispute, he had strong feelings about it."

With a weakened case, Moore agreed to reduce the charge to voluntary manslaughter, whereby Lutgen would serve four to 15 years in prison. Lutgen pleaded guilty, and the case never went to trial.

At the sentencing hearing, Carol's brother, Gene Tranel, said the Lutgen children had been traumatized by their mother's death. One of them "wakes up screaming and crying and talking about the crime," he said. "She has nightmares of her father also trying to choke her to death." (Tranel and his wife Debby cared for the children afterward.)

Nevertheless, Judge Harold Nagel sentenced Lutgen to only four years in prison, with credit for time served in the county jail.

"The certainty of prosecution and punishment is probably, in my judgment, more important than the length and term of the punishment," he said. He also reasoned that Lutgen's greatest punishment rested on the fact that he "must live as long as he does live with the knowledge that his children have been deprived of their mother..." He also said Lutgen was not likely to commit such an act again.

"I think the sentence was wholly inadequate," said Moore, who now works for the U.S. Attorney's Office in Fairview, Ill. "But the judge probably thought he was doing the right thing. He came from a different era and, of all the judges I have appeared before, he was probably the most lenient and had the most difficulty sending people to the penitentiary."

Many people were outraged. However, the light sentence was not the only cause for their anger.

In October of 1986, not even two years after he strangled his wife, Lutgen was released from prison. He then sought custody of his children, and, in 1987, custody was granted.

When Moore was up for re-election, residents voted him out of office. "The case certainly played a role in my loss," Moore said.

Syndicated columnist Ann Landers published a letter about the case and said, "This is worse than outrageous. It's despicable. The people in that town should be up in arms about this horrendous miscarriage of justice."

Meanwhile, area residents were seeing the need for providing services to victims of domestic violence and had started organizing CHOICES Domestic Violence Program. "The case just kicked things into high gear, and, subsequently, CHOICES officially was founded," said Carrie Altfillisch-Melton, executive director.

The Tranel family took the custody case to the Illinois appellate court, where Judge Alfred Woodward upheld the circuit court's decision. He said the law did not preclude a parent who killed his or her spouse from having custody of the children. The Tranels then went to the Illinois Supreme Court, but the higher court declined to hear the case.

There is more. In 1990, Lutgen was charged with assault with injury to his then-girlfriend, after allegedly punching her outside a local bar. He pleaded guilty to a lesser charge and served 30 days in jail.

Then, in 1992, after finding that Lutgen had used inappropriate discipline with the children, the Illinois Department of Children and Family Services removed the children from Lutgen's home and placed them with his brother and sister-in-law. However, 15th Circuit Judge Victor Sprengelmeyer gave custody of the children back to Lutgen. He ruled that the discipline qualified only as "technical abuse."

Lutgen declined to comment.

“You stole away two precious people.”

Lisa Oellerich

I love reading a good murder mystery. But when the crime is real, it is awful and sad.

I spent the worst days of my journalism career covering the sentencing hearing of Robert “Robby” Jones.

Jones pleaded guilty to shooting and killing Rhonda Wurm and Darin Oellerich early the morning of June 19, 1999. He also admitted to charges of rape, home invasion and burglary.

Wurm and Oellerich were in their middle 20s. They had graduated from Scales Mound High School, participated in community sports and lavished their nieces and nephews with affection. They were engaged to be married and were well liked. By all accounts, they made a sweet couple.

I didn’t know them but had spent a day with Rhonda’s younger sister, Melissa, just 18 months before. She was a senior at Scales Mound High School, and I followed her from class to class for a story I wrote about her school. She was quiet yet friendly, pretty and studious. She seemed like a good kid.

Rhonda and Darin lived near Apple River in a farm house owned by Jones’s grandfather. Jones had lived there for a few years as a child. He didn’t know Rhonda and had met Darin only once.

Jones was only 18 and had just graduated from high school when he shot the young couple. Getting through school had been a struggle for Jones, but he had done well in an alternative school program during his senior year. Although Jones sometimes fought with schoolmates, he apparently had a soft side. He once left a thank-you note and a carnation for his tutor, Patricia Homb.

Jones was scheduled to enter the U.S. Army June 29. An Army sargent called Jones an ideal recruit and said he had expected Jones to do well in the military.

Jones confessed to the murders on June 22, three days after the shootings.

The purpose of the hearing, which took place in November of 2000 before Judge William Kelly, was to decide whether to execute him or sentence him to life. Illinois law then called for the death penalty but allowed the court to consider extenuating circumstances.

I dreaded the hearing. I expected that, without the need to prove Jones’s guilt by presenting dry scientific evidence, prosecutors would focus on raw emotion. I was right.

Throughout the hearing, about 30 of Darin and Rhonda’s extended family members clustered together on the right side of the room. I wanted to say something to Melissa and the others, but the group seemed impenetrable, bound tightly by anger and pain, mutual love and support.

On the left, behind the defendant’s chair, sat Jones’s mother Kelly. She appeared to be inconsolable. It was as though I could read the anguish between the small lines on her face.

The only other people there for Jones were his adoptive father, an aunt and uncle and a minister.

“You seem like good, kind people. I don’t blame you for what Robby did,” I thought.

Although I wanted to hug them, I sat down quietly with my note pad and pen.

Among the first witnesses were Jones’s friends, who had been with him during the day and evening before the murders. They said they fished with Jones that afternoon and drank a few beers. A little later, they drove along the county back roads with their hunting rifles looking for raccoons.

It started out as a typical day—just a few friends hanging out together and doing what many teenagers in rural Jo Daviess County do—fish, hunt and, unfortunately, sometimes drink.

But the testimony continued, and no one could change the course of events, to stop what eventually would take place.

"Robby, just go home now and go to bed. If you do, none of this will happen. You and Rhonda and Darin will be safe."

But the evening wore on, and Jones and his friends continued to drive around and drink.

About 2:30 a.m., the others went home, and Jones began to feel depressed. The thought occurred to him that his friends had joined him only because he had a car. He was feeling used.

"Just go home, Robby. Get some sleep. You will feel better in the morning."

But he continued to drive and to listen to the noise in his head.

"Oh, no, Robby. You are on a moving train and can't seem to stop. Go home. Don't get yourself into any more trouble. Give yourself a chance to grow up and deal with whatever is bothering you."

Angry and frustrated, Jones went to the old farm place and parked his car in a shed. He thought about suicide. Eventually he got out of the car, grabbed the .22-250 caliber rifle his parents had given him for graduation, headed toward the house and crawled through a basement window.

"Please, don't do this."

Once inside, Jones crept upstairs and went into the kitchen. He felt a hunger pang, opened the refrigerator door and drank juice from a carton. Next, he walked through the living room toward the bedroom where Darin and Rhonda slept. He lifted his rifle and—

"Oh, my God. Stop!"

—he shot Darin. Rhonda sat up in bed, and Jones fired again, twice. He dragged Rhonda's body out of bed and penetrated her.

"That's it. This really happened. Oh Jesus, oh no. What a waste."

Testimony lasted for eight days. I learned more about Robby Jones than perhaps anyone has a right to know. Psychologists said he suffered from several personality disorders, with symptoms of anti-social behavior, over sensitivity to criticism and paranoia. One psychologist believed he had attention deficit/hyperactivity disorder, causing a tendency toward impulsivity, impatience and trouble dealing with his emotions. He also abused alcohol and took LSD.

I also learned that, when Kelly was pregnant with Robby, her ex-husband (Robby's biological father) beat her in an attempt to abort the fetus. Kelly remained with Robby's father for two or three years after he was born, and Robby witnessed more beatings. Kelly testified that Robby was afraid to visit his father and vowed never to be like him.

I flashed back to a public radio broadcast I had heard. According to researchers, a baby can be affected by the mother's emotional state during pregnancy. I thought about other reports I had heard or read indicating how important the first six months of life can be. I wondered if Robby had much chance, given the cards he was dealt.

"Why couldn't Robby have had a chance to come to terms with his life before he grabbed a gun and killed two people? Will this terrible cycle of violence ever end?"

Robby showed no emotion during the hearing, except to turn his head and look at Kelly several times, as though seeking reassurance from his mom that she still loved and accepted him. During those brief moments, he seemed like a little boy. Kelly barely looked at him, tormented by what her son had done.

"Please, give Kelly some peace of mind."

On the fifth day of the hearing, Rhonda's sister, Angela Koehn, and Darin's sister, Lisa Oellerich, talked about the impact the murders had on them and their families. They described a loving young couple who had been close to their families and who would have made terrific parents.

"They were to become husband and wife, mother and father, and grandmother and grandfather," Koehn said. "But they already were a son and daughter, a grandson and granddaughter, a sister and a brother, and a niece and nephew."

"You stole away two precious people," Oellerich said, addressing Jones directly. "We have lost more than we knew we ever had."

I couldn't help but cry. I dabbed at my eyes with a tissue, hoping no one would notice. But the tears kept coming.

"If I am this sad, imagine how Rhonda

and Darin's families must feel. Please, God—if there is a God—give them some joy in their lives."

On. Nov. 20, Judge Kelly sentenced Jones to death. Later Gov. George Ryan stayed all executions, and Jones remains in prison.

The day following the sentencing, I returned to my normal routine, feeling depleted. I wrote a story about a proposal for a Wal-Mart Super Center, and life went on.

References

Allen, Frederick Lewis, "Only Yesterday," American Studies Department of the University of Virginia at http://xroads.virginia.edu.

Altfillisch-Melton, Carrie, interview, 2005.

Byers, John, "Calaboose: The Life and Times of a Frontier Lawman 1835-1858," pp. 279-292, 2002, Jay Street Publishers, New York, N.Y.

CourtTV Crime Library, "Al Capone—Made in America," www.crimelibrary.com.

East Dubuque Register: "Snowballers in Court," Jan. 17, 1929; "Raid Uncovers Giant Distillery," May 23, 1929; "Prisoners Enroute Escape Sheriff," Oct. 10, 1929; and "Doctor on Trial for Murder of Girl," June 12, 1930.

Elizabeth Weekly News: "E. Dubuque's Soft Drink Parlors Raided by Prohibition Men," Feb. 24, 1926; "Jo Daviess Sheriff Arrests Wisconsin Man on Charge of Bootlegging Near Warren, June 21, 1929; "State's Attorney Rids County of Slot Machines," July 17, 1929; "Elizabeth Prepares against Bank Bandits," Aug. 5, 1925; "County Officers Raid Hanover Liquor Joints," Oct. 9, 1929; "Autopsy and Inquest in Shepard Case," Oct. 17, 1928; "Prisoners Escape from Sheriff Hathaway; Steal Freeport Car and Escape," Oct. 16, 1929; "Escaped Prisoners Located in Iowa Prison," Oct. 30, 1929; "Coolidge and Walker Get Fifteen Years," Nov. 12, 1929; "Prohibition Agents Raid Galena Brewery," March 3, 1930; "Dr. Stilson Guilty: Jury Says 20 Years in Pen," June 18, 1930; "Dr. Stilson Must Serve 20 Years in Pen," September 24, 1930; and "County Officers Raid Elizabeth and Stockton Homes—Arrest Five," Oct. 15, 1930.

The Galena Gazette: "Horrible Murder," May 8, 1889; "Admits His Guilt," May 9, 1889; "Wesley Prisk," May 30, 1889; "Jonathan Skene's Case," Nov. 2, 1897; "Charge Woman with Murder in Fatal Beating at Nora," Nov. 13, 1968; and "Mary Zink Found Innocent," Aug. 6, 1970.

Hawley, May, Miss Rarson and Zoe Lenore Gray, "History of Warren, Illinois: Its People, Industries, Achievements and Growth," P. 59, 1928.

"History of Alcohol Prohibition," National Commission on Marihuana and Drug Abuse, www.druglibrary.org/Schaffer/LIBRARY.

"The History of Banking in Illinois: Building on Our Past ... Shaping Our Future," pp. 84-87, Illinois Bankers Association, 1991.

"History of Jo Daviess County: 1887," pp. 565 and 348-358.

Moore, J. Christopher, interview, 2005.

"The People of the State of Illinois vs. James Lutgen, Case No.84CF57," Jo Daviess County Circuit Court, 1984.

"The People of the State of Illinois vs. James Madison Stillson, otherwise known as J. Madison Stillson, Case No. 20373," Jo Daviess County Circuit Court and Illinois Supreme Court, 1930.

Telegraph Herald: "Ann Landers: Reader Riled by Court's Work," Oct. 11, 1988; "Lutgen Retains Custody of Daughters," Jan. 5, 1989; "High Court Refuses Custody Appeal," April 11, 1989; "Lutgen Held for Assault," March 15, 1990; "Lutgen Gets 30-Day Sentence," Oct. 4, 1990; and "Lutgen Gains Custody of Daughters," Mar. 27, 1993.

Watson, Daryl, interview, 2005.

Schools

Derinda Center School
Back row: Warren Hiring, Durlun Eberly, Robert Reusch, Kathryn Ann McKinley and Leroy Groezinger
Middle row: Johnny Reusch, Betty Reusch, Lois Wurster and Marion Krug
Front row: Frost McBride (teacher), Lucille Krug, Donald Wurster and Lois Miller
(circa 1935, courtesy of Charles and Mardelle Dykstra)

"A lot of people thought we were nuts."

Mardelle Dykstra

Workmen had moved the Derinda Center School, fixed the roof, replaced the windows and siding, put up insulation and drywall, refinished the wainscoting and floors, installed heating, plumbing and air conditioning, built a bathroom and kitchenette, painted the walls and hung an old-time school bell.

The time had come for the people who had worked so hard on the old, one-room schoolhouse to celebrate its completion. The early-evening sun shown brightly through the building's new windows and reflected on its sparkling wooden floors as crew members and their families gathered for dinner.

Charles and Mardelle Dykstra could not have felt more pleased with the results, made possible by a group of fine local craftsmen. They showed their guests the kind of warmth you reserve for those with whom you have completed a tough project and developed enduring friendship and respect.

The Dykstras invited me to the party, too, both to thank me for reporting previously about the restoration and in the hope that I would write a second story for the Telegraph Herald. I did write another, because I'm a sucker for good-natured, hard-working people who do what others say cannot or should not be done. And I appreciated their laughter as Charles "roasted" the craftsmen and they poked fun at the Dykstras. (Part of this story comes from my old TH notes.)

The project began in 1997, when Charles and Mardelle bought the building from the Derinda Township for $1,500. They had it moved a half mile across a field to their acreage 6 miles south of Elizabeth on Derinda Road. They said they did it because both had attended small, two-room schools and still had a soft spot in their hearts for their early education. They also had taught school, which gave the building extra meaning.

By that time the old school house was 110 years old, well used and badly battered. The Derinda Center School had operated until 1962—it was the last country school in Jo Daviess County to close—and Harlan Haug had used it later as a storage shed.

"When they were getting ready to move it, it was election day," said Kenneth Thorsen, a carpenter who worked on the restoration. The township election took place nearby. "Four or five people came up to me and asked why they are wasting their time on it. Of course, you could tear it down and build a new one cheaper, but this is history."

"A lot of people thought we were nuts, but they didn't tell us that to our faces," Mardelle said with a laugh. "But we didn't do this as an investment. We just followed our hearts."

In its day, the school was "deluxe." At 36 by 26 feet, it was larger than most. It featured decorative trim, large cloak rooms and a raised

Charles and Mardelle Dykstra

platform, which held a small library and served as a stage.

The Dykstras hired John Eversoll to oversee the project. Eversoll says proudly that he comes from a long line of carpenters and that his grandfather built his first barn at age 15. "It's still up on Long Hollow Road."

Eversoll and his crew encountered problems from the beginning. The moving company wouldn't give them much advance notice for transporting the building. "I had to get the power company there, sheriff's deputies there and county road people there. I got a call from the company the night before telling me I had to trim a tree. No one told me I had to trim a tree.

"The windows were the biggest problem. They were totally disintegrated." Marvin Company custom-made windows to replicate them.

Replacing the siding and installing wallboard proved to be nearly as challenging. The crew had to scour Jo Daviess County—and beyond—to find siding from the late 19th Century that was still good enough to use. The Dykstras wanted everything to be as authentic looking as possible.

"Then there was a wallboard shortage. Vince Hoskins (who owned Hoskins Building Center in Elizabeth) had to get a truckload out of Canada."

Removing old paint from the doors and varnish from the wainscoting turned out to be no mean feat either, Robert Ertmer said. "It was a dirty mess. I don't know how many gallons of stripper we used." Hard, green paint on the doors nearly gave Ertmer fits.

The building's crowning touch, its bell tower, had no bell. The Dykstras found a heavy, old ringer that looked just like the one in an old picture of the school. "We had to drag that thing up the scaffolding and up the roof to set it in there. It took five of us. It was a gut ripper," Eversoll said.

No part of the project came cheap. "We kept running out of money," Charles said. "We figured it would cost us about 40 grand, but it was about 85 by the time we got done with it."

Despite those challenges—or partly because of them—the project became one of Eversoll's favorites of his long career. "It is so much fun when you can put something back together like that. I have always liked remodeling much more than building something new. The older buildings had more class and style."

Derinda Center School

"I've been doing carpentry work for 22 years, and I loved every single day of it," Thorsen said. "It was done like the way you like to see people do it; we restored it."

Harvey Kloss, who did the wiring, said working on the school took him back to the past. He attended his first four years of school at Derinda Center and remembers how the students helped each other with their lessons and how the older children made sure the younger children put their boots and mittens on before going outside to play.

He will never forget when Russell Beyer blew off two of his fingers. Beyer was playing with some blasting caps that were in a box of junk that someone had brought to school. "Before you knew it, there was an explosion," Kloss said. "The teacher had to pick up the pieces of the fingers."

"Russell came over one day and pointed out where his finger landed," Thorsen said. "Supposedly, it went over by the chalkboard. Of course, he thought Dykstras were really nuts for doing the restoration, too."

Kloss also remembers waiting inside the general store across the road while the school warmed up from the heat of a wood-burning stove. The students who sat closest to the stove were warm, while those who sat farthest away shivered with cold.

During the long restoration, the crew members and the Dykstras got to know each other and their foibles. As Dykstra roasted Eversoll, he called him a "fourth-generation carpenter, gifted craftsman, temperamental artist and itinerant orator." He dubbed Thorsen "an itinerant psychologist and an authority on the modern woman." He teased Vince Toepfer about how much the windows had cost.

Ertmer said Charles was "like a rabbit being chased by a fox."

"We always had such a good time working," Eversoll said. "We had one young guy working there, and we were always riding him. That's Donny Kruger. He is my neighbor and he is one of the most incredible young men I have ever met, I guess because of his personality, his intelligence and his work ethic."

"I would always be joking around with Donny that women like this or they like that," Thorsen said. "Of course, all of it was false."

Thorsen said everyone "meshed."

He also appreciated the fact that the Dykstras wanted to do everything right. "They could have had us put on new asphalt shingles, but they had us put on wooden ones instead, because that's the way the school was."

"The Dykstras are as good of people I have ever worked for," Eversoll said. "I am proud of the work I did, but I couldn't have done it without someone giving me the opportunity. It was the Dykstras's love and money that did it."

"I wouldn't have done it, but I'm sure glad someone did," Haug said.

The Dykstras have furnished the school with an old oak teacher's desk, a Jack and Jill poster from 1912, assorted items from schools throughout the Midwest and the wood stove from the general store. A round top from one of the general store's tables hangs on the wall. (The store is long gone.)

"Derinda Center is Derinda Center again," Ertmer said.

"How is a baby like a banana?"

Kim Thorsen

One spring day Kim Thorsen took one of her middle-school classes out to the old Derinda Center School so students could experience what learning was like for their grandparents. The children also played games that were popular among their ancestors.

Later, they talked about how attending school there differed from what it is like to go to their modern, new River Ridge School.

Instead of riding horses or walking to school, children take the bus. They no longer study just the basics, and activities do not depend as much on the weather. Their teachers don't ask them to carry in wood: A modern thermal system takes care of heating and cooling. And, instead of taking handwritten notes, students can use laptop computers to get lessons and assignments via the school's wireless technology.

"Everything in the bathrooms is automatic!" marveled William Weede, 11.

"Even the lights go on automatically," Tori Groezinger, 10, added.

"Sometimes, when I just walk by the faucet, it goes on," Kayla Miller, 12, noted.

Ben Headlee, 11, said he would like to go back in time, when the Derinda school was still operating, to see what it really was like.

"I think I would like the older way better," Tori said. "They had to walk to school every day, and I like walking. But at our school, you can have a lot more friends."

The children were so interested in the old school house that they raised $100 for it. The Dykstras used the money to buy an antique clock, which hangs near the chalkboard.

Positioned about halfway between Elizabeth and Hanover, River Ridge is a "country school." Like many of its counterparts from years gone by, it sits on top of a hill surrounded by farm fields and woods.

It is early spring, and some children are playing softball—not unlike the stick ball played by generations before—on fresh grass of chartreuse and emerald green. A sharp wind offers a reminder that winter has yet to take its last howling breath, but planting time is near.

However, here the analogy with Derinda and other country schools seems to end.

Opened in 2003 for grades K-12 and built at a cost of nearly $17 million, River Ridge contains 36 classrooms, plus a gymnasium, commons area and technology center. It can hold up to 700 students comfortably. Although it is small by city standards, is the newest, largest educational structure in Jo Daviess County.

In one classroom, Thorsen has invited her sixth-grade students to sit on the floor, which is carpeted rather than finished in wood. A language arts teacher, she introduces them to the idea of personification. She starts by asking them to name 10 things that a "non-human object" can do, which a human can also do.

"Tigers have long fingernails," one student says excitedly.

Encouraged by Thorsen's nod, other students burst in with answers. Soon the class develops a long list.

"I get a kick out of what you guys determine are human things," Thorsen says. "How many of you find that the things that came up at the end of the list are better than the first four or five, which just came off the top of the head?"

Next, she asks, "How is a baby like a banana?" The students eagerly respond, and their answers vary.

"Soft."

"Squishy."

"Curved."

"They can both be alive."

"They can bruise."

"They can grow."

"They both know nothing."

"They come in different shapes, colors and sizes."

"You can play with them."

Soon Thorsen has the children quietly writing sentences using personification. Deep in

Kim Thorsen with Amber Parisi, Kayla Kemp and Morgan Speaker

concentration, they look up occasionally to think about how they want to word something.

Thorsen says later that one of her favorite quotes comes from an Alaskan educator: "In order to teach you, I must know you." She tries to understand the needs, personalities and learning styles of each student so that she can help all of them reach their potential.

"Every student brings his or her individual personality, ideas and experiences to my classroom. Celebrating those differences creates a learning environment where they feel they can safely share ideas."

"If I can give students the tools they need to be successful in other learning environments, while encouraging a lifelong love of learning, then I have done my job to the best of my ability," she adds.

Afterward, I find my way to the teachers' lounge, where special-education teacher Elissa Gunning prepares for her next class. She says she incorporates unusual holidays—such as Pretzel Day, Penguin Day, Tap Dance Day and even Dance Like a Chicken Day—into her daily lessons. "On Dance Like a Chicken Day, we will play 'The Chicken Song.' As sophisticated as middle-school kids are, they still are little kids."

"Whenever food is involved in the holiday, we definitely have food," she adds. "During math classes, kids get cereal or granola bars. Whatever it costs me, it is worth it. I would rather they sit and crunch granola bars and work, rather than sit and complain about how hard math is."

Like other teachers at River Ridge, Thorsen and Gunning will do whatever it takes to promote learning.

Next, I poke my head into the library, where floor-to-ceiling windows reveal the vast countryside below. Several students read quietly in the calming atmosphere. I decide to sit down for a few minutes and go over my notes.

Finally, I pay a visit to Principal Brad Albrecht. (He since has become superintendent.) He says that, like Thorsen and Gunning, most teachers at River Ridge follow contemporary teaching methods by encouraging participation and group activities. "It kind of goes back to the one-room school idea where kids work in groups and help each other out."

Maybe there are more similarities between River Ridge and the old country schools than I realized, I think to myself.

Albrecht says what really stands out about River Ridge is that students receive the kind of individual attention and care they would get in a private school. "I won't kid you, everybody loses kids. But here the teachers really care, and the families really care, which helps the teachers and the staff. I think people are more involved in the educational process than just showing up for the extras like ball games and plays."

"Part of that goes back to the building," he adds.

Before 2003, the district's high school and an elementary school were located in Elizabeth, while the middle school and another elementary school were located in Hanover. When choosing a site for the new, consolidated K-12 school, the board of education made sure it picked a spot halfway between the two towns, in order to prevent stirring up any old rivalries. Although Hanover and Elizabeth lie only 7 miles apart, each has a unique character and engenders strong community loyalty.

By constructing the school in the country, residents in neither town felt they were giving something up in favor of the other.

"People supported the building project, spent a lot of money on it and are proud of it."

Albrecht himself grew up in Elizabeth and attended River Ridge. "In 1973, when I was out of college and looking for a job, the superintendent called me up and said, 'Come on down to the board meeting. We've got some questions for you.'" The board offered Albrecht a job teaching physical education and coaching basketball, and he took it.

"It was a little strange, because some of my teachers were still there," he says. "I had a little trouble addressing them by their first names. At the same time, the seniors had trouble calling me 'Coach' or 'Mister.'"

Apparently, everything turned out OK: He has moved up the ladder, and the school is highly acclaimed. "We're an A+ school again for the fourth year," he says.

I leave his office and head toward the front door. As I do, I notice a colorful mural in the entrance hall. Painted by Pat Holland, a local resident who has a daughter attending River Ridge High School, it depicts Hanover and Elizabeth on opposite sides with farm fields and sky in between. The mural contains the words, "Continuing Our Heritage."

The heritage will continue. As long as Hanover and Elizabeth have existed, there have been students who have been ready to learn and teachers who have made sure they do.

"I liked to learn. I always liked to read."

Violet Rodden

Violet Rodden is the oldest person alive who attended Derinda Center School. She is so old she can remember paying $4 a month for rent and buying 15 cents worth of meat at Bishop's Store and knowing she had enough to feed a family of five.

A slight woman with white hair, she weighs only 88 pounds. She cannot hear very well and she has arthritis in her knees, but she enjoys overall good health and her mind remains sharp.

Born Violet Schaible in 1902 on a farm near Hanover, she received her education in three different country schools, beginning with Derinda Center.

"We had to walk through pastures and fields to get there in the morning. It was a long way. I never learned too much. I only went through eight grades. I never went to high school, because it was 7 miles away."

"But I liked to learn," she added. "I always liked to read."

She still reads. Romance novels are her favorite.

"I liked all the kids, too." During recess, she and the other children played Hide and Go Seek and Drop the Hanky. Sometimes they picked blackberries on a nearby hill.

"It was great if you had a couple of pennies. Then you could go across the road and get candy (at the general store)."

She owned three dresses — one for "good" and two for school. "Everybody was the same. Nobody had any money."

After school, Violet did farm chores. "I helped milk every night. I had to sit under the cows with a stool and pail.

"My dad, he didn't have any boys (until later) and thought I was as good as a boy. I loved it. I loved being outside."

Her growing-up years were good. "My parents were good-natured. I never heard them fighting or anything like that."

Violet loved to dance and, when she was 16, she met her future husband. "I think I ate supper with him." Dances often included a long intermission, during which the gentlemen would ask the ladies out for a late supper. "I kind of fell

Violet Rodden

for him, and I guess he did the same."

Two years later she and George were married.

During their early years of marriage, she and George moved 10 times. They lived in five houses in Hanover and five in Elizabeth. "The rent would always be too high."

The couple had three children, all boys. "They all went into the service. Two of them are already gone."

George worked at the Savanna Army Depot Activity and played the violin and saxophone in a dance band. "I would go and dance. I guess that's why my knees wore out."

Violet waited tables at a restaurant in town. Then she got a job at the Savanna Army Depot Activity. At age 65 she went to work at Eaton Manufacturing Co. in Hanover and stayed until she was 78. (The company now is Invensys Appliance Control.)

"I worked hard always. When I got home from work on Friday nights, I would clean the whole house, up and down. I raised a big garden every year and canned an awful lot of fruit."

But life wasn't all work. She enjoyed cooking and having company over.

George died in 1960. "One morning, he had a terrible time getting out of bed. We got a doctor and took him to Savanna. He was getting along all right for awhile and would sit up in a chair. But, all at once, he slumped over and he was dead."

Violet now lives with her youngest son Jim in Elizabeth. She has lived in the house for 65 years.

Hardly any of the Rodden family is left anymore. "It's just Jim and I." And most of her friends have passed away. "I used to know everybody who lived in every house in this town. Now I don't know hardly anybody."

Life has slowed down for Violet since her days of working and raising a family. "I went to anything that went on in town. Now I can't go to any of it."

But that isn't entirely true, said Margaret Wurster, Violet's cousin and friend. She still plays cards every week, attends church and goes out to dinner now and then. When she turned 103 in the fall of 2005, her church honored her with a cake.

Margaret characterized Violet as a typical German who can be a bit stubborn at times but whose hospitality is legendary.

"Her brother tried to talk her into going into assisted living for the winter. She listened to him for awhile, then she said, 'Are you going to, too?' That stopped the conversation."

Looking back on her long life, Violet feels satisfied. "I did pretty good, didn't I?" she said.

"The other kids, she was mean as hell to them."

Robert Kleckner

Robert Kleckner has boxes upon boxes stored in the back of his garage in Stockton. They are stuffed with old ledgers and other documents from the county's one-room schoolhouses.

Most of the schools are gone — either torn down or destroyed by wind, rain or fire. But Kleckner is hanging on to as much of their history as his garage and his head will hold.

"I have been monkeying around with this stuff since 1983," he told me one day as we sat at his kitchen table.

Kleckner became serious about school history when Nellie Arnold, who taught him during third grade at Neutral Ridge School, gave him a bunch of old school records. Later, he obtained more from the county superintendent of schools. "I've got records from all 118 schools, including lists of all the kids who went to school from 1936 until they closed."

However, he didn't get all the documents he wanted. "Some already had headed to the dumpster." Had he not called the superintendent when he did, they all would have been destroyed.

Now, whenever anyone runs across more school information, they pass it along to him. He sorts it and meticulously organizes it. "I sit here sometimes until 3 o'clock in the morning, writing names down."

He also has written the history of 50 of the schools and has made a study of the Illinois educational system. "The trouble with writing all that stuff down is that people read it and tell you more stuff. Then you've got to rewrite it."

A photocopy machine sits in the corner of Kleckner's living room, where he copies student lists, photographs, teachers' invoices and whatever else he gets his hands on. His wife Shirley types for him on her computer.

Kleckner's memories of his own one-room school days, along with the stories others have told him, could fill his garage.

Each day he walked a mile-and-a-half to school. "It was over fields and uphill all the way. I had to jump fences and go over creeks. When the water was high, I climbed over a dead tree. I was wet lots of times when I got to school."

Later, he bicycled to school and milked cows for a farmer along the way. He said he learned as much on the way to and from school as he did from the teachers, because he would talk to farmers, trap and hunt.

Geography became his favorite subject. "I knew all the goddang countries in the world and all the goddang capitols. The teacher couldn't keep up with me."

Although he never thought he would "get out of those hills" south of Stockton, he has traveled to 59 countries. "I married Shirley Stafford, and she wanted to travel."

In the spring, when the roads turned to

Robert Kleckner in his garage

mud, he would put chains on his teacher's car so she could drive home. "The teacher (Grace Bonjour) always gave me a candy bar, and I got all As from her. But the other kids, she was mean as hell to them."

During the 1941-42 school year, only five students attended his school — he and his four siblings.

"One teacher made my brother stay after school. My brother said he had to go to the rest room — we had indoor rest rooms, because our school was fairly new — and, when he was in there, he crawled out the window and went home."

Several men he talked to later reported that, as boys, they had peaked through their schools' windows only to see their teachers making love to their boyfriends, one of whom was a school director, while standing up against a wall. "That happened at four schools — Massbach, Roes Corner, Yankee Hollow and Robinson. One student had an affair with a teacher at Equal Rights School."

In 1941, Ruth Dawne Whitman, a teacher at Rush Center School, fell through the floor of the outhouse. The pit was almost filled with water, and the teacher had to hang on to the cement foundation with her fingers and feet to keep from drowning.

She called for help, but no one heard her until one of her students, Doris Deyo Plath, went outside for some fresh air. The 13-year-old held on to her teacher's hands until some fellow students got help from some neighbors. They pulled her out with a rope.

"There is no doubt Ruth would have drowned if she hadn't gotten help immediately." Although her entire body broke out in a rash, she recovered and was back in the classroom a couple of weeks later.

From his studies, Kleckner has put together a list of significant dates in Jo Daviess County education. Here are some of them:

1827: The first schoolhouse was built in the county. It was made of logs and located in Galena. Many early schoolhouses served as churches and community centers as well as schools. Before that, the few children who attended school went to private homes to study. They generally paid 3 cents per day, and teachers received about 30 cents per day. Children attended school only up to three grades, but each grade equaled three years of study.

1848: Most of the county's 118 country school districts were formed. Schools were built so that most students wouldn't have to walk more than 2 miles to get there. Log schools cost $150 to $250 to build; wood frame buildings cost $300 to $400; and rock structures cost $600 to $800. There were no written tests or homework. Children sat on logs, and teachers did not have desks. Teachers needed only eight years of education. Usually they lived with families within their districts.

1855: The state of Illinois passed a tax levy and began its public school system, whereby children could attend elementary school for free. Until then, only one-third of school-age children received regular instruction. Within five years, 85 percent attended school. Students still had to pay for their own high school education.

1858: Students were required to speak English in school. Before that, many spoke German.

1865: A fourth grade was added, and each grade became equal to two years. Ten years later, a fifth grade was added, and a new law required schools to hold classes at least 12 weeks per year.

1874: The last log school was replaced.

1892: The seventh and eighth grades were added, and each grade became one year long. Eighth graders studied orthography (spelling), grammer, arithmetic, U.S. history and geography.

1906: The state required classes to be held for 6 months of the year.

1909: Education became compulsory for children ages 7 to 14.

1914: A new law required teachers to have a high school education.

1930: Teachers had to have two years of education beyond high school to teach. Until about that time, women teachers had to quit their jobs when they married. Teachers earned about $100 per month, but, by 1934, their wages dropped to about $35 per month.

1950: By this time, most rural schools had consolidated with those in town.

1962: Derinda Center School became the last one-room school in the county to close.

1964: Teachers were required to earn a four-year college degree.

References

Albrecht, Brad, interview, 2004.

Derinda Center School celebration, 2000.

Dykstra, Charles, interviews, 1999, 2003 and 2004.

Dykstra, Mardelle, interviews, 1999, 2004 and 2005.

Ertmer, Robert, interview, 2000.

Eversoll, John, interview, 2004.

Groezinger, Tori, interview, 2003.

Gunning, Elissa, interview, 2004.

Headlee, Ben, interview, 2003.

Kleckner, Robert, interviews, 2003 and 2005.

Kloss, Harvey, interview, 1999.

Miller, Kayla, interview, 2003.

Rodden, Violet, interview, 2004.

Thorsen, Kenneth, interview, 2005.

Thorsen, Kim, interview and visit to class, 2003, 2004 and 2005.

Weede, William, interview, 2003.

Wurster, Margaret, interviews, 2004 and 2005.

Churches

Pastor Marjorie Drickey

"When you make a total mess of things, God forgives you."

The Rev. Jim McCrea

It was time for the sermon, so Rev. Jim McCrea invited the children to come up to the front of the church and take a seat. After they settled down, he held up a newspaper and started his magic trick. He said he would show them what happened one time when he did something wrong.

Pastor Jim McCrea, Ann Herman and Student Pastor Cindy Serpliss

Slowly, McCrea tore up the newspaper. As he ripped, he said, "I was having a good time tearing away, but then I remembered that I'm not the only one who reads the newspaper."

What was he to do? With the children's help, perhaps he could make the paper whole again. "All you have to do is say the magic word. The magic word is 'block party.'" The congregation had planned to host a block party after the service.

As the children said "block party," McCrea began to unfold the newspaper. It was, to their surprise, in one piece.

"See, when you make a total mess out of things, God forgives you. ... That's all we're doing today—celebrating God's love for us."

McCrea's message—and certainly the manner in which he delivered it—would have stunned the early members of the First Presbyterian Church. They would have heard much more about the evils of drinking, gambling and dancing than about God's forgiveness.

The congregation dates back to January of 1829. The Rev. Aratus Kent had left a thriving parish in New York to preach to people on the frontier. The story has it that Kent wrote to the American Board of Home Missions and asked to be sent to "a place so tough no one else will take it."

That would be Galena. "Those of you, who were here on the first of January 1829, will recollect, that Galena was, at that time, to human view, a God-forsaken place and most repulsive to any evangelical efforts," Kent wrote in a sermon he presented to his congregation in 1862.

Galena had attracted a rough-and-tumble crowd of lead miners who, when not engaged in mining, headed to the saloons. They drank hard liquor, gambled, swore unabashedly, participated in "incessant sleigh-riding" and, God forbid, danced. They did not observe the Sabbath, and some even boasted about their lack of religious affiliation.

His first day in town, Kent swept out the back room of a saloon and preached to about 50 curious people. Soon he developed a faithful following of six people, and they met in the old log courthouse (which is now gone) on Bench Street. The congregation officially became organized in 1831.

Later other people joined, but the membership fluctuated. The congregation built the current church, a sturdy stone structure at 106 N. Bench St., in 1838 and added the vestibule and steeple in 1851. It is the oldest continuously-used Protestant church building of the Old Northwest Territory, McCrea said. The territory consisted of all or part of Illinois, Wisconsin, Minnesota, Indiana, Michigan and Ohio.

The best years in the early church were 1837, 1840, 1842 and 1844, when the church held revival meetings, Kent said in his 1862 sermon.

"At some of these sessions the overshadowing presence of God was so manifest that the impenitent were found ready and willing to converse on the subject," he said. "A scoffing infidel from the country was maddened to cursing, because he could not enter a store except he must be met by these hallowed men. And not merely good men, but even those, who were stout hearted and far from Righteous, were awakened and melted to tears."

Kent lamented "the utter disregard of the Sanctuary by thousands among us." He begged his congregation to visit the unchurched and "persuade them to attend to the means of grace."

Although Aratus Kent sounds harsh and out of date today, he was open to change and open to others, McCrea said. He traveled 30 tough days by steamboat and horse to the frontier and later set up a 100-mile circuit in order to preach at 21 different sites. "I picture him as someone who was willing to set aside his own personal needs to serve the needs of people he didn't even know."

McCrea said that, like Kent, his congregation is open to other people and to change. First Presbyterian was the first church in Galena to have a Web site and among the first to experiment with Power Point presentations during Sunday services.

The congregation consists of about 120 people, mostly retirement age. It is a wonderful, warm group, who make newcomers feel welcome. During the handshake of peace, they flow out into the aisles to talk to one another and to greet strangers. "Sometimes we forget to go back to our seats," one member quipped.

One Sunday I walked into the church feeling angry and bitter. By the time I left, my attitude had completely changed, thanks to McCrea's rambling but gentle and down-to-earth sermon and to the warm reception I received.

Andra Davis put it this way in a letter she wrote to members after she and her family moved out of state: "When we first moved to Galena ... we found ourselves drawn to the First Presbyterian Church because we felt more welcome here than anywhere else and could definitely feel the love and peace of Jesus Christ in the Congregation. ... Brian and I know that we will never find another church like this one because of all the things only this small church has to offer. ... Our son Carson will miss the dozens of 'built in' Grandmas and Grandpas who worship at First Presbyterian and eagerly shake his hand every service."

Lola Gartner, John Stephens, Maureen Willard and Nancy Mangrum

McCrea has encouraged socializing among members ever since he was called as pastor in 1992 and charged with healing a split in the congregation. I can see evidence of the healing in the way members treat each other.

Many meet monthly in small groups for dinner. The dinner groups reorganize every six months so that everyone gets a chance to know everyone else. In the summer they hold a Road Rally and Sundae Sundays. In the fall they get together for a hayride.

They also reach out to the community, volunteering at and donating money to the local food pantry and providing a weekly after-school program for children. They formerly hosted a Fall Tour of Homes to raise money for other local charities. First Presbyterian has worked with other churches to raise money for Habitat for Humanity homes.

In addition, the congregation participates in national and world-service projects. Members raise money for the Heifer Project, which provides animals for poor families in order to help them become self-sufficient. They also raised money for schools in Kenya.

In other words, they go beyond themselves to look out for others. As Pastor McCrea said, if they mess up a little now and then, so be it. They are human. They have earned God's forgiveness.

"Religious worship was known only at the home firesides."

History of Jo Daviess County

When European immigrants first began to settle in Galena during the early 1820s, no public worship services took place. "Religious worship was known only at the home firesides of those who, in distress and privation, had not forgotten their devotion to Him and who had provided their dwelling place," according to "History of Jo Daviess County: 1887."

That changed after a few years. In 1826, a preacher from Minnesota, while passing through on his way back East, held the first known public service. The following year, some lay Episcopalians met at the home of Captain H.H. Gear to read their church's teachings. In addition, a settler by the name of Rivers Cormack held religious meetings of an unknown description.

To the authors of the county history, this seemed like a natural but slow start. They put it this way: "As the transformation of any country from a condition of barbarity to one of civilization is the work of a long time, so that branch of civilization, Religion, must be of slow development."

But soon organized religion came to town.

In April of 1829, The Rev. Aratus Kent arrived in Galena, followed a week later by The Rev. John Drew, a Methodist minister. They had received assignments from their respective church conferences to establish missions on the Western frontier. They wasted no time soliciting church members.

By 1887, twelve churches had organized in Galena, including Presbyterian, Methodist, Episcopal, Evangelical Protestant, Evangelical Lutheran, Catholic and Baptist churches and the Union Endeavor Sunday School.

Each congregation constructed or bought buildings where they could hold worship services or Sunday schools. Many of the churches were small, such as the 25 by 35 foot First Baptist Church, but several of them soon were replaced by larger structures.

Although the First Presbyterian Church's building ranks today as the oldest standing, continuously running church in the Old Northwest Territory, it was not the first one to be built. The Methodists built a church during the summer of 1833, which later burned and was rebuilt.

Today Galena has 12 churches: Church of Jesus Christ Latter Day Saints, First Presbyterian Church, Friends in Christ Church, Galena Bible Church, Galena First United Methodist Church, Grace Episcopal Church, Kingdom Hall of Jehovah's Witnesses, New Covenant Assembly of God, St. Mary's Catholic Church, St. Matthew Lutheran Church, St. Michael Catholic Church and Westminster Presbyterian Church.

"This church has meant everything. It is my fortification."

Lucille Broshous

Dixie and Tony Schubert

The United Willow Methodist Church southeast of Stockton is anything but imposing. Measuring only 40 by 60 feet and set back from Willow Road, it gets lost among the silos and hills of eastern Jo Daviess County. The windowpanes are plain, clear glass and, inside, the furnishings are sparse. A simple wooden cross hangs above the alter.

But the 20 to 30 members of the congregation seem to like it that way. Perhaps too much splendor and glitz would divert them from their real purpose—worshiping God.

Although members would like to see more young people join, they appreciate the coziness that a small congregation in a small church provides. "Everybody is friendly and cares about the other person," Dixie Schubert says. "You don't get lost here."

Humble as it is, the church fills their souls with strength, love and hope. "It has meant everything to me," says Lucille Broshous, a life-long member. "It is my fortification." It comforted her when her parents died, and it helped her get through the terrible summer of 1981, after she lost her brother and three brothers-in law.

Willow Methodist also ties the people of the surrounding farming community together and gives them a sense of continuity, says Pauline Craig. "It brings me closer to my mother (who is deceased). This is something that was very important to her."

The Sunday service usually begins with a short lesson, with members taking turns reading. If someone cannot pronounce a word, such as Artaxerxes, they substitute the word "dog." No one laughs. The important thing is the message.

"Satan brings on depression," The Rev. Marjorie Drickey says one Sunday, summing up the lesson for the day.

"And stops you in your tracks," one woman adds.

Drickey rings a bell when Sunday school is over and the service is about to begin. An energetic, enthusiastic octogenarian, Drickey leads her congregation in a worship service that combines elements of old-time religion with optimism and a sense of celebration. She tells her parishioners that not believing in God is a sin, but that God sent Jesus Christ to Earth to overcome the doubts and fears that Satan spreads.

"I believe in miracles," she says, smiling at her congregation. "Christianity is about God joining mankind and wanting every person to enjoy Eternity with him."

Later she asks everyone to pray for the

Aaron Masters, Elmer Piper, Etola Solt, Mary Blair, Josephine Krise, The Rev. G. Gable, Mrs. John Solt, Sarah Staley, Etta Lawfer, Corrine MacHamer, Mabel Klaus, Lois Gates with baby Betty and Winnie Piper (circa 1925, courtesy of Lucille Broshous)

Supreme Court, Congress and the President to find a "new commitment to Jesus."

Drickey had retired from the ministry before becoming pastor at Willow Methodist, but God called her back into service in 1997, she says. "I came from a little country church in Nebraska. I love little churches. I like the fellowship. This is a very caring community, and we do things together."

"The Lord has a purpose and a plan here," she adds. She prays for each member by name every day. "I pray that each one will have a personal relationship with Jesus Christ and know Him as their Lord and Savior. I preach the Word, but the Holy Spirit has to speak to their hearts."

After the service, church members gather in back for coffee, cookies and conversation. During the summer, the sun streams through open doors, shining on the small group.

The congregation has been meeting in the same building since 1861. Some of the people who attend today descended directly from one of the pioneer families that first settled in Berreman Township and started the church, such as the Schlafers and Krises. Lucille Broshous descended from James Perry and Mary Hager. "Grandpa Perry" moved to the area in about 1830, she says.

She doesn't know who preached the first sermon in the church but she and others have compiled a list of everyone who has ministered since 1863. The list includes notes about some of the ministers. For instance, W.C. Scott, who preached from 1891 to 1893, collected canes and owned 320 when he died. John E. Rogers, who served in 1911, was the first to travel to the church by automobile. Barton Cartwright Holloway, who served the longest (from 1932 to 1940), raised rare iris.

The building itself hasn't changed much. Years ago, a basement was dug under the church, where one can still see axe marks on the roughly hewn walnut beams. Central heat was installed in 1945, and the wainscoting has been replaced by wood paneling. A few years ago, the congregation had cushions made for the pews. In the summer of 2005 the steps in front were removed and replaced with an entrance area.

What has changed most is the size of the congregation. Lucille, who has been attending the country church almost all her life, said many young families with children used to belong to the church. Often the church was full.

Now the congregation is small, with only about 30 members. Like the surrounding community, it consists mostly of retirement-age people. Because it cannot afford a full-time pastor, it has affiliated with Kent United Methodist Church, another country church just a few miles east. The two churches share Pastor Drickey and take turns hosting the Sunday worship service.

However, two children, Brett and Lisa Yeomen, recently became confirmed in the church, and two new families joined within the past year. Members hope enough young people like Brett and Lisa will join, in order to keep the church going.

Meanwhile, the United Methodist Women's group, formerly known as the Ladies Aid Society, still meets on the first Thursday of every month.

Lucille joined in 1954 and keeps the notes from the meetings, dating back to the 1920s. The group raises money for the church and donates items to charities or to soldiers serving overseas.

In 1968, it started the annual Willow Folk Festival. Musicians perform with acoustical instruments, and people gather on the front lawn of the church to listen. Church members bake pies and make sandwiches, salads and stews to sell during the two-day event.

Without the proceeds from the festival, the church could not survive. However, the festival's main purpose is to bring people together for mutual enjoyment. "It is one big project that pulls us all together and keeps us together," Lila Heath says. Admission is only $4.

With an upbeat attitude among its members and a reliable means of support, the church will survive, Lucille said. "We're doing well. Everybody cooperates. We just need more families to move into the community."

"Quilting is something we can do for the Lord." ***Pat Arnold***

Pat Arnold, 87, helped Margaret Marcure, 90, out of her car and into the Schapville Zion Presbyterian Church. They had packed their lunches and planned to spend the day quilting, as they do most Wednesdays.

Soon Evelyn Winmill arrived. Usually Margaret's sister, Molly Hunt, and Adaline Ryder join them, but neither of them could make it that day.

A large frame about as high as a table sat in the back room of the church. It held a larger-than king-size navy blue and white quilt. Someone else had pieced the top in a Basket pattern, a traditional quilt design. Pat, Margaret and Evelyn had the task of hand stitching the top to a plain backing with a layer of batting (a soft, spongy sheet of fiber) in between. They had begun two weeks before, sewing the layers together with curved lines that created an intricate, delicate pattern. Part of the quilt was rolled under along two sides, so that only about one-fourth of it was visible.

The women immediately got to work.

"Let's see, where did I leave off?" Pat said as she sat down at one corner of the quilt and scanned her work from the previous week. She threaded a needle with white thread and began pushing the needle in and out of the fabric.

In quilting, the smaller the stitches the better. It is a tedious job, but the women enjoy doing it.

"For some people, this is nerve-wracking, but for real quilters, it is relaxing," Evelyn said.

"Quilting is serious business," she added. "You really have to concentrate."

"We do the best we can," Margaret said. "I think we do pretty good."

The women chatted amiably as they worked. Pat said her husband descended from Heinrich Arnold, an early settler. Some of the logs for the original Zion Presbyterian Church, built in 1854, (which was replaced in 1886) came from Heinrich's farm.

Small world, I thought. Someone else I interviewed for this book, Tom Arnold, descended from Heinrich Arnold. Tom's grandfather, Arthur Arnold, served as Sunday school superintendent for 26 years. Tom's father, Wayne, was a church officer. More than likely, Heinrich was one of the church's founding members, but no one knows for sure. Fire destroyed the church's early records in 1888.

Heinrich's wife, Augusta, and her brother and sister descended from a German family named Schap. The community of Schapville got its name from them.

The women spoke of their childhoods, when they rode horses to school, and some of the heavy snowstorms they survived. They also talked about some of their projects. They agreed that black fabric is the most difficult to sew on, because the stitches are so hard to see. They find it easier to quilt in straight lines than in curved lines.

After completing a swath about four feet wide on the quilt, they rolled it under and started a new section. Often when the time comes to move to the next sections, someone says, "Are you ready to roll?" The question gets a laugh every time.

The women have been quilting at Zion Presbyterian for more than 30 years. They are not sure just when the quilting group began. "In those days, nobody had been quilting. You might say it was a new thing," Margaret said. "I think we were the ones who broke the ice."

Of course, the art of quilting has been around for a long time — millennia, in fact. European settlers brought the skill to the United States, and women on the frontier found many uses for their patchwork products, according to historian Julie Johnson. "Not only could they be used on beds, they were also useful as covers for doors and windows and as floor mats for the children to play on. In many cases they were also used as currency to pay bills."

At first, women used scraps of fabric salvaged from other sewing projects or cut from well-worn garments, but soon many began to use material they bought specifically for that purpose. They wanted to create works of art.

However, by the late 1960s, few women were quilting anymore. Many of the traditional women's arts, such as needlepoint, knitting, embroidery and applique, had gone the way of the girdle.

During the past 10 or 20 years, however, the crafts have made a comeback.

Pat joined the group at Zion Presbyterian in 1974. "Some time ago, we had a whole slew of ladies here. We used to have two quilts going." But the number of stitchers has dwindled. Some have moved away, some have died, and some have gone to work.

The quilt tops come from people in the community who either have sewn them themselves or have inherited unfinished projects from their mothers or grandmothers. Molly Hunt pieced the navy blue and white quilt top that the ladies were quilting for her daughter. The women give the money they earn to the church.

"I think we do this for the fun of it and for the companionship," Pat said. "It is a good excuse to get away from home, and it's something we can do for the Lord."

Margaret Marcure and Pat Arnold

All three women have been quilting for many years. Pat learned the craft from both her mother and her teachers at school. "I've been quilting quite awhile, and I'm still not good at it." But her stitches looked neat and small.

Margaret learned mostly from her grandmother. She started her first quilt when her first-born, Edmund, was a baby, but left it unfinished for many years. Not until her 11 children were nearly raised and she had retired from teaching did Margaret resume her hobby. Since then, she has made quilts as wedding gifts for each of her 19 grandchildren who have married. Finally, about four years ago, she finished Edmund's quilt. He is 70 years old.

Evelyn began sewing in high school and bought an electric sewing machine with the first paycheck she earned in her first permanent job in the late 1940s. She said she was a "closet quilter," because she learned on her own, through trial and error.

The ladies continued to work and talk. The soft whirring of a well-oiled sewing machine provided soothing background noise, as Peggy Eichmann and Pat Little worked on other craft projects in the next room.

At Noon, Pat Arnold said, "You know what time it is?"

"It's lunch time," Evelyn replied.

Schapville Zion Presbyterian Church

The women got up from their seats and joined the other two crafters at a large table. They munched on sandwiches, cookies and fruit, and talked about their projects.

About a half hour later, it was time to roll, they said.

The women were quiet after lunch, as they focused on their work.

Later, Margaret's two daughters, Corinne LaBrie and Sandra Griffiths, stopped by, livening things up once again. They said Margaret taught them how to sew when they were young.

"The worst words from Mom, which you didn't want to hear, were, 'Rip it out,'" Corinne said. "I wanted to be outside so bad."

Apparently, Margaret's sewing lessons stuck, because the two sisters were making a quilt to be auctioned at the church's 150-year anniversary celebration.

At about 3 p.m. it was time to quit for the day, because the ladies were getting tired. They felt pleased by how much they had accomplished and about having spent another enjoyable day together.

"Women work together pretty good," Evelyn said.

"My first one was just terrible."

Barbara Woodford

One day a couple from Lena, Ill. stopped at Barbara Woodford's house with a quilt to sell. Woodford, a retired chemist, collects quilts from around the country. (This story has little to do with churches, by the way: I am indulging in my interest in quilts.)

"They said they didn't have a clue about where it came from. It was just up in their attic." It turns out the quilt was made by women from the Zion Presbyterian Church in Schapville.

With alternating squares of plain pink and white blocks that are either embroidered or appliqued, it shows off the skills of many women from Jo Daviess County. Each woman made a block and embroidered her name onto it. Names include Marie Eversoll, Bernice Bahr, Louise Dittmar, Hannah Polchow, Mrs. Albert Hammer, Stella Parrott, Annie Mengemer, Shirley Duerr, Meta Stadel and others.

The women must have preceded the current quilting group at Zion Presbyterian. Barbara knows that one of them died in the 1960s, so the quilt had to be made before that. She speculated that the

Barbara Woodford

church raffled the quilt at a bazaar, which was, and still is, a fairly common practice.

Women also have been contributing individual blocks to group efforts for many years, she said. After the Civil War, the wives of fallen soldiers from a given unit would make blocks and then sew them together to commemorate the dead.

During the early 1800s, women used mostly wool and silk in their constructions, because cotton was not readily available. As U.S. cotton production increased, due to the slavery system and the cotton gin, cotton became a staple in quilt making.

One-hundred years ago, as now, women could buy kits with fabrics, patterns and instructions. Now quilters buy them in quilt shops and craft stores. Then they could order them from newspaper ads that featured black-and-white illustrations of the designs.

Barbara did not start collecting quilts until 1994, after she had seen an exhibit of American quilts in England, of all places. She bought her first one at an auction and, since then, has bought and sold dozens.

She doesn't see much distinction between quilts made in the Midwest and those made in other parts of the country, except that Midwest pieces tend to be brighter. However, historians likely will make more distinctions soon, now that they are taking greater pains to find out where individual quilts were made.

Over the years, Barbara has seen some ugly quilts, as well as some stunningly beautiful ones. Some crafters had a good sense for color and design, while others didn't pay much attention to aesthetics, or had strange taste.

Barbara herself has made three quilts. "My first one was just terrible, so it was OK with me when I saw that my son had put a cigarette hole in it." The other two turned out better, and she keeps one of them on a bed in a guest room. But she prefers to collect, she said.

References

Arnold, Pat, interview, 2004.
Broshous, Lucille, interview, 2003.
Craig, Pauline, interview, 2004.
Davis, Andra, letter to the First Presbyterian Church in Galena, 2003.
Drickey, Marjorie, interview, 2004.
Heath, Lila, interview, 2004.
"History of Jo Daviess County: 1887," pp. 498-508.
Johnson, Julie, "History of Quilting," www.emporia.edu.
Kent, Eratus, sermon, 1862, www.firstgalena.presbychurch.org.
LaBrie, Corinne, interview, 2004.
Marcure, Margaret, interview, 2004.
McCrea, The Rev. James, interview, 2003.
"Our Hundredth Anniversary: 1854 - 1954," pamphlet of the Schapville Zion Presbyterian Church.
Schubert, Dixie, interview, 2004.
Winmill, Evelyn, interview, 2004.
Woodford, Barbara, interview, 2005.

Pioneers and Indians

Re-enactors Rob, Brandi Louise and Amanda Ernst at Apple River Fort

"I thought, 'Oh God. It's a fort.'"

Susan Gordy

Susan Gordy grew up in the suburbs of Cincinnati. She had never tended farm animals or gathered eggs.

But she loved the outdoors and was involved in sports. She also had a passion for history, clothes and food.

All these interests have come together at the Apple River Fort in Elizabeth, where she is director. Some days you can find her wearing a long work dress, apron and bonnet like those worn by the pioneer women of the 1830s.

On those days, she also wears a corset and feels surprisingly comfortable in it. "I bend over, cook food, fire guns and garden." It gives her back support.

Susan Gordy

Susan began to find her niche in life during the late 1980s when she was in college. Thinking she might want to work in recreation services, she accepted an internship at the Land Between the Lakes, a museum and park owned by the Tennessee Valley Authority.

"They had this place called Home Place 1850. At first it looked like a standard museum. Then I walked outside, into the park, and, as I came around a bend, a whole valley opened up."

Then she saw a sheep pasture and someone walk out of a building wearing period clothing. "I probably saw myself there. This is what I had been looking for my whole life."

The site director was a pioneer in the living-history movement, which was new to her.

After finishing her degree, she became an apprentice at the park. "I cared for livestock, cooked on a wood stove and made clothes. I got 'married' to another apprentice and did all the research on 1850s weddings. It is one of the favorite times in my life.

"I had these great mentors who set such good examples and high expectations."

Milking cows by hand didn't bother her in the least.

After a year there and a brief stint at a historic park in Minnesota, she enrolled in grad school at Eastern Illinois University. During school, she worked as an interpreter at Lincoln Log Cabin State Historic Site in Charleston.

"I became Matilda 'Tildy' Hall, Abe Lincoln's step sister."

Soon Susan became director of the interpretation, education and livestock programs.

"After spending eight years in 1845, I got itchy to move on. I felt as though I was done and had taken the program as far as it could go."

A co-worker told her about a job opening at the newly constructed Apple River Fort and its interpretive center.

"I thought, 'Oh God, a fort.' I'm not crazy about wars and military life." She was more interested in agrarian and everyday life.

But she visited the fort and realized there could be so much more to it than telling the story of war. It could involve the stories of the Sauk and Fox Indians, of the first pioneers who settled in northwest Illinois and even of lead mining.

"The fort was there, but it was part of a bigger picture. ... There was a lot more happening in the sense of things one could talk about."

Susan began working for the fort in December of 2000 and to steep herself in the 1830s. With only a small staff, she had to train volunteers to re-enact local history. She has organized countless lectures, encampments, scouting experiences and demonstrations and has managed the fort complex itself. Under her direction, the fort has enacted 1830s weddings, funerals and spring cleaning days, as well as the 1832 battle at Apple River Fort during the Black Hawk War.

"I have a great respect for and cannot even fathom the physical labor these people had to do to survive." She also respects the democratic social structure of the Sauk and Fox.

She tells the story of both the pioneers and Native Americans with compassion and understanding, but she doesn't varnish over the mistakes that both groups made. She acknowledges that the white settlers could be imperious land grabbers and the Indians could be vicious fighters. They both had a history of negative experiences with each other.

"When interpreting all this, there is so much to keep in mind. Everyone had their own cultural baggage."

As much as Susan has done to bring the 1830s alive, she would like to do more. "Eventually, I would like to have people in those buildings (doing living-history interpretations) five days a week. The buildings have a story to tell, but you have to give a voice to it."

"I was of the opinion that the white people had plenty of land." ***Black Hawk***

Apple River Fort has quite a story to tell—several stories, actually.

"It is the story of Native Americans who tried to maintain their way of life. It is the story of the frontier. And it is the story of women," said Carl "Skip" Schwerdtfeger, a founding member of the Apple River Fort Historic Foundation.

The stories, in abbreviated form, go something like this:

The Sauk and Fox Indians had lived east of the Mississippi River, in what later became northern Illinois and southern Wisconsin, for more than 100 years. They lived a stable existence, planting crops during the summer and hunting on the west side of the river during the winter. Some mined for lead.

The United States takes ownership of the Indians' land

In 1804, a chief and three Sauk and Fox braves, having no authority from their tribe, signed a treaty ceding the land—50 million acres—to the U.S. In return, the Indians received $2,000 and were promised a $1,000-per-year annuity, as well as the right to continue to live on the land until it was sold. Black Hawk, a warrior leader in the Sauk band, did not sign.

"I could say much about this treaty, but I will not at this time," Black Hawk said later, when he dictated his autobiography. "It has been the origin of all our difficulties."

Black Hawk's people continued to farm and to hunt where they had for more than 100 years. The Sauk and Fox called their villages Saukenuk and Mesquakanuk, but today we know the area as Rock Island, Ill. It lies about 60 miles south of Apple River Fort.

Around 1820, with encouragement from the government, white miners began buying land leases and moving to northwestern Illinois, mostly in the Galena area, to prospect for lead.

The lead-up to the war

When the Sauk and Fox returned to Saukenuk for planting in the spring of 1830, they learned that some whites had settled in their village. Chief Ke-o-kuck, a civil leader, went back to Iowa, but Black Hawk and part of the tribe remained and planted their crops. The Indians and whites co-existed, but their relationship was shaky. Black Hawk complained later that the whites would get his people drunk and cheat them out of their belongings.

Black Hawk thought he could talk Ninian Edwards and John Reynolds, the governor and past governor of Illinois, into giving the Indians their village back.

"I was of the opinion that the white people had plenty of land, and would never take our village from us," Black Hawk said. "My reason teaches me that land cannot be sold. The great Spirit gave it to his children to live upon, and cultivate as far as is necessary for their subsistence; and so long as they occupy and cultivate it."

The governors said they could not help, but seemed genuinely sorry, Black Hawk said.

The following winter he learned that most of the land had been sold to George Davenport. In the spring, the Sauk and Fox women tried to work new ground west of the Mississippi but found the going tough and the corn yield low.

"The women were very upset that they had to start over with farming," said Susan Gordy, director of Apple River Fort. "And Black Hawk felt strongly about not wanting to leave his ancient land."

The land had been good to his people. Black Hawk described Saukenuk as follows: "We had about 800 acres in cultivation, including what we had on the islands of Rock River. The land around our village, uncultivated, was covered with bluegrass, which made excellent pasture for our horses. Several fine springs broke out of the bluff, near by, from which we were supplied with good water. The rapids of Rock River furnished us with an abundance of excellent fish, and the land, being good, never failed to produce good crops of corn, beans, pumpkins and squashes. We always had plenty – our children never cried with hunger, nor were our people ever in want."

In 1831, he got together a group of 1,200 warriors, women and children to move back. The women planted their crops wherever white settlers had not built fences. General Gaines ordered the Indians to leave, but the group refused.

Eventually, however, Black Hawk agreed to leave, under the condition that the government would give his people corn to replace what they had planted.

"I touched the goose quill to the treaty, and was determined to live in peace."

The government did not send enough corn to meet the Indians' needs.

Meanwhile, a Winnebago prophet sent word to Black Hawk that, if he and his people came to his village, the Winnebago would help the Sauk and Fox. At least, that is what Black Hawk later claimed.

"This is one of those things, whereby we may never know all his true motivations," Gordy said, "and it makes me wonder about the Winnebago prophet. Black Hawk was also under the impression that the British were going to come and support him." (He had supported the British during the War of 1812.)

In the spring of 1832, Black Hawk and his band again crossed the river, back into Illinois, to farm.

Gov. Reynolds took Black Hawk's action as a sign of war. He sent the militia to Saukenuk to forcibly remove him and his people. By the time the army arrived, the Indians had gone, and the militia burned the village. Thus began the Black Hawk War.

Between May and August of 1832, the Indian warriors engaged in skirmishes and battles with the Illinois militia, the U.S. Army and white settlers between Rock Island and present-day La Crosse, Wisconsin.

The battle at Apple River Fort and the three Elizabeths

Meanwhile, white miners had begun to build cabins near what now is the village of Elizabeth. In May of 1832, they heard that Black Hawk and his warriors were on their way. In a panic, they built a fort for protection, accomplishing their task in just a couple of weeks.

"Trees were felled, split, and about one hundred feet square of ground was enclosed by driving these rough posts down, close together, leaving them above ground about twelve feet," according to the 1887 history of Jo Daviess

County. "One corner of the fort was formed by the log house in which one of two stories, with the upper story projecting over the other about two feet, so that the Indians could not come up near to the building for the purpose of setting it on fire, without being exposed to the guns of the settlers from above. On one side of the yard were built two long cabins, for dwelling purposes, and in the two corners not occupied by houses, benches were made to stand upon and reconnoitre."

Forty-three men, women and children took refuge in the fort. Three of the five women were named Elizabeth—Elizabeth Winters, Elizabeth Armstrong and Elizabeth Van Volkenburg.

On June 24, Black Hawk, then age 65, and about 200 warriors attacked.

"The people talked about surrendering," Schwerdtfeger said. "Elizabeth Armstrong said, in rather profane terms, 'If you won't fight, I will.' She headed to the wall with a gun and the others started firing."

The women molded musket balls and helped the men reload their guns. As the lead for ammunition ran out, Elizabeth Van Volkenburg and Rebecca Hitt volunteered to sneak out of the fort to a nearby smelter for lead. With their help, the men were able to keep up a steady barrage of fire.

After 45 minutes, Black Hawk and his forces retired. One white settler died, and Black Hawk reported that none of his men died.

Over the next five weeks, the army and the militia pursued the Indians. Many of Black Hawk's people died in battle or starved. The war ended Aug. 2, when many of the Indians were killed at the mouth of the Bad Axe River, where it flows into the Mississippi in southwest Wisconsin. Black Hawk escaped but later was captured. About a year later he was released and, in 1834, dictated his autobiography. He died in 1838.

This is what Black Hawk said about European Americans: "I had not discovered one good trait in the character of the Americans that had come to this country! They made fair promises, but never fulfilled them! ... it appears that their feelings are acted upon by certain rules laid down by their preachers!—whilst ours are governed only by the monitor within us."

A few people continued to live in the Apple River Fort, and it remained standing until 1847, when the farmer who owned the property tore it down and used the wood to build a barn.

Elizabeth Winters went on to build a tavern. Her children, Martha and Theodore, were the first two white children born in the village of Elizabeth, which was named after her.

Joyce Potter can trace her ancestry back to Rebecca and Thadeus Hitt. She said Rebecca Hitt was pregnant with Mary Hitt while she was in the fort. Later Mary married and gave birth to Alice Rebecca Hunter. After Alice married, she gave birth to Francis John Kevern, who is Potter's father.

The Apple River Fort in Elizabeth

"I don't think much about that but I must be proud of this, or why do I tell it? My biggest regret is that I didn't listen to my grandmother's stories. She would have been so happy about the fort."

Rebuilding the fort

Local historian Gordy Kilgore found evidence that, as early as 1931, area residents were talking about rebuilding the fort. Periodically, people brought up the idea, but nothing happened until 1994.

That year members of the Galena Rotary Club and the Elizabeth Chamber of Commerce, including Kilgore, Schwerdtfeger and the late Paul Kindig, formed the Apple River Fort Historic Foundation.

"We had two ideas in mind," said Dick Harmet, another founding member. "One was to find it and rebuild it, in order to learn its history. The second was to provide economic benefit to Elizabeth."

No one was sure just where the structure stood, but Schwerdtfeger believed he had confirmed the location while researching his Masters Degree thesis. So, the group hired Floyd Mansberger, an archeologist from Fever River Research in Springfield, to poke around on Maurice Berlage's farm, just north of Elizabeth. As Mansberger started to dig, Schwerdtfeger held his breath. "My blood pressure must have shot up to 300 over 200."

Mansberger found pottery shards dating back to the pre-Civil War era--a good sign. Later he disked the site, turning up more than 500 artifacts. Then serious digging began. Archaeologists found the impressions of three walls and more artifacts, including a musket ball.

"That was very exciting. We had found the fort!" Harmet said. "We found more than 2,000 artifacts."

In 1996, the reconstruction work began. "We moved the new fort a little up hill so we didn't ruin the fort site.

"That was a wonderful period. We had all kinds of volunteers up there to help strip logs and cut shingles. To the extent possible, we tried to build with the same tools the settlers used. We would be up there working every weekend. The local churches took turns bringing us lunches."

Keith Arnold, owner of Arnold Construction and Wood Products in Stockton, volunteered to supervise construction. He examined some old log cabins and toured several forts to learn more about 1800s construction techniques. "I guess I came to the conclusion that I didn't want to build something with telephone lines and air conditioning. I wanted people to feel like they were there at the actual place and not at a substitute.

"The thing I remember most is how everybody dug in and wanted to see the project happen. I think it brought a sense of community to the people there and a sense of pride that everybody had a part in it. We built the structure, and Susan Gordy came and put life into it."

He particularly noted Helen Kilgore's contribution. "She would do any thankless job that needed to be done."

The fort was dedicated in October of 1997, and an interpretive center opened in September of 1998. The center is located on U.S. 20 in downtown Elizabeth.

"This is a life-time dream come true," Schwerdtfeger said. "After talking about the fort for all these years, to actually have this happen is beyond belief."

"A lot of kids my age wouldn't do this."

Amanda Ernst

Amanda Ernst swept a floor in one of the small cottages at Apple River Fort, while her younger sister, Brandi Louise, helped two women stuff straw into blue-and-white striped "ticking," to be used as a mattress. Meanwhile, their dad, Rob, split rails for fences.

It was March at Apple River Fort, and this family of volunteer re-enactors was demonstrating to the public what pioneers in 1832 did to get ready for spring.

"A lot of kids my age wouldn't do this," Amanda, a teenager, admitted. But she enjoys it. "I get to go back in time. I get to say how people actually lived. And I get to meet new people."

She thinks living back in the 1830s would have been "more of an adventure" than life today.

"I get to wear old clothes and a bonnet," Brandi Louise said. She also likes washing dishes the old-fashioned way. Her family owns a dishwasher. She wouldn't mind living in the 1800s. "I bet if I grew up and was, like, 15, in those days, it would be pretty fun because I would get to clean and cook and sweep and do the dishes."

Rob said "curiosity" got him started with re-enactments. He grew up near Apple River and wanted to see just what the Apple River Fort, which bears his home town's name, was about. "The whole time I was in school, I learned about stuff that happened in the 15th Century, but I didn't learn about what was going on in our own backyard.

"I would like the younger generation to understand their background, their heritage." He also would like visitors to learn more about the "neighborliness and togetherness" that existed in 1832, when families worked hard and neighbors helped one another.

"Also, this is a chance for us—"

"—to do something together," Amanda said, finishing Rob's sentence.

"Everyone seems to enjoy it, and we get along well together down here. It's a good opportunity to—"

"—learn together," Amanda said, again finishing her father's sentence.

"I am getting to appreciate the things that people made by hand," Rob added.

From her experiences at the fort, Brandi Louise has learned things that other children her age do not know, such as what kind of clothing the Indians wore. "I'm pretty happy about knowing this stuff. I'm one of the smartest kids in my class for this stuff."

All three would like to learn more. Amanda wants to learn how to shoot a musket, "even though girls back then didn't do that." Brandi Louise would like to know more about how people cooked Thanksgiving dinners.

"I would like to learn more about maintenance, like chinking cabins," Rob said.

"I just like learning stuff," said Ian Urven, a teenager from Fond du Lac, Wisconsin. Urven did odd jobs for his "parents," such as fetch water and clean out the chicken coop. As un-glamorous as that sounds, he was having fun.

Rion and Ian Urven at Apple River Fort

"I'm interested in history in general. I like seeing what it was like back then."

Yet, he yearned to get into the militia and shoot a flint-lock rifle.

"He is a little young for the militia," said his mother, Betsy. "But he likes to fall in and practice drills." (Urven had to wait a year or two, but he became a member of the Michigan Mounted Militia and now re-enacts battles at the

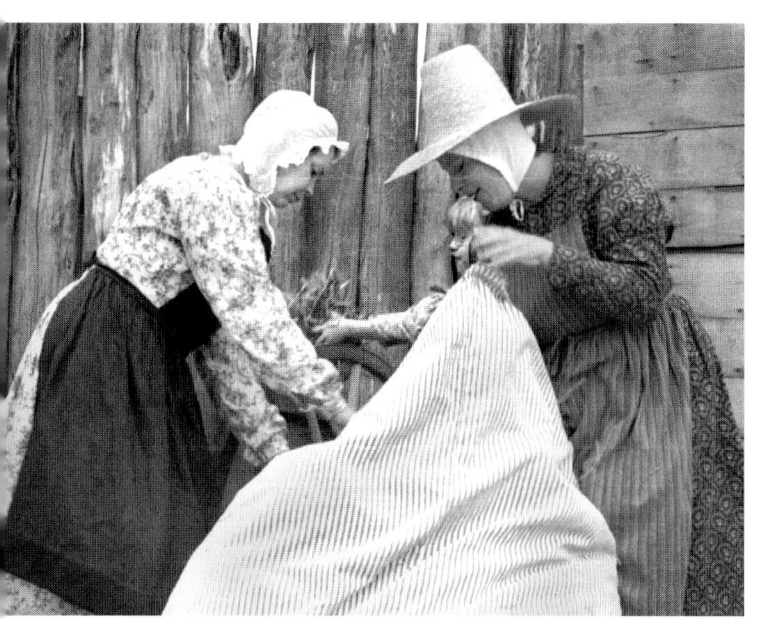

Sharon Nolan, Brandi Louise Ernst and Sheila Cottral

Apple River Fort.)

As much as she loves learning about domestic life in the 1830s, there are days when Sheila Cottral, fort site interpretive coordinator, feels she knows as much as she would ever want to know about cooking back then. "Cooking could be very dangerous. Women had to be very careful with their skirts, because of the embers that would roll out of the hearth."

During spring clean-up day, she made bread pudding in a cast iron pan and tried to keep from burning her fingers. "It's not setting up," she said as she gingerly removed the heavy lid. "These fingers should be playing the piano."

The recipe she used wasn't very clear. "It called for bread, eggs, sugar, milk and butter. That's it. It didn't say how much of them to use."

She also made a sausage stew with potatoes and onions.

"Women basically cooked all day long in those days. They would no sooner finish breakfast, when they would have to start on dinner (the Noon meal). After dinner, they would have to work on the evening meal, which was called 'supper.'"

There was another drawback to pioneer life. "I'm not crazy about those day caps women wore. They were not very flattering."

But she doesn't mind the rest of the clothing. "It is breathable. It almost acts as an insulator from the heat. People can get used to almost anything. But don't tell me that women didn't tie their skirts up around their waists sometimes!"

After spending several years immersed in the life and culture of the 1830s, Cottral probably could write "Hints from Heloise" for the 19th Century. "I have learned that corn cobs make great Brillo pads. You learn how hot food is by placing your hands near the Dutch oven."

In the end, her bread pudding turned out just fine.

"The pioneering spirit is to stay, build and plant."

Cathy Townsend

Jerry Townsend is the sixth-generation Townsend to live on the family homestead near Stockton. His great, great, great grandfather, George N. Townsend, built the big stone house in which he and his wife Cathy live. The family has traveled far, both literally and figuratively, to get where it is today.

George grew up in New York State. In 1826, at age 20, he headed west with his brother Absolem and his father. They traveled the last 180 miles to southwest Wisconsin by foot, over rugged terrain. George worked for awhile in a couple of lead mines and, in 1828, went back to New York. He married Mary Miner and they had three children.

In 1836, he returned to the "West" and squatted on land in eastern Jo Daviess County. He built a cabin there and soon brought Mary and the children out to live. For nearly two years, they were the only white settlers in that part of the county. Soon others, including George's brother Halstead, joined them. Later, George registered his claim, paying $1.25 for each of 800 acres. He and Mary had 10 more children.

Halstead later wrote that the early settlers were generous and hospitable. "If you had visited one of these settlers, you would have been made heartily welcome, and would have been received in the most friendly manner. In their log cabins a bountiful meal would have been set before you, of venison and corn bread, or mush, the meal for which was ground on a tin grater. This was the best that could be had short of Galena. To purchase luxuries, we needed money, and that was an article we did not possess."

To change the money situation, George and many others from Jo Daviess County headed to California to look for gold. It was 1850, and the Gold Rush was in on. Despite trying times, George fared well. He returned in 1851 with enough gold to build a new home. It took five years to build and cost $4,500, a healthy sum at the time. Today the house, a large, sturdy structure made of wheat-color limestone rock, makes for a pleasing picture in its rural setting. Inside is an open stairway with black walnut banisters.

(Another one of George's brothers, Ira, traveled with Jasper Rosencrans to California. They started home in 1851 but were never heard from again.)

George was a Whig who admired Abraham Lincoln and supported the abolition of slavery. According to an article published in 1932 by "The Warren Sentinel Leader," he was part of the Underground Railway that helped black slaves get to freedom in Canada. "All who knew George N. Townsend became a friend," the paper said.

Mary also earned the love of the community. "No one could have been more devoted to home, children and neighbors. Nurses were unknown, and physicians were scarce. No day was too cold, and no night was too stormy, and she was never too busy to go, near or far, to the sick and distressed and grief laden."

Two of the couple's sons and five of their sons-in-law fought in the Civil War. Mary, "a woman of faith," prayed for their safe return, Cathy said. "Every single son came back. That was evidence of how prayer worked in their lives."

One of the sons was Samuel Townsend, the next in Jerry's line. He inherited the family home, along with about 400 acres, and devoted his life to farming. Like George, he became a successful, respected member of the community. "During his long residence here he has acquired and maintained the confidence and esteem of every resident of the Township, and his word is implicitly trusted by every person with whom he has ever had a business transaction," according to the "Portrait and Biographical Album of Jo Daviess County, Illinois."

He married Rebecca Borthwick, and they had 10 children.

But all did not remain well. In late May of 1891, Asher and Rebecca's daughter, Rena, and her boyfriend, Elmer Foster, took their own lives. They poisoned themselves with strychnine, Rena told Rebecca as she was dying.

"About 2:50 o'clock Monday morning the most agonized shrieks which human ear ever heard aroused every sleeper in the Townsend homestead. The dying groans and wild yells came from the bedroom adjoining the upstairs living room," one of the local papers reported. "There was no evidence as to how the poison was taken as no vial or paper could anywhere be found. It is the theory of the family that the poison was drank down in the drawing room and that they went immediately in the bedroom and sat down on the bed to await death together."

"Rena's suicide was hush-hush. Due to pride and stubbornness, it wasn't talked about," Cathy said.

Next in Jerry's line came Samuel A. Townsend, Jr., Rena's brother. He was the youngest in the family and pampered too much, according to Jerry. "My great grandfather was always up town messing around and wasn't taking care of the farm. He neglected the farm and nearly lost it."

Cathy and Jerry Townsend

"You can see the family start to decline then," Cathy said.

Nevertheless, it hosted a large family reunion in 1929, and four generations of Townsends came. They dedicated a granite boulder inscribed with these words: "To the memory of George and Mary Townsend, Arrived in Illinois 1827, Took possession of land 1834, Humility, Hospitality, Patriotism, Erected by their descendants 1929." The boulder sits in a prominent spot on Jerry and Cathy's lawn, where it always has been.

Samuel's son, Claude T. Townsend, worked the farm for a short while, but the Depression hit, and he couldn't do much to undo the years of neglect.

In 1950, the family pooled its resources and signed off on the farm so that Jerry's dad, Harlan R. Townsend, could take it over. "The ground was so poor that clover would hardly grow on it," Jerry said. Harlan worked hard to refurbish the land. "Now it is some of the richest soil in the county."

But he didn't have the means to give the house the care it needed. "When we moved into the house, there was just one cold-water faucet," Jerry said. "I was 8 years old when we moved in. After 20 years, the house looked terrible. The shutters were gone and the windows were cracked. It looked as though nobody was home."

For a while, the home was empty. Then, in 1989, Jerry and Cathy bought the farm. They modernized and restored the house, pruned the orchard and planted flowers. They have worked hard to keep the property in the family. Unable to make a living in farming, they sold the barns across the road and all but 155 acres. Jerry went to work as an information-technology specialist, and Cathy has a few part-time jobs. They want to keep the house in the family, if possible.

"But the house isn't that big a deal," Jerry said. "We are trying to rebuild the farm spiritually, which is more important."

At first the couple didn't have a strong spiritual base to go on, they said. They were "children of the '60s" and were "a little wild." But, during the mid-1970s, Cathy became involved in the charismatic movement.

"I really did get born again. I was filled with the Holy Spirit, along with a whole bunch of other people from Stockton. Jerry did too, five years later."

"In 1979, I got born again, like Cathy."

Now they are active in the Assembly of God Church in Galena and try to live their lives according to Christian principles. By doing so, they believe they are reconnecting with faith that

Mary and George lived. "It's real simple if you follow what Jesus Christ and the Bible have to say about life," Cathy said. "You do reap what you sow."

They also are trying to preserve the pioneering spirit of the earlier Townsends. "The pioneering spirit is to stay, build and plant," Cathy said.

For the Townsends specifically, it also means "humility, hospitality and patriotism," Jerry said.

"The road out here has been there since the 1820s," Jerry said. "I think of all the generations that walked up and down this road and I think, 'What were they thinking when they walked on this same road?'"

Recently the couple placed their home on the National Register of Historic Places.

"We saw a number of men sick and some dying and some dead."

George N. Townsend

Although a few people, including George N. Townsend, made a small fortune panning for gold in California, it was tough going. Some miners returned to Jo Daviess County poorer than when they left and worse for the wear. Some didn't make it back at all.

Besides facing bad weather and exceedingly rough terrain, the miners encountered sickness and price gouging. Letters moved slowly back and forth between loved ones, and the loneliness was often hard for the miners and their families back home to bear.

Below are excerpts from letters that Townsend and Arthur Tyrell, a man from the rural Stockton area, sent back to family members and friends. (I have changed some of the wording, punctuation and spelling to make them easier to read.) Like Townsend, Tyrell returned and must have done all right for himself. His body is buried at Willow Cemetery near Stockton and is marked with a large stone.

Letter from Townsend to his daughter Jane

"Absolem lost one of his men after he overtook us; one of the Roberts' steers died on the sweetwater; and the Haskel oxen failed. I left them at Salt Lake. I got $27.50 for them. Old Spot had cracks come in her heels that made her lame, and I left her on the Humbolt. Then our cattle got frightened and run off. About 20 teams, 4 and 5 yoke to the team, and you may believe it was a dreadful sight to see—men, women and children screaming and running to get out of the way, and teams running against teams and smashing down the wagons, some sick in the wagons. ...

"To undertake to tell you anything of the misery on the latter part of the journey would be too great a task now. We would see lots of men trying to bet or buy something to eat, men who had lost their teams and had been obliged to leave all except what they could pack on their backs—and that from 500 to 600 miles. And when he gets a blanket or a few clothes on his back he has not much room for provisions, and many of them sick, and in so high a country. The tops of the mountains are covered with perpetual snow, which was the case after we came near the pass of the Rocky Mountains until we got over the Civioavodo, a distance of 10 or 12 hundred miles. The days will be hot and the nights so as to freeze ice, and men half sick without blankets or provisions and no place to stop, not as much as a tree for shade. ...

"We saw a number of men sick and some dying and some dead left by the wayside with a boot or a shoe full of water to drink, and they not able to raise themselves up enough to drink. We were so situated that we could not take them in or assist them, except as we passed along, and they did not have as much as a blanket to cover them. ..."

"The cholera has been very bad in Sacramento City and in San Francisco. Sacramento City is the nastiest place I ever did see, it stands on a low spot and all the streets are covered with filth. All was full of old bacon, dead rats and all kinds of nastiness. The back streets are filled with dead horses, cattle and mules, and when cholera got there it made a sweep. There is a population of from 6 to 7 thousand, and 100 to 120 died per day for a time."

Letters from Arthur Tyrell to family members and friends during his journey

"The Company is all well. I am now 522 miles west of the Missouri River. I commence where I left off. Above Wood River is a small stream, but a hard rain had raised it. The water was 10 feet deep or more. We cut two logs 30 feet long and fixed them like eave troughs and put them across so that the wheels run on them and drawed the wagons over by hand. The oxen swam. We had good luck and a very good road except for some sand. When we was 306 miles from the Missouri River, our oxen ran away from us and was gone over two weeks. We could not find them. They got scared at the buffaloes and run off in among the bluffs, and we could not track them."

"The 3rd of September we camped at night. Hentuck Phillips' wife gave birth to a daughter, but we was not detained a minute by it. We started the next morning as early as usual on our journey. She and the child are both doing fine."

"The Mormons told us we would not have any snow, but the 27th of Nov. at night the snow fell about 4 inches deep. We had no more bare ground, except in some very few places where it had blowed for 250 miles. It has been very cold and snowing frequently. The snow was from 2 to 24 inches deep. Our cattle could get nothing to eat except what they picked out of the snow until the 20th of Dec. ... We frequently had to camp at night where there was no water and no wood but wild sage to make a fire and melt snow for water."

"We expect the mail every hour from Salt Lake. It is the last chance for it to go through this fall to the States, and this is the last chance I shall have to send to you until spring. I do no know where I shall be then. I have not heard a word from you yet."

Tyrell's letters from California

"Many men I have seen have spent all they had to get to California, so that they curse the country and wish themselves back home. Any man can make money here, who has his health and works and goes into no speculation. Trying to get more is a little like a lottery. Last week a man got 150 dollars in one bucket of dirt not 10 rods from where I work, and I can't get over 8 cents to the bucket."

"I once more take my pen to inform you that I am well and in good spirits at this time. But I have had a hard run of the diarrhea. ... It lasted me four weeks. I was able to be up most of the time but was weak and could not work any and did not doctor much. ... I met Halstead Townsend in the street. He told me his brother George and Ira Bowker was camped out of the city half a mile and that I must go with him and stay all night. I was pleased to see them, being the only ones I had seen of my old acquaintance."

"I am well and have a good appetite to eat but have not much to eat at present. ... Flour is selling at 75 and 80 cents per pound and salt pork 45 to 50, hams 50 to 55, side bacon 50 to 55, potatoes 30 to 35 per pound, no meal, no beans nor rice here, beef fresh 30 to 35, pork fresh 50 to 75, grizzly bear 25 to 50, venison 25 to 30, sugar 25 to 35, coffee 40 to 45, tea 100, butter 100. Everything edible is scarce and hard to get."

"I must say Mrs. Rice died last summer. Mr. Rice buried three of his children before she died. Ira Benton is dead."

"I will now tell you what I have done and intend to do, as I have stayed over the time I was to come back. The first summer I had bad luck. I did not make much in the fall. I was not able to work much in the winter. Hirum boarded me in the spring. I was in debt to him. The 3rd day of August 1851, I had made enough to pay him up. Then I wanted to go further north but had no money. Hirum furnished me with 160 dollars, and I started leaving him at Nelson Creek. In 3 weeks I arrived at Shasta Flats. Some of the company was taken down with the chills and fever as soon as we arrived. ... Then it came my turn. It being the ague (fever), I didn't fear it. I did not employ a doctor, but after shaking 2 times, I took 2 tablespoonsful of cayenne pepper in one dose. It burned all the chills out of me and, in two weeks more, we was able to start back to Shasta City, where we arrived in October. I made preparations for winter, and I bought some tools to work with. The $160 was all gone. ... I have been unlucky about finding gold and I am in hopes my luck will turn better. ... Don't think hard of me for staying away. You would hate to have me come back on your account and have nothing. I want to try. If I cannot make anything, I will go to work by the month and get money and come home."

Letter from Eliza (Tyrell's wife) to Tyrell

"O Arthur, how I wish you was here. Remember you said you would not stay but three years at the longest, but it is almost four and you are not here yet. It seems to me as if this last year was almost as long as the other three, and, if I thought it would be three or four years longer before I could see you I would as live or die at once, if it was not for our children, for what comfort is to be taken here, not but what we are well and well provided for. ... I have seen more sad hours and days since you went away than I thought my body could have."

Letter from Tyrell to Eliza

"... I do not know what is going on there and I cannot tell you what to do, only to say as I did before that do as you think best. I wish you was here and the children because I don't see as I can get money to come home and pay your father and Nation. If I get money enough I shall come home in the spring, if not, I shall send some money and stay longer. Don't think because I stay away that I have forgotten you and the children, or that I don't care anything for you and them. Time and distance from you cannot erase the affection that I have for you and them. There is not a day passes by but a part of my mind is there and I look forward to the time when I shall meet you and other friends once more. I cannot describe the anxious feelings that I have for fear that things may go amiss with you and the children."

"There was nothing I liked better than listening to those trains at night."

Wendell Lewis

The building of the railroads brought new people to Jo Daviess County. It helped change the rural area from a challenge to be overcome by a smattering of pioneers to one with settled communities that offered many of the amenities of normal city life. The railroads made an impact on farming, the economy, social structure and the location of population centers.

Local railroading officially began in 1850, when the federal government gave the Illinois Central Railroad a swath of land consisting of nearly 2.6 million acres from Cairo (in the southern tip of Illinois) to Chicago and to Jo Daviess County. The IC could sell the land it didn't need and use the proceeds to pay for track construction and rolling stock.

The company got its charter in 1851 and didn't waste any time completing the project. It laid tracks across Jo Daviess County in 1852 and 1853 and began operating in 1854.

To find buyers for its land and to create a demand for its services, the company advertised in Europe and in other parts of the nation, enticing people with cheap land. It encouraged the development of towns five to 15 miles apart, or the distance that farmers could haul grain to town for shipping.

The advertising worked. Within 10 years, the county's population grew almost by one-half—from 18,604 in 1850 to 27,325 by 1860—in part because of the railroad's promotional efforts. (Galena also grew.)

The line resulted in several population shifts. Millville, which was on the Frink and

Walker Stage Line to Galena, had been a small but thriving community with its own post office, a mill, a blacksmith shop, a dry good store, several groceries and a tavern. It quickly lost people and businesses to Nora, Warren and Apple River, which were on the Illinois Central line.

Council Hill, which also was on the stage line, still exists as an unincorporated community, but now it includes only a few houses, a township hall and a wedding chapel. Some of the trade that took place in Council Hill moved to Council Hill Station, just a mile and a half south, where a stockyard, general store, homes and a church quickly sprang up. (The stockyard and most of the buildings are gone, and today Council Hill Station is nearly abandoned.)

"The town of Elizabeth moved to the railroad," said Gerald Speer, director of the Chicago Great Western Railway Depot Museum in Elizabeth. "There were a lot of miners' cottages down in the valley. When the railroad came in on the top of the hill, the houses literally were moved up the hill."

The railroad also led to the development of Dunleith (now East Dubuque). Not until 1853, after the construction of the Illinois Central began, did George W. Sanford, Jonathan Sturges, Morris Ketchum, George W. Jones, George Griswold and Charles Gregoire file a plat for the city with the county clerk. The IC had bought land to build a freight house and depot in the area, which prompted the action.

"In 1849, there was but one house and one fishing shanty at Dunleith, but by the time the road was complete, June 1, 1855, as many as fifty substantial buildings, many of them graceful brick structures, had been erected and were in waiting for the business the road was expected to bring," according to an 1887 history of Jo Daviess County.

Businesses started cropping up. More than 50 of Dunleith's residents found employment by ferrying passengers and goods from Dunleith, then at the end of the IC line, across the Mississippi River, to Dubuque, Iowa.

The 50 people lost their jobs in 1868, after a railroad bridge was built over the river. However, Dunleith did not die. By that time, it had a market house, which contained City Hall, a fire department and a grade school. Burt Machine Works was already off and running, making farm machinery and shingles, and Cultivator Works made both riding and walking cultivators.

The Grand River Excursion of June of 1854 also gave the county a boost. The Chicago & Rock Island Railroad had recently completed a line to the Mississippi River at Rock Island, about 70 miles south of Galena, becoming the first to reach the river from the East Coast. To celebrate—and, more important, to interest people in investing in future lines—a group of people affiliated with the Chicago & Rock Island treated up to 1,000 people to a free train ride from Chicago to Rock Island and then a steamboat ride up the Mississippi River from Rock Island to St. Paul, Minnesota.

Pres. Millard Fillmore promoted the idea and participated in the excursion. Invited guests included industrialists, bankers, politicians, journalists, artists (who painted pictures of the scenery along the way), philosophers and other "notables." A few "no-bodies" received invitations, too, just to add variety. (The invitation list did not include many people from the slave states, for fear of transporting slavery to the "West.")

The excursion was a big deal because of its size, and newspapers across the United States reported on it. Press coverage was mostly complimentary, despite the fact that the boats were overcrowded, and some people got sick from drinking water from the Mississippi River. The scenery and the novelty of the experience seemed to make up for any inconveniences. Writers praised the beauty of the bluffs and let readers know that the West was, at least to some extent, civilized.

Meanwhile, the communities along the river got to show off their stuff. Although Galena was not on the Mississippi itself, it became a major stop along the way. The steamboats chugged up the Fever River (now called the Galena River) to the thriving community, where cannons were fired and citizens waved and cheered.

A few writers found the town too muddy for their liking, but most wrote favorable accounts. They saw Galena as bustling and prosperous, due to its lead industry, large wholesale trade and steamboat access. They also liked the hills with the cottages that cascaded down to the river.

More railroads came to Jo Daviess County.

In 1885, The Chicago, Burlington and Quincy laid tracks from Quincy, Illinois to St. Paul, Minnesota, The line roughly follows the Mississippi River through western Jo Daviess County. (Later it became the Burlington Northern Railroad.)

In 1888, the Chicago, St. Paul and Kansas City line (which later was sold and became the Chicago Great Western Railway) made its first run between Chicago and Dubuque, Iowa, creating a third major route through Jo Daviess County. The tracks went through the middle of the county and junctioned with the Burlington Northern south of Galena.

Building the line was no easy feat. The company had to blast out a tunnel a half-mile long through some of the roughest terrain in the Midwest. The Winston Tunnel, as it came to be known, was a thorn in the Chicago Great Western's backside. There were drainage problems, which caused the supporting timbers to deteriorate. The company had to fortify it after a few years and, in 1902, rebuild it altogether. In 1947, it made major repairs.

The CGW also found that ventilation was a problem. To prevent people from passing out while going through the tunnel, the company installed a huge fan on the west end, which cleared out the steam and smoke. (The men who operated the fan worked 12-hour shifts alone in the fan house, seemingly miles from civilization. Some believed it was haunted. They called it "Hell Hole.")

In 1887, the company announced it would build a station at what now is the village of Stockton. At the time, Stockton included only five homes, plus the Shoo Fly School. Soon Septimus T. Eade built a brick building and moved his general store from Nora to Stockton. Merwin K. Hammond built a grain elevator, and Peter M. Rindesbacher started a bank. Other businesses and residents followed.

In 1912, the CGW built a large railroad yard just East of Stockton, where crews changed, cars were switched and engines were repaired. It employed up to 400 people.

In addition to the three major lines, several smaller railroads served local communities. One short line went from Warren to Mineral Point, Wisconsin. In Hanover, a group of businessmen built a 2.5-mile railroad to the Chicago Great Western tracks.

Unknown railroad employee (back) and Roy Dresser at the Chicago Great Western Railway Depot in Elizabeth (circa, 1930, courtesy of the Chicago Great Western Railway Depot Museum)

Besides influencing the population, railroads changed the way farmers operated. With access to larger markets, farmers could ship grain to Chicago. Instead of growing crops to feed themselves and to sell locally, farmers began growing large "cash crops" to sell regionally or nationally. Later, they raised livestock, which they sent to the stockyards in Chicago.

Local companies, such as Hanover Manufacturing, also benefited. Hanover

Manufacturing, also benefited. Hanover Manufacturing wove and shipped hundreds of thousands of yards of cloth every year via rail.

The railroads also brought visitors to Jo Daviess County, who needed places to eat and stay. Entrepreneurs in towns such as Stockton and Elizabeth built restaurants and hotels to accommodate them.

In addition, the railroads connected county residents with the outside world. Now people could travel, see other places and learn new ideas. They could mail-order consumer goods and even order the materials to build a house or a barn.

Each town—and some spots in between—had a railroad station. The depots became centers of cultural and economic activ-

Gerald Speer of the Chicago Great Western Railway Depot Museum

ity, where people from all stations in life crossed paths and embarked on exciting adventures. Townsfolk would send messages via telegraph from the train stations, pick up packages and ship out goods. Little happened in towns that did not pass through the depot in some manner.

Young boys dreamed of becoming railroad engineers or of working as telegrapher/agents at the local stations. They loved the thugga-thugga sound of the hulking locomotives as they came into town, like monsters bearing down on their prey, and the rat-a-tat-tat of the telegraph machines that conveyed a raft of information, often to places unknown.

"When I was a youngster, all I wanted to be was a trainman," said Wendell Lewis, who grew up near the train station in Elizabeth.

Perhaps not many young girls saw a future for themselves in railroading, but they, too, got caught up in the mystique. "I lived east of town about 10 miles," said Faye Heidenreich. "Every time a train would go by, I would have to run up the hill, because I couldn't see it from my house."

"You knew the station agents," said Joyce Kevern Potter. One agent, Roy Dresser, worked at the Chicago Great Western Railway Depot in Elizabeth for several decades. "He wore a wig, and his wig was always crooked."

"He would let the kids fool around with the telegraph machine," said Gerald Speer. "In a little town like this, the depot was the happening place for kids."

"The railroad was my backyard," Lewis said. "When I was a kid, it was in the '30s, and we had no money and no place to go. I almost lived at the depot. Without the railroad, I don't know what we would have done as kids. ...

"One of the things I used to really enjoy was, during the wintertime in a snowstorm, some of the men would have to ride out (to the switching cabin) to keep the switches cleaned out. My dad, he worked for the Great Western and would be called out, mostly at night. They would bundle me up and take me along. My dad would build a fire, and we would stay out there all night for the trains that came through.

"There was nothing I liked better than listening to those trains at night, having those wheels go click, click, click."

But, even when people like Lewis were kids, railroads were losing passengers to automobiles and buses. Ridership dipped after reaching its height in 1920. The East Dubuque Register reported in early 1929 that "American railroads carried fewer passengers in 1928 than in any other year since 1905." That year only 787 million people took the train, compared to nearly 1.3 billion in 1920.

The Great Depression didn't help. In late

November of 1929, the Great Western laid off 50 to 60 workers at the Stockton roundhouse. In 1931, it discontinued two of its passenger trains. By the end of the Depression, the roundhouse had closed, due to the introduction of the diesel engine as well as hard economic times.

World War II temporarily brought passengers back. Railroads advertised how clean, modern and efficient they were, but ridership declined again after the war. Not only was the U.S. building a super-highway system, but people were beginning to rely on air travel. Soon railroads scaled back their passenger service and eventually cut it out completely.

On May 2, 1971, the Burlington Northern's Empire Builder made its last run from Seattle, through East Dubuque, to Chicago. That marked the near end of passenger service in Jo Daviess County. Between 1974 and 1981, Amtrak made a daily trip between Dubuque, Iowa and Chicago, but it discontinued the service because of insufficient ridership.

Freight business fell off for awhile but now is going strong. Trains haul semi trailers loaded with goods to trucking transfer stations throughout the nation and to major seaports. The Illinois Central (now part of the Canadian National Railway) and the Burlington Northern (now part of the Burlington Northern & Santa Fe) make numerous trips daily across the county.

But the Chicago Great Western is gone. For awhile the company talked about rebuilding Winston Tunnel or rerouting the line, but it backed off. In 1968, it merged with the Chicago & North Western Railway. Within a few years, the C&NW abandoned most of the line. Its last run through the county occurred in 1971. The C&NW later tore up the track and sold it for scrap metal.

In 2000 and again in 2001, I got to see the Winston Tunnel and the old fan house. It lies on private property in a heavily wooded area. A few old railroad ties remain, but the path is overgrown. As I stood in the silence—except for the rustling of a few leaves—I could hardly believe that as many as 25 trains roared through the area each day. Parts of the tunnel had caved in, and chunks of the entrance had fallen way. The roof of the old fan house was nearly gone, and trees were beginning to grow inside.

But one part of the Chicago Great Western remains—the old train depot in Elizabeth. The village used it for storage after the railroad left town. Then, in 1997, the Elizabeth Historical Society opened a museum there.

The building was in poor shape, so, in 1999, the society began to apply for grants and raise money for repairs. It replaced windows, repaired the roof and floor and painted the building, inside and out. "It hadn't been painted since the '40s. It took 50 gallons of paint," curator Speer said.

The depot now is listed on the National

Chicago Great Western Railway Depot Museum

Register of Historic Places. It contains the old telegraph machine, plus photos and other memorabilia from the Chicago Great Western.

Parents and grandparents now take their kids and grand kids to the depot to teach them a little about history. The children seem as fascinated by the telegraph machine as Lewis and his playmates were during the 1930s. But the depot is much less active now than it was then, because there are no passengers waiting for trains, mail deliveries or whistles blowing.

It seems strange to Lewis to see what a quiet little place the depot has become. "I went to Korea in '51 and didn't get back here until '82, so I missed out on the end of the railroad. You couldn't have made anybody believe (in 1951) that the railroad would disappear."

"At this time saloons seem to have been very profitable investments."

History of Jo Daviess County, 1887

I used to associate ghost towns with places like Colorado and Wyoming, but Jo Daviess County has ghost towns, too. It also has small settlements that have shrunk from thriving little communities to spots in the road with just a few houses and maybe a church.

The fortunes of these communities ebbed and flowed with mining, lumbering and various modes of transportation. Even Galena, which once contained 9,000 to 14,000 people—estimates vary—now has only 3,500 residents.

These are some of the communities that have come and gone—or almost gone—during the past 185 years:

Council Hill: Locals say Black Hawk met with Col. Henry Gratiot beneath a large white oak tree during the Black Hawk War of 1832, in order to come to peace terms. In 1844, Henry Branton cut the tree down in order to expand his tavern. Close to nearby mines, Council Hill became an important stop on the main stagecoach line between Chicago and Galena. By 1840, it boasted several saloons and a hotel. "At this time saloons seem to have been very profitable investments," according to the 1887 history of Jo Daviess County. Eventually the community included other stores, a church, a school and a post office. Now the hotel and saloons are gone. The Methodist Church, which served the community for many years, was disbanded in the 1990s. Beverly and Larry Stabenow restored the church building and made it into a wedding chapel called The Little Church on the Hill Celebration Church. In addition, there are a few homes and the Council Hill Township Hall.

Council Hill Station: As mentioned earlier, Council Hill Station began with the building of the Illinois Central Railroad through the county. Several houses, a church and a school sat on the hill behind the Council Hill Station General Store, but now the hill is a hayfield. Also gone is the stockyard, where local cattle farmers brought their livestock to be shipped to the stockyards in Chicago. The Council Hill Station General Store still stands, looking much like it did during the 1930s and '40s. It is open several hours each week.

Derinda Center: There never was much to Derinda Center—a school, a few houses, a general store and a church—and there is little left of it now. However, it was important enough for people to still say they grew up at Derinda Center. Trinity Lutheran Church still stands and has a small but faithful congregation. Charles and Mardelle Dykstra bought the old Derinda Center schoolhouse, moved it to their property nearby, and restored it.

Guilford: There never was much to the settlement besides a general store and a post office, and there still isn't much there today. Francis and Joanne Wachter bought the store from Francis's grandfather, George Wachter, and remodeled it inside and out. Tthere still were cigarette burns on the floor from when the building was used as a dance hall, Francis said. Nearby there is a mini-storage facility, a junkyard and the ruins of an old stone house.

Massbach: Signs point the way to Massbach, and locals still identify themselves with the community, but there isn't much left except for St. John's Lutheran Church and a few homes. It was never very large, but it was big enough to have a wagon shop, a blacksmith shop and a general store. At one time, Massbach had an auto dealership and a cheese factory. "Years ago, you could buy shoes, clothing and groceries there," said Glen Albrecht, who grew up about 2 miles away.

Millville: As mentioned before, Millville was on the main stagecoach line through the county. "For a number of years it was the only town of any importance between Freeport and Galena." When the Illinois Central Railroad went north, many of the townspeople left. In 1892, a violent storm, accompanied by heavy rainfall, caused a dam near the village to break.

Ruins at Guilford, Guilford Road

Water rushed into town and destroyed almost all the buildings that remained. In 1932, the state of Illinois bought the land on which Millville stood and incorporated it into Apple River Canyon State Park.

Morseville: Morseville, which lies about 3 miles south of Stockton on Curtiss Road, grew up during the 1870s, after folks discovered that the area held what they believed to be a large lead reserve. Soon there was a church, a hotel, a cheese factory, a general store, a drug store, two blacksmith shops, two wagon shops, a harness shop and a tin shop. Although the lead soon gave out, businesses remained for quite some time. Now Morseville consists of a few homes of various ages and states of repair, plus a small white church and cemetery.

Pleasant Valley: Like many communities in Jo Daviess County, Pleasant Valley began as a mining community, with several people establishing claims. In 1828, Col. James Mitchell built a cabin at the approximate location of the settlement, but the cabin was burned during the Black Hawk War. After the war, Mitchell built a new home and started a tavern. Other settlers followed, and Pleasant Valley became a stop on the Galena and Dixon stagecoach route. However, it never became a very large settlement. About all that is there now is the Pleasant Valley Church of God, a plain white building with a single cross.

Vinegar Hill: The area around Vinegar Hill was among the first to be mined, and Michael Burns built a saloon and store there in 1826. Three men each built other stores between 1853 and 1857 and, in 1851, a post office was established. The 1887 history of Jo Daviess County includes this tale about how the settlement was named. "The derivation of the name Vinegar Hill was, probably, from a town of the same name near Wexford, Ireland, from which a number of miners emigrated to this vicinity. Michael Burns afterward told Mr. Harvey Mann, that he himself, John Furlong and Thomas Carrol, with others, while in a state of 'spiritual hallucination' at Burns' saloon, christened an Indian mound near there, by pouring whiskey over it and declaring that 'henceforth and forever, this place shall be called Vinegar Hill.'" Virtually nothing remains of the settlement. Nearby Vinegar Hill Mine was open for tours until recently.

Weston: In 1842, miners found lead in what briefly became Weston. About a year later, they built a smelting furnace. Soon nearly 1,000 people rushed to Weston, building cabins along what still is known as Lone Street. A church, various stores and even a race track sprang up to serve and entertain residents. But soon the miners depleted the surface minerals and many headed to California during the Gold Rush. Others remained but turned their attention to farming. By 1860, Weston was nearly abandoned. All that remains is a graveyard, which lies just west of Ill. 84 and south of U.S. 20.

Willow: Willow was and is only a tiny settlement. At one time, there were a couple of general stores, along with a few homes and a church. Now there are just a few houses, along with Willow United Methodist Church. Church services take place only every other Sunday, since the congregation joined with another church nearby.

"We had to cut the trees down and cut out the stumps one by one."

Jeff Trannel

God only knows how many hours people like Jeff Trannel, Francis and Pearl Rosemeyer, Gerry Oliver, Bob O'Brien and Rus Stewart spent cleaning up Gramercy Park. Although they are not pioneers, they sure must have felt like ones, as they cut down trees, hacked away at heavy undergrowth and planted new "crops" of perennials.

"I mostly do this for future generations, so they don't lose their historic roots," O'Brien said.

Gramercy Park, which spans the bluff overlooking downtown East Dubuque and the Mississippi River, was inhabited long before white settlers came to the northwest Illinois. The Hopewell Indians lived in North America, from Iowa to New York, from 100 B.C. to 500 A.D. Those who lived in northwest Illinois probably mined for lead and traded it for seashells (from which they made beads), precious metals and flint. They were part of a large trade network that extended as far south as the Gulf of Mexico.

Gerry Oliver and Bob O'Brien

Archaeologists have found evidence elsewhere that the Hopewell grew crops, fished, hunted animals and gathered food. They also made fine jewelry, pottery and ceremonial ornaments.

"The Hopewell disappeared with little explanation around 500 A.D., leaving many more questions than answers about their culture," according to the Northeast Ohio Areawide Coordinating Agency. "Their demise has been attributed to either unknown conquerors, epidemics or a cooling of the climate that drastically affected their corn and squash crops."

The Hopewell, also known as the Mound Builders, left behind 26 burial mounds in what now is known as Gramercy Park. To construct them, they cleared off large, roughly circular areas and then covered the circles with soil or clay. Then they built wooden crypts and placed the bodies of the deceased inside. Finally, they mounded over the burial sites with dirt. This involved the work of several people, perhaps over many years.

Archaeologists found scant evidence of habitation in 1989, when they sampled ground near the mounds. That was not surprising, because the Hopewell probably lived closer to the water, Trannel said.

However, during an excavation during the late 1800s, archaeologists found numerous structures and remains, including an unusually large skeleton that still has scientists guessing.

It was during the 1930s when Gramercy became a park. Pres. Franklin Roosevelt had established the Works Progress Administration to put people back to work during the Depression. The WPA built a beautiful pavilion and council circles out of native limestone.

Over the years, however, the park went to

seed. It became so overgrown with weeds, thorny brush and saplings that it was almost impossible to tell where the Indian mounds were. What little playground equipment there was had broken, and some residents had dumped junk there.

During the early 1990s, a group of community-minded people got out their axes, rolled up their sleeves and went to work. They cleared the mounds, making them visible from the river below, and carved out hiking trails.

"Because of the mounds, we couldn't take a bulldozer and pull out the trees," Trannel said. "We had to do it by hand. We had to cut the trees down and cut out the stumps one by one.

"But one of the toughest jobs was building those trails. Laying those railroad ties—whoa! You more or less had to drag them."

Scouting groups and other organizations pitched in to help. Local contractors, construction companies and other businesses donated materials and labor for a new pavilion, a scenic overlook, rest rooms, interpretive signs and flower beds. They also paved the trails and parking lot. Individuals donated picnic tables and benches. Others, such as Tom Berryman, researched the history of the park and worked on fund raising.

Jeff Trannel

Today Gramercy Park is one of the most pleasant spots in Jo Daviess County.

"It's gratifying to see all the changes. It didn't happen fast enough for some of us, but it's coming together," Trannel said.

References

Arnold, Keith, interview, 2006.

Bale, Florence Gratiot, "The Branton Tavern."

Black Hawk, "Life of Black Hawk," Dover Publications Inc., New York.

"A Brief Historical Sketch of the Illinois Central Railroad," Illinois Central Historical Society, www.icrrhistorical.org.

Carson, May Hawley, and Zoe Lenore Gray, "A History of Warren, Illinois: Its People, Industries, Achievements and Growth," 1928, reprinted in 1993 by the Jo Daviess County Republican Central Committee.

Dreyfus, Benjamin, W., "Railroads and Their Influence on the Growth of Chicago in the 1850s" in "The City Transformed," 1995, Benjamin W. Dreyfus, www.hcs.harvard.edu.

East Dubuque Register, "Railroad Passenger Business Falling Off," Jan. 10, 1929.

Elizabeth Weekly News, "Great Western Cuts Many Men from Payroll," Nov. 29, 1929.

Ernst, Amanda, interview, 2004.

Ernst, Brandi Louise, interview, 2004.

Ernst, Rob, interview, 2004.

Fleming, Ruth, Leone C. Anderson, Martha Parker Kuhns and Patricia Nagel, "Discovering Our Past: Volume I," 1990, Whippoorwill Publications, Inc.

Galena Gazette, "Marker Dedicated at Townsend Family Reunion," Sept. 5, 1929.
Gordy, Susan, interviews, 2003.
Harmet, Dick, interview, 2004.
Hassen, Harold, "The Dunleith Mound Group, East Dubuque, Illinois: Part 2," in "The Living Museum," Vol. 52, No. 1.
Heidenreich, Faye, interview, 2004.
"History of Jo Daviess County: 1887," pp. 546, 547, 548-552 and 583.
Huddleston, Jerry L., "The Hole in Stickney's Pocketbook—CGW's Winston Tunnel" in "North Western Lines," Summer 1998.
"Illinois Central Railroad," Encyclopedia of Chicago, www.encyclopedia.chicagohistory.org.
Illinois Historic Preservation Agency: "Unearthing a Nineteenth-Century Fort," in "Historic Illinois," February 2000.
Keillor, Steven J., "Grand Excursion" Antebellum America Discovers the Upper Mississippi," Afton Historical Society Press Publishers, 2004.
Lewis, Wendell, interview, 2004.
Michigan History Magazine, "The Hopewell" in "The Mitten," Sept. 2003.
Nolan, Sharon, interview, 2004.
Northeast Ohio Areawide Coordinating Agency, "Pre-Recorded History," www.noaca.org.
O'Brien, Bob, interview, 2003.
"Portrait and Biographical Album of Jo Daviess County, Illinois," 1889.
Potter, Joyce Kevern, interview, 2004.
Schwerdtfeger, Carl "Skip," interview, 2005.
Speer, Gerald, interview, 2004.
Stratton, Christopher and Floyd Mansberger, draft report "An Archaeological Resource Management Plan for Millville, Apple River Canyon State Park, Jo Daviess County, Illinois," January 2001, Fever River Research, Springfield, Ill.
Telegraph Herald: "Trains Reach End of the Line," May 2, 1971; "Scouts Help Refurbish Park," Oct. 2, 1994; "Playground on Site of Ancient Indian Mounds," Oct. 2, 1994; "Archeologist Digs up Original Site," July 2, 1995; "Apple River Foundation to Fortify Historical Spot," July 27, 1995; "Researcher Finds Hopewell Indians Were in Park," Jan. 3, 1998; "Restoration: Hundreds of Volunteers Assist," July 14, 1999; "A Flash in the Pan, Weston: Lead-mining rush took place in the 1840s," Dec. 12, 2000; "Towns Formed, Thrived Near Railroads," Sept. 28, 2001; "Short Lines Kept Smaller Communities Connected,: Sept. 28, 2001; "Railroads Brought Together Many People and Cultures," Sept. 30, 2001; "Advent of Automobile Signals Demise of Passenger Service," Oct. 1, 2001; "Time Fades Traces of Railroad Heritage," Oct. 2, 2001; and "Freight Trains Still Carrying a Hefty Load," Oct. 4, 2001.
Townsend, Cathy, interview, 2004.
Townsend, George N., letter to his daughter Jane Crowell Townsend, Nov. 18, 1850.
Townsend, Holstead, paper (date and title unknown), www.rootsweb.com.
Townsend, Jerry, interview, 2004.
Trannel, Jeff, interview, 2003.
Tyrell, Arthur, letters to family members and friends: Aug. 26, 1849; Oct. 12, 1849; Oct. 13, 1849; May 9, 1850; Sept. 15, 1850; Nov. 2, 1850; Jan. 23, 1852; May 4, 1852; Oct. 20, 1852; and Dec. 17, 1852. www.rootsweb.com.
Tyrell, Eliza, letter to Arthur Tyrell, Jan. 2, 1853, wwwrootsweb.com
Urven, Ian, interviews, 2004 and 2006.
The Warren Sentinel Leader: "The Townsend Family, Early Settlers," Nov. 2, 1932; "Two Rush Lovers: They Take Poison and Die Together," June 1, 1891.

Working

John Becker

"I really am odd and a different kind of person, but that's just fine."

John Becker

I first met John Becker in 1997. He, my husband and I and a few other friends occasionally meet after work on Monday nights for tacos at the Paradise Bar on Main Street in Galena.

John, or "Johnny," walks in wearing his work boots, a T-shirt dotted with holes, rugged jeans like those you would buy at a Farm and Fleet store and a thin layer of cement dust. His hands are calloused, and his face is permanently red from the sun.

He tells whoever is behind the bar, that he would like three orders of tacos and some of that green sauce he likes so much. A bricklayer and a stone mason by trade, Johnny has worked up an appetite.

As he approaches the table—usually two square tables pulled together to make an oblong one—his mouth goes a mile a minute. Although Johnny is over 60 and has a bad back, his thin, wiry body bounces with energy.

Once his tacos arrive, he quiets down to eat, wolfing his meal down with gusto. "Man, there's nothing like these, especially if you haven't had 'em for awhile," he says as he chews his last bite.

The main idea behind the get-togethers is to have a few laughs and relax. Often Johnny breaks into a fit of laughter, sometimes at his own jokes. His laughter combines high wheezes with gut-rumbling chortles.

We also talk about what's going on around town and what our other friends and acquaintances have been up to. Sometimes we discuss local politics. Once in awhile, we talk about life. Then Johnny becomes serious. He is the most likely of the group to say something bordering on philosophical.

"All the possessions in the world don't mean a thing if you haven't got good health," he says. Or, "It's astonishing how incredibly good we all have it in this country."

We don't stay long. Most of us have things we need to do. Johnny needs to get home and go to bed. He needs his rest because he gets up early in the morning—really early. He likes to get something substantial done before he goes to work, such as mowing the weeds on his farm, repairing a roof or fixing the carburetor on his motorcycle. Hardly a waking moment goes by that he isn't in motion.

"I really am odd and a different kind of person, but that's just fine," he told me once. "I don't go by the world's standards."

At work, the bricklayer is both fun loving and serious. He must pay close attention to what he does, he says, because a miscalculation can jeopardize an entire project.

"In this trade the last thing you want is to have to do something over. It isn't easy to rip out a brick wall."

Recently I spent some time with him on a job site. He and his business partner, Dave Hahn, were measuring for brick work on a big home in rural Galena. Rows of bricks would span two-and-a-half stories above a stone foundation. The partners had to space each row precisely, so that they would come out evenly at the top and match on all sides of the house.

Dave stood on the ground, while Johnny stood on a plank about 15 feet above him.

"Hey, Dave, it would take no effort at all to take this square and hang it so you can see it from down there," Johnny yelled.

Dave peered through a transit and yelled back up. "I'm reading 184 and five-eighths. Why don't you put a nail in that mark there?"

Johnny did so. Then he pulled out a folding rule, took some measurements and made

John Becker

some mental calculations.

"This soffit's up 5 or 6 inches, Dave. Do you want it around the corner or the other way?"

"I want to check this back with the soffit now, to see how close everything is," Dave replied.

"This time, I'm going against an existing soffit," Johnny shouted. With his measuring tools in hand and a pencil behind his ear, Johnny continued to work.

"You're going to have to go on the ladder," Dave said after a bit.

Johnny swung onto a ladder and climbed, looking more like a 25-year-old than a 61-year-old with a bad back. Then, with one foot on the ladder and one on the scaffolding, he reached out to his side to mark the house for more measurements.

"We're reading 180 and 3/4," Dave said. The height of one side had come within an eighth inch of the other side of the wide house. Now they knew exactly what they needed to do.

"You don't want big mortar joints," Johnny told me. "The mortar joints shouldn't be more than three-eighths of an inch. We've discovered that we need to lay on four-and-a-half inches on center from where we are."

I nodded, not really understanding what had just occurred.

The most difficult part of the project was done. The tradesmen would check their work after setting in three courses of brick. If everything worked out, they could relax and get into a steady rhythm.

"It's a good feeling once you are mixing the mortar and start laying the bricks. It's somewhat of a relief. When I take the trowel, I feel relaxed."

Dave and an apprentice mixed some cement and hauled it up the scaffolding. I stood on the platform with them, trying to stay out of the way, yet remain close enough to ask questions.

What has kept Johnny in the profession so long?

"It's Davey," he said without hesitation. "He is such a craftsman. He is taking an age-old trade to the next level. He is a master tradesman. It is such an honor to work with a master trades-man. ... He is a problem solver extraodinaire."

Johnny talked about how Dave had designed a device they use to keep corner bricks perfectly straight.

The two met while they were working for another contractor and, in about 1985, they formed their own business.

"John and I kind of feed off each other," Dave said. "It's kind of neat to come up with different ways of doing things."

Earlier Johnny had told me how he got into the trade.

He had graduated from high school just a year before and had managed a small dairy herd on his parents' farm near Galena. When he realized he couldn't make a decent living as a dairy farmer, he paid a visit to Frank Einsweiler, who owned V & E Construction, where Johnny's dad worked. All he knew was that he probably wanted to work outside.

"When I was young, I don't think I could have spent my career indoors or in a factory."

It was 1963, when schools and colleges were rebuilding or expanding, and Einsweiler had plenty of work. He told Johnny he could become an apprentice and learn either the cement finishing or the bricklaying trade. Johnny chose the latter.

"When I went down there, I never had a clue as to what I wanted to do. Something might have registered that buildings go up in the air and some are beautiful. Perhaps something appealed for me there."

He can hardly believe that a brief meeting in 1963 set the course of his life. "It was one sentence from him and a sentence from me, not even a paragraph. That is how little I knew about either one of the trades."

Johnny had much to learn. "I didn't even know how to build a scaffold. They told me to build a scaffold and, after I did, the bricklayers wouldn't get on it."

But he liked figuring out how things work. Whenever a mechanic would come to his parents' farm to repair a piece of equipment, he would watch closely so that he could learn how to make his own repairs. He also worked like a son of a gun.

On the other hand, he didn't exercise much caution.

"I was on a dead run all the time. When I was on my first job, the cement finishers had just poured the floor, and, you know what I did? I ran right onto the finished concrete. As soon as my feet touched down, I knew it was the wrong thing to do.

"I got chewed out so terrible, and in front of everyone else. I would just like to have started bawling, but I couldn't do that on the job. That kind of was the beginning of my maybe trying to use my head a little bit more."

Over time, he learned the basics of the trade and graduated from helping other bricklayers to becoming one himself. He says he still is learning and that he faces new challenges on every job. Recently, for instance, he had to use slivers of bricks only five-eighths inch wide to fill in narrow spaces between some sun room windows.

"Any time you take a piece of brick that's no wider than this," he says, holding up a small piece of plastic, "and set it next to another, it just doesn't want to stay."

Many of the beautiful, large homes in the Galena Territory feature some of Johnny's exacting work.

But he is humble about his skill. "I want to be the first to credit the other tradesmen, particularly the carpenters. You are not alone in your trade. What makes a job turn out well is the other trades." They provide the foundation and structure on which bricklayers build.

In addition, Johnny has learned stone masonry. Once I watched him and Dave cut and lay stones of different sizes and shapes, so that they would appear random. They were anything but random. The stones had to come out even on top and work nicely around the windows and doors. The craftsmen also chiseled into the stones to make them look old and weathered.

They could have fooled me. The house looked as though it had been built during the 19th Century.

"Stone masonry is one of those trades where you never fully get it. Sometimes I still get stymied and puzzled."

Johnny said the home was one of his favorite projects, because of the interesting juxtaposition of brick and stone. "But it really stands out because of the great owners. They are such good people, good for tradespeople to work with and very humble."

Brick and stone masonry require stamina and strength, as well as precision. After more than 40 years, the work has taken its toll. Johnny suffers from chronic lower back pain, both from carrying heavy loads and from working in awkward positions. Sometimes he gets a stabbing pain in his right shoulder. Periodically he takes a short break to bend backward and try to straighten his spine. But, by the end of each day, his body is bent like a hinge on a door.

Yet, he is grateful for being able to make a living doing work he loves. He derives satisfaction from finishing a job and seeing everything look "real nice."

"All these years it has been absolutely rewarding."

But there are one or two or three more things Johnny would like to do. "If I ever have the chance again, I would like to teach young people. It would be wrong and sinful in God's eyes if you had some expertise and didn't help young people learn."

Outside of work, Johnny enjoys a fairly quiet life. He loves antique tractors and muscle cars, so he occasionally enters "tractor pulls" at community fairs and does some drag racing.

He also is a devoted Catholic. "My faith is Number 1 for me. But, believe me, I don't always do everything like I should."

Recently he rebuilt an outdoor fireplace, converting it into a shrine, and placed a statue of Mary inside.

Although Johnny has dated a number of women, he has never married. "I have had some beautiful ladies in my life."

But he never found the time or the energy to take his relationships beyond the dating stage. "I like to drag race and I like tinkering with stuff, so I just wasn't able to continue finding time. And now at my age, in this trade I'm in, I can get so worn out. I think my relationships suffer because of my weariness."

He still lives on his parents' farm. (His parents died many years ago.)

"I've been here since the spring of 1957. I just haven't left, you know. This is where I probably ended up forming my opinions about things and learning how to deal with life and think about life."

Johnny has never remodeled or redecorated the house. "I don't want any missing paint on a barn, but I couldn't care less about the inside of the house. I don't have any use for any interior style or decorating. But that's not to say I don't care about cleanliness."

In most ways, he lives frugally. He probably would laugh at the thought of buying a computer, an espresso machine or many of the other trappings of contemporary life. He takes few vacations and seldom buys new clothes. Yet he owns a late-model Harley Davidson, which he bought new.

In 1968, he built a garage for storing and repairing his vehicles. After nearly 35 years, it looks as clean as a hospital surgery room.

"If you are working in a clean environment, you are happier and do nicer work."

Johnny said he wants to continue to work as long as he can, but he might work in some other field besides masonry. "I love people. I would like to do more things for other people."

Whatever he does, he will go at it with all he's got. "I will hit it hard. That's the way I've been all my life."

"I've been hit by a lot of rocks."

Tom Golden

When Tom Golden was about 12 years old, he was buried alive.

Golden was with a Boy Scout troop and had jumped into a ditch to dodge rocks being hurled by another scout troop. The ditch collapsed, and he was covered with dirt.

"I was in total darkness. I couldn't move and I couldn't breathe.

"I could hear other people scream, but I knew I couldn't panic because I knew if I did, I would vomit. If I did that,there was no place for the vomit to go. Then I would just suffocate."

Golden began to hallucinate and then went unconscious. He was unconscious when rescuers pulled him out.

"After that, I was extremely afraid of having anything over my head."

So, he became a miner.

"I got into mining to get over my fear. It was a monkey I had to get off my back."

In 1968, while earning his way through college, Golden started working part time for the Eagle-Picher Company, which operated several zinc mines around Galena.

He made good money. Mainly, he trimmed loose rock off the walls of the mine with a crowbar.

"There is a lot of thought involved in trimming. It's not just about grunting out the rock. You have to find the right part of the crack. I would size it up, pull a little bit and see what wiggled. There is a lot of finesse involved."

He also drilled and blasted, loaded trucks and worked as a security guard. Tall and muscular, he could handle the heavy work.

After earning his degree, Golden moved to Bauxite, Arkansas, where he worked as a foreman for Reynold's Metals Company (now Alcoa). He also worked as a mining engineer for a company in North Dakota. He spent much of his time underground.

"I was a little nervous at first, but the mine was bigger than I thought, so I was OK. I just focused on the tasks at hand."

It turned out that he liked mining much more than he feared it. "First off, there was that machismo thing. You got dirty. You worked hard. There was a respect and camaraderie with miners that you don't' see with other people, like stock brokers. Also, you are always part of a team.

"There was no color. You worked side by side with people of different races and with different backgrounds. I had one guy beside me who couldn't read.

"Nobody kids anybody. They tell it honestly and then they're done with it. There is respect all the way around.

"Miners are very pragmatic. They keep things in perspective."

But mining is noisy and dangerous. Golden suffers from a permanent ear injury. "I have constant ringing in my ears."

Over the approximately 20 years he spent in mining, Golden sustained several injuries and experienced his share of close calls. "I've taken a lot of falls and broken a few bones, but I haven't had any serious injuries."

"A guy knocked a rock on me about the size of that dresser," he said, pointing to what would be small for a dresser but huge for a rock that landed on you. The rock rolled into his legs, and his legs fell out from under him. No bones broke as far as he knows, "but it hurt like heck."

"Another one that size hit me when I was in the bucket of a front-end loader. It fell into the bucket by me.

"I've been hit by a lot of rocks."

"There also was the time I was working on a drag line. The chain that was holding up the cross tie broke, and the tie hit me right between the legs." Golden was catapulted into the air and landed on a heater. As sore and bruised as he was, he merely cut his hand.

Yet another time, when he was drilling

the last round in the Birkett Mine near Galena, he ran out of oxygen. "There was a fan to push the air in, but they were getting ready to close the mine and pulled the fan out. I went unconscious and, when I woke up, I found myself draped over a ladder."

Golden no longer works in mining. Now he is a consulting engineer. However, he retains a good measure of respect for the mining industry.

Tom Golden when he worked for Reynold's (courtesy of Tom Golden)

"Say what you want about mining, but it is, arguably, the oldest profession. When the first caveman took a rock and threw it, that was mining. If you just go back and think about it, everything we use is a direct result of mining or an indirect result of mining— even the fillings the dentist uses, your glasses and the cloth that we couldn't sew without needles.

"You would have nothing. We all use it. We all need it."

"It seems the people were crazy and rushed to the mines."

Illinois Governor John Reynolds

Lead sulfide – galena – brought the first white settlers to the Galena area. For a few decades, mining ranked as the Number 1 occupation.

Back in 1804, the federal government bought 15 square miles from the Sac and Fox Indians, later to be leased to prospectors. By then, more than 20 years had passed since Julien Dubuque cut a deal with the Fox Indians to mine lead just west of the Mississippi River. Word had gone out that the east side of the river also contained the sought-after ore.

Not much happened, however, until in 1819, when Col. R.M. Johnson led a group of 100 men, including some black slaves, up the Mississippi River from St. Louis to what now is known as the Galena River. (Then it was called the Fevre, Bean or Fever River). He negotiated a treaty with the Indians enabling him to mine. (The Indians had been digging lead from just beneath the ground's surface for many years. They used it for ceremonial paint.)

In 1822, the U.S. government began to promote the mining industry by offering 320 acres to anyone who would employ upward of 20 people and give 10 percent of the smelted lead to the government.

Lead mining got its biggest boost in 1823, after the first steamboat, The Virginia, made it through the rapids on the Mississippi at Rock Island, proving that there was an efficient way to transport ore and smelted lead.

Soon miners were over-stepping the bounds of the Upper Mississippi Lead Mine District established in 1804, but no one seemed to care except the Indians. They tried to maintain a stronghold, but virtually abandoned Jo Daviess after the Black Hawk War of 1832.

Meanwhile, white prospectors kept coming. By the fall of 1826, 550 were working in the area around Galena, according to a report prepared by Fever River Research in 1996. By 1827, the U.S. government had issued 2,384 lease permits.

"For several years, down to 1834, the whole earth, north, east, and south of Galena was covered with people, prospecting, digging, and looking for lead ore," said Illinois Gov. John Reynolds, who was quoted by Fever River Research. "It seemed the people were literally crazy, and rushed to the mines with the same blind energy and speed, that a people would in a panic flee from death."

Miner, Ginte Mining Co., Galena (courtesy of the Galena Public Library Historical Room)

The "blind energy" affected all classes, the Governor wrote, and created a "mysterious medley of people."

Some writers characterized the miners as harsh, rough and reckless. The miners also were transient. Not knowing that the Mississippi River Valley was rich for agriculture, they did not settle there at first. Instead, they spent much of the year at their homes in Kentucky and Missouri, tending to their crops, and traveled up North to work the mines the rest of the year.

At first, they scooped the ore out of the ground, much as the Indians had done, but after the easily-mined surface lead was gone, they began to dig crevasses, following veins of lead horizontally. Later, they dug mine shafts and went well below the earth's surface.

Lead mining increased rapidly until 1848, when the Upper Mississippi Lead Mine District produced 28,000 tons. In 1886, Harper's New Monthly Magazine reported, "Twenty-five or thirty years ago, four out of every five men in the country [the Galena area] were connected directly or indirectly with mining operations."

"There were 238 mines in Jo Daviess County—and that's just those with names," Tom Golden said. "Maybe there was one name for every 100 shafts."

In addition, traces of "sucker holes"—small depressions where miners dug from the earth's surface—still dot the landscape.

Production dropped off severely for about 20 years. The price of lead had gone down. Local miners had caught gold fever and headed for California. And the U.S. dropped its tariff on imported lead. But production increased later again and hit its peak in 1898, with 50,468 tons produced. In 1900 most lead was used to make paint, tamping/trimmings and pipes.

Meanwhile, people discovered they could farm the area around Galena, and many made it their permanent home. The population increased dramatically, and other businesses and industries began to pop up. Harper's estimated in 1866 that "not one in twenty men has any connection with the mining interest."

During the 20th Century, lead decreased in importance. Manufacturers no longer make lead pipes or lead-based paint. Now gasoline is lead-free.

But another ore began to find a place in manufacturing in during the late 19th Century—zinc. Zinc is used to galvanize iron, to protect it from rusting. It also is an important component of brass, and zinc chloride is used as a wood preservative. The Upper Mississippi Lead Mine District contained plenty of zinc. (Often lead and zinc are found together.)

U.S. zinc production reached its height during World War I, when Germany controlled the European zinc market and the U.S. began to supply its allies. It dropped off dramatically after the war but experienced a resurgence during and after World War II.

Like lead mining, zinc mining was dangerous. As late as 1970, 19-year-old Charles

Miners, Ginte Mining Co., Galena (circa 1945, courtesy of Galena Public Library Historical Room)

"Chuck" Miller, of Hanover, died in an industrial accident at the Bautsch mine south of Galena. He had been employed there only four months.

The demand for U.S. zinc began to dry up during the 1970s, because it was cheaper elsewhere. "It always gets down to economics," said Tom Golden, a former miner.

Today no mines operate in Jo Daviess County. They all have been sealed.

Local residents earn their living much differently than they did before. According to the U.S. Bureau of Labor Statistics, the largest employment sectors as of 2004 were: accommodations and food service, with 19 percent of all employment; manufacturing, with 18 percent; and retail sales, with 11 percent. Service-sector jobs continue to increase.

According to the Galena/Jo Daviess County Convention and Visitors Bureau, 20 percent of all 8,274 jobs are related to tourism.

"People were skinnier back then. Plus, my family is pretty short."

Ruth Ann Einsweiler

Ruth Ann Einsweiler grew up playing Cowboys and Indians with her siblings and cousins at the Vinegar Hill Museum and Lead Mine. "I was one of the younger children, so I always got one of the crappier parts."

Nevertheless, she would badger her parents about when she could go back to the mine to play.

During high school, she worked summers there. "I was looking for a summer job, and they (the owners) were looking for people to give tours. I figured I might as well go ahead and do it."

But giving the tours became more than a summer job. It brought her closer to her family's history.

Ruth Ann explains that her great, great, great, great grandfather, John Furlong, became a lead miner after fighting in the battle of Vinegar Hill in Ireland in 1798. He had been captured by the British and later escaped to America and settled in the Galena area. In 1818, he bought the land where the mine is located. Six years later, he and three of his friends struck lead at Cave Ranch, now known as Vinegar Hill.

Furlong's son, John, worked the mine in 1882, and his great grandson, Thomas, worked it in 1934. In 1967 Furlong's great, great grandson Earl opened it to tourists, and now his great, great, great grandson, Mark, owns it. Ruth Ann is Mark's niece.

Ruth Ann starts her tours by showing visitors the windless—a bucket on a rope with a crank, which lifted lead from the mine shaft—and other mining artifacts. "A one-cylinder gasoline engine replaced the windless," she says.

Then she asks them to put on hard hats and takes them down into the mine. She shines a flashlight onto the cave walls to show what lead ore looks like before it is mined and smelted. It comes in grayish-pink, cube-shaped crystals.

The tourists must walk single file in some spots and crouch in others if they are much more than about 5 feet tall. "People were skinnier back then. Plus, my family is pretty short."

The teenager has given the tour so many times that her voice can become a bit sing-song. "You are 50 feet underground right now and 40 feet under the hill. ... This red, flaky substance is called ochre."

But she responds naturally to questions, and shows feeling when she tells tourists, "Miners were tough but fun people. They were there to support each other. Everyone learned to work together."

Because mining could be dangerous, even life-threatening, they had to be able to trust one another, she says.

Perhaps that is why trust is so important to Ruth Ann. "Friendship is all about trust," she said one day after finishing a tour. Good friends will keep your secrets and will be there for you when you have a bad day. "They are there to drop their boyfriends for a couple of minutes in order to talk to you."

Like miners, she said, she also is fun loving and determined. "It's the going out and doing it."

During her senior year in high school, she did a lot. She worked out at the gym, was editor of the yearbook, participated in several sports, played the leading role in her school play, worked part time and maintained good grades. It was stressful, but she didn't lose sight of the fact that she and her classmates wanted to enjoy their final year together. One day she and her friends showed up for class in their prom dresses.

Ruth Ann Einsweiler

"Our goal was to be known as 'the fun class.'"

She said her friends probably would describe her as "goofy at times but has her serious moments," as well as "very well organized and busy."

Working at Vinegar Hill has given Ruth Ann confidence. "When it comes to meeting new people, I used to be pretty shy. Now it's easy."

The knowledge she gained also helped her with at least one homework assignment. "I had to do a history research project, so I wrote about Vinegar Hill and got an A."

References

Becker, John, interviews, 2004 and 2005.

Einsweiler, Ruth Ann, interview, 2003.

Galena Gazette, "Youth Dies in Mine Accident," April 16, 1970.

Golden, Tom, interview, 2003.

Hahn, Dave, interview, 2004.

Harper's Magazine, "Galena and Its Lead Mines," May 1866.

Mansberger, Floyd and Tim Townsend, "'The People Were Literally Crazy': The Lead and Zinc Mining Resources of Jo Daviess County, Illinois," 1996, Fever River Research, Springfield, Ill.

U.S. Bureau of Labor Statistics, Quarterly Census of Employment and Wages, www.bls.gov.

The Arts

Carl Johnson

"It's the love of my life, I'll tell you."

Carole Koester

Turner Hall has provided the stage on which much of Carole Koester's life story has played out. As Carole grew up during the late 1940s and '50s, she roller skated and danced at the community gathering place.

After graduating from college, she returned to Galena and has directed plays there for the Galena Art Theatre and the Galena Public Schools. She met her best friend, the late Sue Corbett, through her involvement in theater at Turner Hall.

About 30 years ago, she helped form a committee to save it.

Carole remembers what it used to be like to direct plays at the 131-year-old facility. "It was a challenge. We had a light box back then, which was one where you had to pull the handles down. The roof leaked, and there would be puddles on the floor. There were times when people in the audience actually sat there with umbrellas. It was cold during the winter, and people had to wear jackets. During the summer, it was beastly hot."

Turner Hall

The German Turner Society of Galena built the large stone facility in 1874 to promote physical and mental well being through exercise programs, sporting events, debates, lectures, theater and musical performances. The Society opened its doors to everyone "without regard to politics, religion, or nationality."

As its immigrant founders died, the Society died out, too. At some point the Galena Opera House Association bought the building and, in 1925, sold it to the Galena Lodge of Eagles.

Early in 1926, a fire broke out. Soon the large cupola at the front of the building and a loft at the rear were engulfed in flames. Firefighters worked feverishly to put out the fire and to prevent sparks and falling debris from igniting nearby buildings. Meanwhile, members of the Eagles rushed in to save what furniture they could.

The building was gutted, which shocked Galena residents. They had considered Turner Hall impervious to fire. Fire officials said faulty wiring probably was to blame.

The Eagles restored the hall and installed beautiful woodwork, which remains today.

Later, the city bought the building.

For awhile, Turner Hall again became the center of the community. If the walls could talk, they would describe friendships made, hearts broken and young love begun. The walls might even reveal the mystery of Spencer, Turner Hall's ghost.

By the 1960s, when Carole began to direct, the much-revered and sometimes-maligned gathering place had fallen into disrepair. The amount of money needed to fix it went far beyond what the Galena Art Theatre could earn from its productions. So a group of people, including Carole, formed the Save Turner Hall Foundation to raise money for remodeling and repairs.

"We did everything we could to raise money, from selling sandwiches at auctions to working bingo every week."

Through the money raised, grants, donations and thousands of hours of volunteer time, the group

Carole Koester at Turner Hall

During the early 1990s, an architect drew up plans for an addition. The Save Turner Hall Foundation had torn down a house and poured a foundation in preparation. Having met several times with the Galena City Council, members expected the council to approve the project and city funding to help pay for it. But new council members were elected, and plans were dropped.

"As the council changes, the mood changes," said Tracy Jenkins, former building manager.

Some council members saw it as a money pit. At that time, the city was losing about $20,000 per year on Turner Hall. One council member half-jokingly suggested selling it for a dollar.

In 2000 residents pleaded with the council to retain and maintain the building. "This is a part of our heritage, just like Grant's home," said Tom Golden.

Keith Ahlvin called it his "second home." "If the council supports only those things that have an immediate financial benefit, then this community is in for a very dark future," he said.

Jill Millhouse said it has a special place in her heart because she met her husband Bill through her work with the Save Turner Hall Foundation.

The city did keep the building and eventually installed air conditioning. Lately it has been running about $10,000 per year in the red. It is booked most weekends, but seldom used during the week.

Despite its flaws, most people love Turner Hall, including those involved in theater. "I think it is amazing," Chrissy Hogue said. "The versatility of the space is incredible." Groups have performed theater in the round and partial round, as well as on stage.

Ron Eichstaedt is in awe of the fact that people have been performing on the same spot for more than 100 years. "So much has happened here. So many people want to go on stage, just like I am doing now."

"I love the building. I love the balconies," Phil Jackman said.

Matt Zanger called it "a classic beauty."

"It's the love of my life, I'll tell you," Carole

repaired the roof, re-plastered the walls and installed new flooring and lighting.

With its curved balcony and box seats, oak floor and cream colored walls, the hall exudes dignity, warmth and grace. Besides hosting school and community plays, it has become a popular venue for weddings, dances, meetings, auctions and small trade shows.

Some people, including members of the Chicago Symphony Orchestra who performed chamber music there, say its acoustics are the finest around for musical instruments.

But there still are problems. Some actors and directors believe the acoustics do not work well for the speaking voice. In 2003, when Mike Willis directed a comedy called "Dearly Departed" for the Main Street Players, he had to constantly remind his cast to speak loudly and clearly.

"You have to over-enunciate, over-project and slow down so that people can hear you," said Phil Jackman, a frequent performer on the theater circuit. "That's not easy to do. You cannot act like you would in another setting."

City fire alarms can drown out the action. "Turner Hall is next to the volunteer fire station, so you have to be prepared to freeze when the alarm goes off," said Emily Painter.

There are no rest rooms back stage. "We have to run to the house next door to use the bathroom," Matt Zanger said. There is no work room, storage room or kitchen. Parking is inadequate.

Koester said. "It's wonderful. It's beautiful. It's historic."

"Besides Spencer, it's really nice," Katie White said.

Oh, yes, back to Spencer.

Carole had heard other people talk about Spencer but was skeptical about the ghost. Then, one night, she and a few others were ready to lock up and leave, when they saw someone walk past the dressing-room door. They called out, but no one answered. "We sent someone up there, but there was no one there."

She said there have been other strange appearances, unexplained crashing sounds backstage, chilly drafts, flickering lights and even a voice that ordered a local minister to "get out of here."

"You tell people these stories and they look at you like you are out of your mind," she said.

Many people believe it is the ghost of Charles Scheerer that has been creating the strange disturbances. The treasurer of the Turner Society, Scheerer was Turner Hall's first manager. He took care of the building for many years. On March 14, 1910, his body was found inside the hall. He apparently had died of natural causes.

"Those who believe in such things feel that Charles is still watching over Turner Hall, making his presence known from time to time, as the need arises," Daryl Watson wrote in his book, "Ghosts of Galena."

Over the years, Scheerer's name has evolved into "Spencer."

Although Spencer seemingly haunts the old hall, he has never harmed anyone.

"We laugh and call him Spencer the Friendly Ghost," Carole said.

"I love to paint." *Carl Johnson*

"I'm a saver." *Marilyn Johnson*

Carl and Marilyn Johnson are dedicated to the arts, to historic architecture and to each other.

They both grew up in the Chicago area. She studied history, and he studied art. They married, had four children and lived in Hinsdale, Ill. He worked for an advertising agency and later started his own graphic design business. She taught for a year and then stayed home with the kids.

On weekends Carl etched copper plates and painted. She loved to read and knit. They both loved to travel.

During the summer of 1969, they went to Italy and Greece. "I got to Greece and discovered architecture," Carl says. "I came back with 65 drawings and paintings."

That same summer, they took the family to Galena for a weekend and saw that Galena also had architecture to die for.

Before long, they decided to sell their house and move to Galena. "We were living in suburbia, and I guess I was climbing the walls," Marilyn says. "The history was here and, of course, the beauty was here."

"When you're in the ad business and getting to be 40, you start looking over your shoulders at the young turks," Carl says.

Although they had four kids to support, that didn't stop them. Carl would paint and make prints, and Marilyn would continue to focus on raising the kids. They figured they had enough money to survive for three years. If things didn't work out, they could move back to Chicago and Carl could resume his graphic design business.

They never had to move back.

Soon after their move, the Johnsons met Zelma Wilson Clark, who owned a small art gallery downtown. Zelma invited Carl to show his work there. They sent out a press release, and the Telegraph Herald in Dubuque, Iowa sent over a reporter and photographer. The paper ran a full-page story.

"The place was jammed," Carl says. "I had babbled on to the reporter, and I guess people wanted to see the kook from Chicago."

Some of the right people showed up. Walter

Peterson, then president of the University of Dubuque, liked Carl's paintings and invited him to show his work at the U. Wayne Norman, who was influential in the business and cultural communities, bought several pieces.

"I think the reaction was, if Wayne Norman thinks my paintings are OK, then they must be OK."

In 1972, the Johnsons moved into a downtown storefront, and Carl painted watercolors of local architecture. (A year later they bought a downtown building.) The store attracted walk-in trade from tourists who were re-discovering Galena. People loved his work.

"People came in and bought stuff!" Carl says with a mix of incredulity and humor.

In 1975, Wayne Norman asked Carl to design and illustrate the book, "Heritage of Dubuque." That increased Carl's exposure, and, during the years that followed, Carl broadened his scope. He painted scenes throughout the Midwest and Europe.

At one point, he tried to paint what he thought people would buy. "When I force myself to do something, it doesn't turn out well. I got — what's the preamble to ulcers? — gastritis." He went back to painting what he likes to paint.

But Carl was disciplined. Every weekday he painted and many weekends he worked in the store. Now that he is 74, he is cutting himself a little more slack, but he still works most days. "Only a small percent of us get a talent for painting, or for whatever. I am lucky enough to have the talent, so I ought to be serious enough to do it."

Carl Johnson with his old printing press

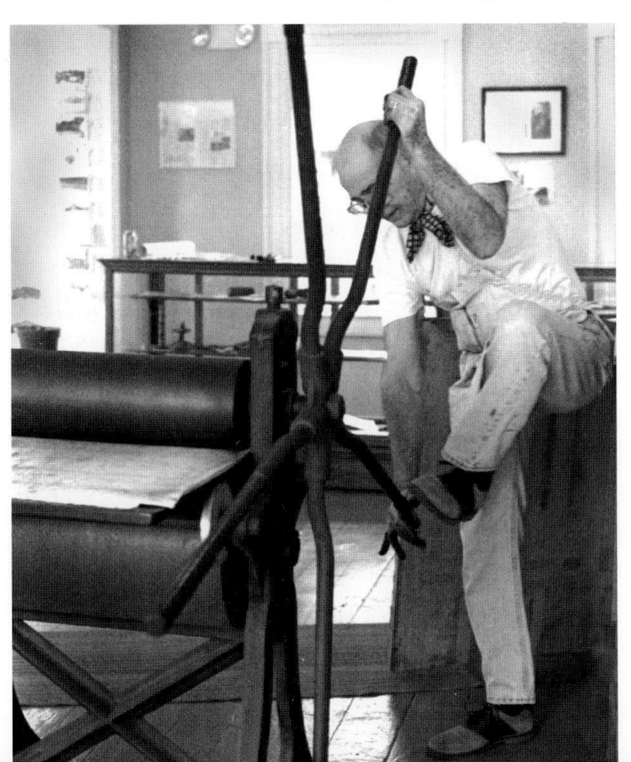

Meanwhile, Marilyn took some business courses and began to manage the store. "I got to about Page 5 (in the first textbook) and discovered you're supposed to make a profit! I thought, 'Please, please can we just at least break even?'"

Carl says the two have complemented each other. "Marilyn has a mind that leaps and makes connections. I don't have a mind like that. I get focused, and there I am."

As business progressed, the Johnsons bought the building next door and the one next door to that. Their son Adam, a restoration architect, helped them with the renovation, and now they live above their store. "We love to use these buildings. Restoration is part of being a Galenian," Marilyn says.

Carl and Marilyn are among my favorite people. They dive into life with enthusiasm and maintain a lively interest in each other. They speak respectfully about each other's work and laugh about the times they have shared. Carl's voice goes up when he tells a funny story. Marilyn's thoughts tumble out in delightful disorder.

Marilyn says a successful relationship "is about each of you finding your passion and also supporting your partner." When Carl wants to go off someplace to paint, she goes with him, taking along her knitting or exploring the local history. When she wants to do historical research, he goes along. "Carl is always accepting and encouraging me, and he can always find something to paint."

Carl says he has learned at least two things about relationships: "If it doesn't make any difference to you, don't argue. And treat your wife as a girlfriend part of the time."

Marilyn and Carl also have immersed themselves in the community. Carl was president of the Galena Area Chamber of Commerce, and Marilyn promoted tourism. She also served on the board of the Galena Community Foundation for many years. It was her idea to build a foot bridge over the Galena River.

Together the couple worked on passage of a

county hotel/motel tax. The tax won voter approval, and the county has been using the tax proceeds ever since to promote tourism. They also were active in the Save Turner Hall Foundation.

"You kind of gather together with people who have goals like yours and sink your teeth in," Marilyn says. "You can always find something that needs to be done."

Although she had a lot going on, Marilyn was missing something to call her own, Carl says. "I think she always had a bit of jealousy because I had my painting."

That changed in 1998. Marilyn had been encouraging her dentist to buy the building known as the Old Stockade, which is one of the oldest buildings in town. She bemoaned the fact that it would crumble if someone didn't fix it up. "Then he said, 'If you are so interested in it, why don't you buy it?' I walked down to the real estate office and got the papers. The next day Carl and I made an offer."

Since then she has made the building's history her passion.

The building did not start out as a stockade, as many people think. Marilyn is not sure who built it or just when, but it was constructed before 1828. She found an obscure record showing that Samuel Muir, a trader, sold the property to George Davenport that year. Marilyn believes they used the building for storage.

Soon Amos Farrar went into partnership with Davenport and, in 1831, Farrar bought out Davenport's interest. Farrar, who had married Sophia Gear, Galena's first female teacher, converted the structure into a home.

In May of 1832, when the Black Hawk War began, a stockade was built around Farrar's building, and it became an emergency refuge for townspeople.

The war did not last long, but Sophia's troubles lasted several years. After Amos died in 1832, she had to fight to save her home. "The county made a move on Sophia to take this over as a jail — a widow with kids!" Marilyn says angrily. "In 1838 they finally let her have her own house."

After Sophia's death in 1883, Mary Gardner and her grown daughter, Margaret, bought the building at auction. Margaret cut openings into the walls and fitted them with glass, exposing the timbers of the original structure.

Marilyn learned that Margaret taught first grade for more than 50 years and wrote a history of the building. In 1932 Margaret held a celebration commemorating the Black Hawk War. After she retired from teaching, she held kindergarten classes at the Old Stockade.

Marilyn quotes from a piece that Margaret wrote for the Galena Gazette: "I'm very proud of my home and have had many opportunities to dispose of it. But those who would buy it would tear it down and build a more modern structure in its place."

"Margaret never married," Marilyn says. "She was the kind of teacher who corresponded with her students long after they were gone. I taught first grade for a year and I wonder what happened to my kids. It gets 'ya."

In 1941, after Margaret died, her niece, Mary Isabella Rouse, and Rouse's brother took over the home. Mary Isabella ran a tea room and owned a small historical collection.

Later, Elsworth and Ruth Glick bought the building and, from 1965 to 1995, operated the Rootin' Tootin' Indian Museum there.

The building then sat vacant until the Johnsons bought it. With a little help from a state tourism loan, they restored the building to Margaret Gardner's vintage. The project took two years.

Marilyn says she has something in common with the building's previous owners. "They were persevering."

She loves telling visitors about the history of the place. Often she veers into other aspects of Galena's history, having collected other information and memorabilia.

"I am kind of a saver. I would be an archivist if I were that organized. I have a ton of things on Ulysses Grant. I'm scattered. I'm kind of all over."

One of her documents lists the mothers and widows of soldiers who died during World War I and were buried in Europe. "This kind of thing knocks the stuffing out of you — or it does me."

"It has been nice to see Marilyn be so passionate about something," Carl says. "It's just been a pure pleasure to do this together."

Carl now uses part of the Old Stockade as

a print-making studio, an art he had neglected for 18 years. Print making has become a welcome departure from painting. It is much more painstaking.

He begins by coating a copper plate with an acid-resistant ground. Then he draws on the copper with a dry-point needle, scratching its surface. Next, he dips the plate in acid, which eats away the metal where the lines have been drawn. He repeats the process several times until he is satisfied with the etching.

"What happens when you throw the plate into acid is not an exact science. Things happen. I am always excited to pull off my first proof."

To make a print, he spreads ink onto the plate with a piece of cardboard, then wipes off the excess with a soft cloth. He fusses with it until the ink is even. "Some people wear gloves when they print, but I like to get my hands dirty."

Then he lays the plate on a flat bed and covers it with a damp sheet of paper and three felt blankets. Then, cranking a large wheel, he rolls the plate and print through an 1854 printing press. He bought the press 40 years ago. He can make only one print before he has to ink the plate again, but he doesn't mind the tedium.

"This gives me a different kind of solitude than I have when I'm painting. It gives me time to, I don't know, evaluate my life or something," he says with a chuckle.

But he hasn't given up painting and probably never will. "My first love, I suppose, is watercolor. Even after all this time, I don't have any trouble getting the juices going. I just love to paint."

Marilyn Johnson

"Pottery really is a kind of exploration of yourself." Charles Fach

I first met Charles Fach at a public forum I covered for the Telegraph Herald during the mid-1990s. He expressed concern about the semis that were roaring into town and using their screeching "jake brakes" (low gears) to slow down for the stoplight in the center of town. The screeching was occurring in front of his home on U.S. 20. He thought the Illinois Department of Transportation ought to install yellow flashing lights, reduce the speed limit and put up signs prohibiting jake brakes.

I asked a transportation official how the department's standards for speed limits could possibly apply to Galena's unique geography, and he couldn't provide a satisfactory answer. IDOT later dropped the speed limit — at least temporarily — and Charles became a fan of mine.

Occasionally he called me about an issue he thought I should write about. A potter and sculptor by profession, he struck me as a quirky, intelligent and complicated man, as well as an opinionated one. I didn't know many people who made their living as artists, and I enjoyed talking with him. But I never knew whether to call him Charles or "Charlie," as many people call him. I still don't. He seems too cynical and funny to be a Charles but too serious about his art to be a Charlie.

In 2002, I interviewed him for a story about a studio he built on the foundation of an old brewery. I saw that, as Charles was transforming clay into objects of art, he was elevating a crumbling stone structure to something of beauty and usefulness.

Later, I also learned of his personal transformation from a young, green craftsman to an accomplished potter and sculptor. I began to wonder how his political ideas evolved.

Charles, a thin man with a bemused smile, grew up in Galesburg, Ill. He studied industrial design in college but, after taking just one course in pottery, he changed his career objective. Once he graduated in 1962, he set up a studio in his parents' home. He built his own potter's wheel and kiln.

"I had seen a kiln maybe once," he says. "I cranked it up and almost burned the garage down. I look back at it now and chuckle at the kind of innocence I had."

Charles made mostly tableware. "I remember taking a load of cups into Chicago and selling some to Crate and Barrel, which was just starting out. They probably bought four boxes, and I thought I was in Seventh Heaven."

At the time, he saw himself more as a manufacturer than as an artist.

"When I started, I thought my speed would only get greater and, therefore, in a kind of elemental way, I thought I would only increase my income. But, guess what. It doesn't work that way. You do become adept, but you also become more aware of the challenges in your work. Your awareness becomes more refined. You see more there and you become very particular and, ironically, even slower sometimes."

"You want to change," he adds. "You want to feel like you have grown."

Meanwhile, he joined the Army Reserves and helped train young soldiers bound for Vietnam. But he began to see the Vietnam War as a mistake. "If I had known then what I know now, I think I would have become a conscientious objector."

Soon he married and, in 1969, started graduate school. "I decided I needed to learn more."

He and his wife Sandra looked for a place where Charles could work and they could live and sell his pottery. "I didn't want to keep hauling stuff into Chicago."

In 1971, they bought their old stone home on U.S. 20. Built in 1850 to age beer, the building was a mess inside. Charles restored it and made pots while Sandra taught school. They opened a sales room in one of the stone-vaulted basement rooms and called it Stone House Pottery. (Now it is on the main level and called Spring Street Gallery.)

The history of the building intrigues Charles. It was constructed by Conrad Wetzel and John Gund, who were in the brewing business together. Gund later sold his interest to Wetzel.

In 1855, Wetzel died, and, in 1856, his wife Marie married Rudolph Speier. The couple gave birth to two children who died in infancy and later had three daughters and two sons. But Marie live only until 1876, leaving two young children behind.

Charles believes it is the ghost of Marie whom he sometimes hears open the second-floor door and walk in. "Many, many times I have gone up the steps to see who has come in, but no one was there."

Once one of his friends saw a female figure walk through his home. The ghost had tears in her eyes. Charles wonders whether the ghost was Marie, and if her tears were tears of grief from leaving her children behind, .

"I didn't believe in ghosts before."

In 1918, the Blum family bought the building. During the Prohibition, they ran a pop bottling operation.

By 1934, one the daughters, Marie, was running a tea room there. Late one afternoon, so the story goes, a fellow stopped by for supper and left a generous tip. Two days later, as Marie was reading the newspaper, she noticed a picture and a story about a bank robbery that had occurred March 13 in Mason City, Iowa. She then realized that the stranger was John Dillinger. "He had stopped for supper on the way to robbing the bank."

The years have gone by. Charles has fine-tuned his craft to the point where he can make pots that are almost paper-thin. His cups feel comfortable and light, yet keep coffee steaming hot. He finishes his pieces with delicate designs and subtle glazes.

By contrast, some of his abstract work is heavy and bold.

"He takes pottery beyond utility," says Larry Priske, who has been learning the art from Charles. "It's not that he just throws pots. It's a deliberate

Charles Fach

takes to develop and refine your skills."

After awhile, he realized something: "I was never happy with my abstract work unless I could see a figurative element. I thought, 'Why not do figures?' Now I do figures, but that's a lot more complex than I imagined."

Charles's political life has taken various turns, too. During the early 1990s, he organized an effort to place three gambling-related questions on the primary ballot. Opposed to gambling, he felt pleased when a large majority of voters said no to helping those who wanted to establish a casino. But the referendum was non-binding and, a few months later, the Jo Daviess County Board of Supervisors voted to build water and sewer lines to the Silver Eagle Casino.

"The board didn't say hardly anything about the referendum. It was like nothing had happened."

Charles then became the plaintiff in a lawsuit filed against a board member whom he felt had a conflict of interest, but the case was dismissed.

The potter learned a bitter lesson: "If this can happen at the county level, what happens on the state and national levels? Now I am a lot more sensitive to people's statements and to reading between the lines."

Charles also has become involved in the peace-and-justice movement. "I don't support violence and military solutions." When Pres. George W. Bush announced plans to invade Iraq, Charles organized a rally in downtown Galena. Demonstrators held up large letters, which he had painted. They spelled: "Support the troops, oppose preemptive wars."

In 1981, Charles and Sandra bought the property next door to them. It consisted of an 1876 building that was used as a cooling house for beer and a shed that had been built over the foundation of the old brewery. The couple converted the cooling house into a bed and breakfast inn. But Charles wanted more studio space.

In 2001, he hired an architect to design a

exercise in creating a piece of work. He is not only a talented artist, but a great mechanic — whether in welding, forging or machinery. He seems to understand the connection between how a piece flows and its function, and how they support each other."

"He is always thinking about his craft," Larry adds. "He doesn't have a lot of patience for not trying to do it correctly."

Often, when Larry completes a piece, Charles looks it over, weighs it in his hands and says, "It's too heavy."

"I don't see a linear progression in my work," Charles says. "A lot has to do with my surroundings, the people I am with, what I am reading, what is going on politically and what is going on artistically. Some of the pieces I'm making now I couldn't have made five years ago.

"Pottery really is a kind of exploration of yourself. You're always questioning whether you're really being honest with yourself."

"I really don't know where I am with the sculpture," he admits.

Besides working in porcelain and clay, Charles casts sculptures in bronze. He worked with Dubuque sculptor Tom Gibbs to learn the craft. "We just cast and cast and kept on casting. That's what it three-story, multi-use facility on the old brewery foundation. He asked the architect to incorporate the two barrel-vaulted limestone chambers that had remained intact. Charles acted as general contractor, and everything went smoothly, almost too smoothly.

"I don't believe in a God that can intercede, but this was just weird. When we were digging and doing a lot of earth moving, it never rained. When we were done with that, we were facing winter, but we put on the roof before the first snow of the winter. We just kept going. Many a time, when I needed a board, one the exact length I needed would be right there. When I was worried about something, bam, the next day or so, there would be the answer. It was creepy. The project was blessed. I'm telling you, things just kind of fell into place."

Charles called the new building the Artists Annex and moved his studio into the first level. He works in natural light that flows in from large windows. Every Saturday and Sunday he demonstrates pottery making for anyone who is interested. His hands work steadily as he transforms lumps of clay into cylindrical shapes, or patiently trims excess material from partly dried pots. He explains the process and jokes lightly with the onlookers.

He doubts whether he could have done that 20 years ago. "I'm getting better at it, but I've always been an introvert."

"I am just amazed by the interest," he added. "I didn't realize how marvelous this craft is to people."

The top two floors of the building consist of artists' lofts. Patricia Lehnhardt holds cooking classes in one, and a wine bar has moved into another. The arrangement works well, Charles says.

But Charles worries about the future. Around the time he turned 60 and began work on the Artists Annex, he was diagnosed with rheumatoid arthritis. "Everything changed. I would eat breakfast, then come down here to work. But I was always tired, so I would have to go back upstairs to nap. It was terrible. I got very depressed. I couldn't even hold on to my pottery."

Charles stopped working for awhile. Then he tried a new medication that took away the pain. But its effectiveness later diminished, and Charles stopped taking it. Now he works through his pain.

He would like to continue for many more years. "It has been wonderful being in this craft. I have no regrets. Absolutely none." His only regret would be if he had to stop working.

References

Eichstaedt, Ron, interview, 2003.
Fach, Charles, interviews, 2004 and 2005.
Galena City Council Meetings, March 27, April 15 and May 9, 2000.
The Galena Weekly Gazette, "Fire Ruins Turner Opera House; Was Eagles' Lodge New Home, Was Insured for $8,000," January 11, 1926.
Hogue, Chrissy, interview, 2003.
Jackman, Phil, interview, 2005.
Jenkins, Tracy, interview, 2004.
Johnson, Carl, interview, 2004.
Johnson, Marilyn, interview, 2004.
Koester, Carole, interview, 2004.
Painter, Emily, interview, 2003.
Priske, Larry, interview, 2005.
Prinz, Harvey, "A Misplaced Turner Hall in Galena, Illinois," Infoblatt, Winter 2001.
Telegraph Herald: "Galenians endorse Turner Hall," March 28, 2000; and "Turner Hall's past provides impetus for discussion about future," April 16, 2000.
Watson, Daryl, "Ghosts of Galena," 1995, Galena/Jo Daviess County Historical Society.
White, Katie, interview, 2003.
Zanger, Matt, interview, 2004.

Index